SWEDISH CRIME FICTION

Manchester University Press

For Leigh, and my parents

SWEDISH CRIME FICTION

NOVEL, FILM, TELEVISION

Steven Peacock

Manchester University Press
Manchester and New York
distributed in the United States exclusively
by Palgrave Macmillan

Published by Manchester University Press
Oxford Road, Manchester M13 9NR, UK
and Room 400, 175 Fifth Avenue, New York, NY 10010, USA
www.manchesteruniversitypress.co.uk

Distributed in the United States exclusively by
Palgrave Macmillan, 175 Fifth Avenue, New York,
NY 10010, USA

Distributed in Canada exclusively by
UBC Press, University of British Columbia, 2029 West Mall,
Vancouver, BC, Canada V6T 1Z2

British Library Cataloguing-in-Publication Data
A catalogue record for this book is available from the British Library

Library of Congress Cataloging-in-Publication Data applied for

ISBN   978 0 7190 8695 3   hardback
ISBN   978 0 7190 9069 1   paperback

First published 2014

Edited and typeset
by Frances Hackeson Freelance Publishing Services, Brinscall, Lancs
Printed in Great Britain
by Bell and Bain Ltd, Glasgow

CONTENTS

ACKNOWLEDGEMENTS

Thank you first and foremost to Matthew Frost and Kim Walker at Manchester University Press for their support, guidance, and enthusiasm for the project. Thank you to Barry Forshaw for sharing time and expert knowledge of the field, as well as our many pleasurable and illuminating conversations. Special thanks go to all at Yellow Bird Productions, particularly Eric Hultkvist, Mikael Wallén, Ole Sondberg, and Jon Mankell for the generosity of their time during our correspondence and interviews, and for such a warm welcome in Stockholm. Heartfelt thanks to Left Bank Pictures and in particular to Andy Harries. I am very grateful to Swedish scholars Johan Wopenka and Daniel Brodén, and authors Mari Jungstedt, John Ajvide Lindqvist, and Johan Theorin for their invaluable counsel on the subject of Scandinavian crime fiction. An earlier version of Chapter 5 appeared as 'The Impossibility of Isolation in *Wallander*', *Critical Studies in Television* 6: 2 (2011), and parts have previously appeared in Steven Peacock (ed.), *Stieg Larsson's Millennium Trilogy: Interdisciplinary Approaches to Nordic Noir on Page and Screen* (London: Palgrave Macmillan, 2012). I am grateful to Manchester University Press and Palgrave Macmillan respectively for permission to reprint this material. Thank you to Brandon Pazitka for the cover design. I thank my colleagues at the University of Hertfordshire for their enthusiastic backing, and the QR Research Group for its source of financial support.

INTRODUCTION:
A POST-MILLENNIUM
PHENOMENON

The 2000s saw an explosion of interest in Swedish crime fiction. Between 2008 and 2010, in the UK, digital television station BBC Four hit upon a winning formula of screening double episodes of Swedish detective series.[1] First onto the channel came the Swedish *Wallander* (dir. various, 2005–2010), based on the characters of Henning Mankell's bestselling novels, the *Wallander* mysteries.[2] A wintry sort of *Inspector Morse* (dir. various, 1987–2000), *Wallander* focuses on an eponymous loner detective (played by Krister Henriksson) and replaces Oxford's dreamy spires with the ice-blasted terrain of Southern Swedish city Ystad. At the same time in 2008, BBC One aired a new, English language co-production of *Wallander* (dir. various, 2008–ongoing), starring Kenneth Branagh in the title role, and focusing on stories from the original Mankell novels.[3]

Flushed with the success of these two hits, the BBC took more steps in quick succession, building the momentum around Scandinavian crime drama. BBC Four picked up another Swedish series with the same name – *Wallander* – an earlier production (dir. various, 1994–2004) starring a different actor (Rolf Lassgård) and adapting the Mankell novels. Then, confident that the climate was right for more subtitled Scandinavian serials, it aired the Danish series *Forbrydelsen* (*The Killing*, dir. various, 2007) to universal acclaim. The series garnered a cult-like following of UK fans, with members of the British media falling over themselves to cover *Forbrydelsen*'s popularity. The curious apogee of this frenzied interest was the launching of a competition in UK TV listings magazine *Radio Times*, inviting readers to send in photographs of themselves wearing knitted sweaters in the style of those favoured by *Forbrydelsen*'s lead character Sarah Lund (played by Sofie Gråbol).[4] The series' place in the nation's hearts was also represented by Gråbol's knowing cameo appearance (as Sarah Lund) in one of the 2011 Christmas episodes of Jennifer Saunders' sitcom *Absolutely Fabulous* (dir. various, 1992–ongoing). The sequel to the crime drama – *Forbrydelsen II* (dir. various, 2009) – followed, again shown on BBC Four, and was quickly pursued by another Danish thriller investigating the seedy underbelly of the political realm, *Borgen* (dir. various, 2010). This too was met with widespread praise.[5] Following two more successful imports for BBC Four – the Swedish/Danish co-produced police procedural *The Bridge* (dir. various, 2011) and Swedish detective drama *Sebastian Bergman* (dir. various, 2012), of which more later – television critic for *The Guardian* Sam Wollaston was moved to write about Scandinavia, 'That part of the world seems to be this bottomless treasure chest of bleak, wonderful character-led thrilling drama. Nordic noir, the gift that keeps on giving.'[6] And, like a bass-line reverberating across all of these successes, was Stieg Larsson's *Millennium* trilogy, in novel and filmed forms: *The Girl with the Dragon Tattoo*, *The Girl Who Played with Fire*, and *The Girl Who Kicked the Hornets' Nest*.[7]

The term 'Nordic noir' merits qualification. Debates about the constituent elements of film noir fill shelves in academic libraries.[8] We can hopefully agree that crime features as a central component in the majority of films categorised as noir.[9] In many studies, the specificity of the protagonists' nationalities and the setting of the films are also of paramount importance. Film noir is most often thought of as a quintessentially American form and discussed as such. As Michael W. Boyce notes, 'One of the few consistencies in the widely divergent critical work on film noir ... is the emphasis placed on the American roots of film noir – the novels of James M. Cain, Raymond Chandler, and Dashiell Hammett – and the American classic film noir – for example, John Huston's *The Maltese Falcon* (1941), Billy Wilder's *Double Indemnity* (1944), Edward Dmytryk's *Murder, My Sweet* (1944)'.[10] Mark Bould extends an invitation for studies of film noir beyond its traditionally American denomination:

> [O]utside of the main period of American film noir the terrain is still lacking any kind of critical consensus. There is still work to be done on film noir before noir, film noirs after film noir and film noirs in other national, linguistic and international contexts ... Questions of omissions and additions inevitably return to questions of definition, and any attempt at definition restructures the genre, drawing in or casting out particular titles. It is through such complex feedback processes that genres form and reform.[11]

This book takes up Bould's invitation, exploring the modern phenomenon of Swedish crime drama within Nordic noir and considering its national context. It follows Boyce's most useful understanding of noir as 'a particular sensibility or mood, one of alienation, pessimism, and uncertainty'.[12] As Wollaston's review suggests, there is a particular and particularly 'bleak' aspect to Nordic noir, a certain strand of Scandinavian sensibility that the crime drama can tap into more than any other genre. In turn, *Swedish Crime Fiction* considers how the bleakness of this country's noirs reflects the historical moment, indicating an 'increasing scepticism about both the possibility and effectiveness of human attempts to direct a future course of events'.[13] In particular, as we shall see, this fatalism is much informed by the fractured dream of the welfare state.

Whereas global interest may now have finally been granted to Swedish crime fiction, the form is not a recent development. Swedish crime fiction has a rich history, its keystone period, in which many of its central tropes and concerns calcified, occurring in the 1960s. Moreover, there is an equally pronounced history of international adaptations, for film and television, of Swedish crime novels. The intricacies and complexities of these histories are matched only by those of Swedish socio-political affairs, deeply embedded in many of the crime texts. This book unpicks the knotty ideological threads running through the fictions, to understand better both the crime dramas and their country (or countries) of origin. Above all, it explores the popularity and achievements of Swedish crime fiction. Why the appeal? What makes them distinct from other stories of detection and murder?

Crime fiction has for a long while been a staple genre in both the home nation and neighbouring Scandivanian countries. As Karen Klitgaard Povlsen notes about iterations on the small screen, 'Scandinavian crime fiction on television has become popular inside and outside the region. In most Scandinavian countries, the nationally produced crime series have more viewers than any other fiction.'[14] The recent, larger-scale interest from the USA and the rest of Europe simultaneously augments Sweden's cultural position globally and highlights its 'small nation' status when placed in the context of these bigger states. In the introduction to *Scandinavian Crime Fiction*, Andrew Nestingen and Paula Arvas illuminate this fundamental paradox:

> Scandinavian crime fiction has become a familiar brand in North America and Europe since the 1990s. Its prominence stands in contrast to the diminutive size of the region. Roughly twenty-five million citizens inhabited the nation states of Scandinavia in 2009 – making it equivalent in population to the US state of Texas or slightly smaller than Saudi Arabia, Afghanistan or Malaysia. Yet crime writers from Scandinavia are comparatively well-known, having sold millions of books, having had their works translated into many languages and having also made an impact through influential reviews of their work and receipt of literary prizes.[15]

In the wake of Larsson's *Millennium* trilogy, there is a great deal of attention surrounding contemporary Swedish crime fiction – yet little of length (as yet) has been said in Film and Television Studies about the growing trend of translating the material for the big and small screen. Moreover, since the much-lauded work of Peter Cowie in the 1980s, Scandinavian cinema has received scant scrutiny in academia. Recently, studies in the niche subject of Scandinavian crime fiction and its adaptations have started to emerge, including Andrew Nestingen's *Crime and Fantasy in Scandinavia: Fiction, Film and Social Change* (2008) and the aforementioned edited collection *Scandinavian Crime Fiction* (2011), Barry Forshaw's *Death in a Cold Climate: A Guide to Scandinavian Crime Fiction* (2011) and my own *Stieg Larsson's Millennium Trilogy: Interdisciplinary Approaches to Nordic Noir* (2012). Outside of this specialist area, the keystone reader *Swedish Film* has also appeared (2010), edited by Mariah Larsson and Anders Marklund. Placed next to these publications, Mette Hjort and Peter Schepelern's series Nordic Film Classics is particularly valuable as it not only helps redress the shortage of contemporary work on Scandinavian cinema, but also makes space for detailed studies of individual films.[16]

This book aims to redress the limited appearance of currently available literature. It extends further than the study of the most popular titles to explore other lesser-known works of Swedish crime fiction. As noted and as key to this work's parameters of scrutiny, alongside the recent cycle of fictions, there is a rich history of Swedish crime fiction as novels, films, and television series, extending back across the decades and beyond Sweden, in international forms. Going beyond the recent phenomenon, surveying a wider territory and placing the works in larger contexts allows the books, films, and programmes to open up in new ways. Patterns and variations of generic, stylistic, and structural tropes can be discerned, as can sets of distinguishing features, accomplishments, and meanings. At the same time, the chosen focus on *Swedish* crime fiction (rather than Scandinavian) allows for an important delimitation of interest on one country's output, in turn creating an opportunity to look in detail at particular examples in a series of close readings. *Swedish Crime Fiction* explores critical achievements in different art-forms (books, films, TV programmes) and attends to significant intersections and distinctions. Its overarching methodology is one of a combination of approaches not normally united in the fields of Film and Television Studies. It brings together stylistic criticism – an interpretative examination of *mise-en-scène* and inherent expressive meanings coming from the works' fusion of form and content – with socio-political readings. This approach aims to uncover the texts' significance and appeals from both inside (in terms of points of style such as camerawork, performance, and décor) and outside (surrounding political climates and social circumstances) the work itself.[17] In its appeals to close critical analysis, the book follows Jonathan Bignell's appreciation of the relationship between television style and impulses in crime drama in his piece on 'The Police Series':

> Ultimately, this study argues for the significance of an evidence-based analysis of television aesthetics, which is particularly appropriate to the thematisation of pursuit, discovery, witness, explanation and justification that organises the visual and aural components of police series fiction. For police drama is always about what can be seen and evaluated, and how conclusions are drawn from evidence. This study has indicated that some police series reflexively meditate upon the activities of seeing and interpreting, to the extent that they become thoughtful and sometimes critical works about television itself ... As fictions set in a contemporary world, the series discussed in this study each address their audiences' lived experiences, though in different ways. Their visual styles have been shown to be fully integrated into these modes of address, and in fact to be inseparable from them.[18]

The following comprises the key texts (and central protagonists) under scrutiny throughout the book. All are novels that have been adapted into Swedish films and/or television series, and many have been remade for international audiences. The various versions of Henning Mankell's *Wallander* mysteries have already been introduced.

The *Millennium* trilogy

Beginning with *The Girl with the Dragon Tattoo* ('Män som hattan kvinnor'), Karl Stig-Erland 'Stieg' Larsson's work in its written, filmed, and televised versions has become a worldwide phenomenon, calcifying and intensifying the modern global interest in Nordic noir first raised by *Wallander*. This book's analysis concentrates on the versions and concerns of the first part of the trilogy, *The Girl with the Dragon Tattoo*. Rather than attempt a summary of the trilogy's many successes here, an extensive quotation from the novelist Edward Docx may serve us better at this point, as encapsulating the widespread impact of *Millennium*. In a somewhat sniffy piece for *The Observer* newspaper – bemoaning the 'amateurish' writing of Larsson and Dan Brown, as well as rehearsing, once more, the age-old and deeply suspicious debate about 'true literary works' as superior to genre fiction – Docx begins with a humorous account of *Millennium*'s almost unprecedented popularity:

> On my way back to London the other day, I was clawing my way toward the buffet car when I noticed with a shock that more or less the entire train carriage was reading ... novels. This cheered me up immensely, partly because I have begun to fear we are living in some kind of [Simon] Cowellian nightmare, and partly because I make a good part of my living writing them ... My cheer modulated into something, well, less cheerful (but still quite cheerful) when I realised that they were all, in fact, reading the same book. Yes, you've guessed it: *The Girl with the Dragon Tattoo* who *Played with Fire* and who, some time later we are led to believe, *Kicked the Hornets' Nest*. ... And when, finally, I arrived at the buffet car, I was greeted with a sigh and a how-dare-you raise of the eyebrows. Why? Because in order to effectively conjure my cup of lactescent silt into existence, the barrista would have to put down his ... Stieg Larsson. In terms of sales, 2010 has

> been the year of the Larsson. Again. His three books have
> been the three bestselling fiction titles on Amazon UK.
> Along with Dan Brown, he has conquered the world.[19]

It is hardly a controversial statement to note that Larsson's writing is not comparable to that of Shakespeare, or Flaubert, or Bellow. But in contrast to Docx's critique of Larsson as a 'bad genre writer', Heather O' Donoghue's essay in the edited collection *Stieg Larsson's Millennium Trilogy* traces the trilogy's skilful engagement with central structural elements of the detective and thriller novel.[20] One of the most striking aspects of the *Millennium* trilogy is each entry's affiliation with different sub-genres of crime drama. *The Girl with the Dragon Tattoo*, in introducing post-punk cyberhacker Lisbeth Salander and investigative journalist Mikael Blomkvist, soon settles into a variation of Agatha Christie's 'locked room' mysteries, with a family's secret murky history playing out on their own private island. The second book, *The Girl Who Played with Fire* expands the mythos of the *Millennium* universe to detail a government-led conspiracy against Salander, harking back to Cold War political thrillers and antics akin to James Bond's brand of derring-do. The third and final novel, *The Girl Who Kicked the Hornets' Nest* continues in this vein before moving towards a courtroom finale of the kind more often seen in Hollywood legal thrillers.[21] Due to his early death aged fifty in 2004, Larsson never witnessed the publication or tremendous success of his novels, the first of which was released in Sweden in 2005, and the UK in 2008. His estate is now held by his partner, Eva Gabrielsson, who has published her own account of their time together, *'There are Things that I Want You to Know': About Stieg Larsson and Me*.[22] Rumours abound of a fourth novel in fragments on a laptop locked away by Gabrielsson, though at the time of writing, it remains private and I for one hope an unfinished draft manuscript stays that way.[23] Sarah Niblock offers a useful and concise description of the novels' adaptations for film and television:

The Swedish film versions of the *Millennium* trilogy were released in Scandinavia in 2009. Made by Yellow Bird, they were co-produced with the Danish Nordisk production company. Only the first film, *The Girl with the Dragon Tattoo* (dir. Niels Arden Oplev), was intended for theatrical release, while the subsequent films, *The Girl Who Played with Fire* and *The Girl Who Kicked the Hornets' Nest* (both dir. Daniel Alfredson), were planned as TV movies. However, the tremendous success of the first film prompted their cinema release. In 2010, the films were shown in an extended version of approximately 180 minutes per film as a six-part mini-series (each film divided into two parts of 90 minutes) on Swedish television. This version was released on 14 July 2010 on DVD and Blu-ray in three separate sets and, on 24 November 2010, as a complete *Millennium* trilogy box set with an extra disc. All three films feature Michael Nyqvist as Mikael Blomkvist, an investigative reporter and publisher of the magazine *Millennium*, and Noomi Rapace as Lisbeth Salander.[24]

The first US remake of the trilogy, *The Girl with the Dragon Tattoo* (dir. David Fincher, 2011), met with a lukewarm critical and commercial reception.[25] The relationship between the Swedish and American films becomes particularly complex and fascinating when we consider that the director of the 2009 Swedish film – Niels Arden Oplev – is on record as stating his intention to draw heavily on the style of none other than American filmmaker David Fincher.[26] The dragon is in danger of chasing its tail!

Inspector Martin Beck/The Story of a Crime

Most often, the pioneering police procedural novels of Maj Sjöwall and Per Wahlöö featuring homicide detective Martin Beck are seen as the archetype of modern Swedish crime fiction.[27] This husband and wife writing team produced ten novels under the collective banner of 'The Story of a Crime', beginning with *Roseanna* in 1965, and ending with *The Terrorists* (*Terroristerna*) in 1975. All of their books have been adapted as films in different parts of the world. As Jakob Stougaard-Nielsen notes, 'These were not only the first truly modern and popular crime novels in Scandinavia, but also the first to be adapted for film and TV both at home and abroad.'[28] *Roseanna* was made into a Swedish film for cinematic release in 1967, directed by Hans Abramson, and starring Keve Hjelm as Martin Beck (for Minerva Film AB). In 1973, an American film version of their fourth novel – *The Laughing Policeman* (*Den skrattande policen*) – starred Walter Matthau as the Martin Beck figure (now called Jake Martin), and was set in San Francisco instead of Stockholm.[29] Itself heavily influenced by William Friedkin's US crime thriller *The French Connection* (1971), *The Man on the Roof* (*Mannen på taket*) is a 1976 Swedish film directed by Bo Widerberg, and based on the 1971 novel *The Abominable Man*. In 1993, *The Locked Room* (*Det slutna rummet*, based on the novel first published in 1972) was made into a Belgian-Dutch film with the setting moved to Antwerp.[30] Between 1997 and 2009, a tele-film series of the novels and original stories was produced for Swedish television (by Nordisk Film, TV4 and ZDF Enterprises), starring Peter Haber as the eponymous hero.

The *Van Veeteren* series

Nine of Hakan Nesser's ten *Van Veeteren* detective novels have been made into a 2005 pan-European TV series (international in terms of production and broadcasting) – an apt fact when one considers the setting of the works: a fictional country and city called Maardam with shades of, variously, Sweden, the Netherlands, Poland, and Germany.[31] The distribution company Arrow Films, under their umbrella grouping 'Nordic Noir', released the films on DVD with English subtitles in 2012.

Sun Storm

This 2007 Swedish film based on the first novel of Åsa Larsson – *Solstorm* (2003), UK title *The Savage Altar* – introduces us to one of many female protagonists in Swedish crime drama:

attorney Rebecka Martinsson. While starting in the urban setting of Stockholm, the film and novel move to the far Northern terrain of Kiruna (also Åsa Larsson's homeland). Two further novels featuring Rebecka Martinsson have been translated into English: *The Blood Spilt* (2007) and *The Black Path* (2008).

The Irene Huss and Annika Bengtzon mysteries

Alongside their international success with film/TV versions of *Millennium* and *Wallander*, the Swedish production company Yellow Bird has also had more local (German, Scandinavian) hits with adaptations of contemporary crime dramas written by women and featuring another two strong central female characters: Detective Inspector Irene Huss from the novels of Helene Tursten, and Annika Bengtzon, from the novels of Liza Marklund. Four of the Irene Huss novels have so far been translated into English: *Detective Inspector Huss* (*Den krossade tanghästen* 1998, translated and published in the UK 2003), *Torso* (*Tatuered torso* 2000, 2006), *The Glass Devil* (*Glasdjävulen* 2002, 2007), and *Night Rounds* (*Nattrond* 1999, 2012). In collaboration with Illusion Films, Kanal 5, ARD Degeto and Film I Vast, Yellow Bird have made two series of *Irene Huss* mysteries: the first (2005–2007) including all of the above titles, and the second (2012) featuring *The One Who Keeps Watch in the Dark*, *A Man with a Small Face*, and *The Deceitful Web*. All of the tele-films star Angela Kovács as Irene Huss (also one of the actors of the Swedish *Wallander* series, appearing as the character Ann-Britt Höglund).

As Yellow Bird's website suggests, 'If Sjöwall/Wahlöö created the modern Swedish police procedural in the 60s, journalist Liza Marklund revolutionized it in the late 90s with *The Bomber*, the first instalment in a series that would become the most successful ever from a female Scandinavian writer.'[32] Marklund's cycle of works features crime reporter Annika Bengtzon. Two novels from the cycle have been filmed (for cinematic release) in Swedish by the English director Colin Nutley (both starring Helena Bergström as Annika Bengzton): *The Bomber* (*Sprängaren*, also known as

Deadline, novel published 1998, English translation 2011, film version released 2001) and *Paradise* (*Paradiset*), novel published 2000, English translation 2012, film version released 2003). Yellow Bird has the rights to bring six more Annika Bengzton novels to the small screen: *Studio 69* (1999), *Prime Time* (2002), *The Red Wolf* (*Den Röda Vagen*, 2003), *Nobel's Last Will* (*Nobel's testamente*, 2006), *Lifetime* (*Livstid*, 2007), and *A Place in the Sun* (*En plats I solen*, 2008). All but the last two novels have recently been translated into English. Yellow Bird's tele-films star Malin Crépin as Annika Bengzton, and the first – *Nobel's Last Will* – and last – *A Place in the Sun* – were released theatrically. Both are directed by Danish filmmaker Peter Flinth, also responsible for directing the acclaimed tele-film episode of the Swedish *Wallander*, *Mastermind* (2003). Marklund's work is already globally acclaimed and transnational in design, as best illustrated by her collaboration with the American crime writer James Patterson on the novel *The Postcard Killers* (2010).

The *Stockholm Noir* trilogy

Jens Lapidus's epic trilogy of noir novels surveying the contemporary Stockholm criminal underworld – *Easy Money* (*Snabba Cash*, 2006); *Never Fuck Up* (*Aldrig Fucka Upp*, 2008); *Life Deluxe* (*Livet deluxe*, 2011) – is the latest Swedish work to gain Hollywood's interest. At the time of writing, Warner Bros. is currently producing a big-budget American version of *Easy Money* to be directed by Daniel Espinosa (and rumoured to be starring Zac Efron). A Swedish film version of *Snabba Cash,* also directed by Espinosa and co-written by Lapidus, was released to great commercial and critical success in 2010. Espinosa received initiation into Hollywood via direction of the 2012 Tony Scott-produced CIA thriller *Safe House*. The high-octane Scott aesthetic is much in evidence throughout both *Snabba Cash* and *Safe House*, as well as, especially in the former film, an homage to Martin Scorsese's blend of excoriating violence and the giddy perspective of an outsider looking into a closed (under)world. The Scorsese connection continues, as the Italian-American director's enthusiasm for and patronage of Espinosa's *Snabba Cash* led to the film receiving a theatrical, subtitled release in the USA in the summer of 2012. A Swedish film sequel – *Snabba Cash II*, directed by Babak Najafi – was also released in 2012. Although the sequel departs from Lapidus's novels, a planned third film returns to the source trilogy, as an adaptation of *Life Deluxe*. The history presented within and without *Snabba Cash* is acutely expressive of Sweden's global positioning. The film's plot revolves around the intertwined lives in modern-day Stockholm of a Swedish opportunist, Serbian hitman, and Chilean drug-dealer. Its industrial and aesthetic life – as a Scandinavian work influenced by Anglo-American forms and artists, the film versions helmed by Chilean-Swedish (Espinosa) and Iranian-Swedish (Najafi) directors – reflects its transnational status and appeal.

Sebastian Bergman

Daniel Espinosa is also the director of this latest offering from SVT, shown on BBC Four in June 2012 and released on DVD in July 2012 by Arrow Films. The eponymous anti-hero – a criminal profiler recovering from the loss of his wife and child in the 2004 Indian Ocean tsunami – is played by Rolf Lassgård (the 'original' Kurt Wallander, thus taking us full circle). The two-part tele-film – *Den fördömde* or *The Cursed One* – is based on novels by (duo) Hjorth Rosenfeldt: Michael Hjorth, a writer on Lassgård's *Wallander* and Hans Rosenfeldt, creator and head writer of the television series *The Bridge*. The first episode is based on the first novel in a planned series, *Dark Secrets* (2010, re-titled *Sebastian Bergman* for its publication in English in July 2012). The second episode is based on the second novel *The Disciple* (not yet available, at the time of writing, in English). The relationship between novel, film, and television becomes even closer in *Sebastian Bergman*, more tightly involved. Here, TV writers adapt self-penned novels for the small screen, calling in film directors to shoot the series.

A note on the selection of novels, films, and series for detailed study. Wherever possible, I have used only those primary texts that are readily available in print or DVD for the general reader to access. This is important to a project engaging in, and encouraging, an open critical debate about a shareable object. It leads, with a tinge of regret, to the omission of Jan Guillou's Coq Rouge series of novels and films, most of which remain unfathomably inaccessible to a non-Scandinavian audience.[33] Then, the chapters comprise extended analysis and close readings of sequences from those films or series that I consider *exemplary*, and that offer opportunities to discuss different registers of expression, distinct arrangements of style and structure, and that allow the achievements of this cycle of works to emerge most clearly. As suggested here, the book's analytical emphasis is on interpretative readings of film and television adapted from Swedish crime novels. Passages from the novels will also be placed under scrutiny, and receive detailed attention, but the focus, as might be expected from my work in the field of film and television aesthetics, is on the image over the written word.[34]

Across the chapters, certain moments from television episodes and film sequences have been returned to, opening up in different ways through the distinct topic informing each section. In some cases, only the Swedish or US/UK remake has been referred to, with close stylistic scrutiny of one version privileged over a compendious account of all versions. The examples and moments chosen are those which best reflect the expressive possibilities of the form. The book does not provide encyclopaedic reference to all episodes, films, or novels that could be seen to comprise the category 'Swedish crime fiction'. Unapologetically, to get into the details and make critical claims for certain works' (and certain moments') achievements in style and meaning, it makes selective discriminations. For example, more time is spent on David Fincher's 2011 film version of *The Girl with the Dragon Tattoo* than the lacklustre Swedish film offerings of the Larsson trilogy. The ninety-minute tele-films of *Wallander* starring Rolf Lassgård take precedence over the Swedish series featuring Krister

Henriksson, and Bo Widerberg's film *The Man on the Roof* is given priority in discussions of the Martin Beck cycle of works.

A number of central concerns underpins the following readings, as particularly compelling cross-over points of interest in the works of Swedish crime fiction as novels, films, and television series.

Form

This book interrogates the popularity of Swedish noir via its internal mechanisms. It parses exemplary works of fiction to understand (a) their handling of genre (b) their use of a specific medium of expression and (c) their particular artistic accomplishments. Central to these issues are the choices made by writers and filmmakers/television showrunners in their 'modus operandi': the crimes and mysteries themselves, the forms and facets of characterisation on display, the ways in which the works convey the protagonists' feelings and sensibilities, the handling of their environments and surrounding communities.

Equally, for the most part, the books, films, and series under consideration are particularly alert to the possibilities and parameters of the crime genre. That is to say, much like the cinematic auteurs of the Hollywood Golden Age – Alfred Hitchcock, Nicholas Ray, Howard Hawks, Vincente Minnelli – were able to find expressive freedom precisely from within the contraints of the Studio System and regimented generic models of melodrama, Western, musical or noir picture, the creators of these crime fictions find particular artistic possibilities within the mainstream form. I'm compelled by the texts' understanding of their status, as crime dramas operating in a particular mode. They are adept at locating the expressive potential of mainstream fiction, finding the generic and industrial constraints liberating rather than inhibiting of their creative imagination.

Nation

What is the 'Swedishness' of these Swedish crime fictions? How do particular fictitious evocations of the characters' experiences, emotions, and actions echo national concerns and sensibilities? The generic conventions of the crime drama/novel afford certain routes into socio-political iterations. First and foremost, the majority of Swedish crime fictions are set in worlds readily associable and understandable by the rules and forms of our own contemporary realities: bound by tenets of verisimilitude and realism, the texts place a mirror against the real world, the 'here and now'. They magnify particular social scenarios and states of being, presenting a fresh perspective from which to view certain ideological and political tendencies, and the impact of these factors on ordinary people. Secondly, in dealing with crime and criminal underworlds, the works necessarily break the veneer of the social status quo, getting under the surface of Sweden's daily business and into the heart of darkness. Such a trajectory is particularly fitting, and revealing, in the case of Sweden: a society mourning the failure of its utopian dream of the welfare state and living in the shadow of Prime Minister Olof Palme's assassination in 1986. In the Foreword to the 1999 collection of short prequels to the Wallander cycle, *The Pyramid* (*Pyramiden*), Henning Mankell suggests that a suitable subtitle to the series 'naturally had to be "Novels about the Swedish Anxiety"'. He continues by asserting that the books 'have always been variations on a single theme: "What is happening to the Swedish welfare state in the 1990s? How will democracy survive if the foundation of the welfare state is no longer intact? Is the price of Swedish democracy today too high and no longer worth paying?"'[35]

World

If the breakdown of the utopian vision of a Socialist past and the welfare state represented a certain loss of innocence and idealism in Swedish society, echoed in the moods, polemics, and politics of the country's crime fiction, then it is also informed by a larger struggle, of the country negotiating its position in the world in the light of globalisation. Historical flashpoints will be considered in detail in Chapter 1; as a snapshot, we can note at this stage how the ratification of the European Union in 1994 would instrinsically affect Sweden's previously homogenous sense of itself, moving from a putatively 'neutral', protectionist and insular nation to one slowly and uncertainly negotiating its place in the global collective.

Borderlines

Bringing together all three of the above concerns, the book explores the ways Swedish crime fiction crosses distinct borders: moving from the page to screen; moving from Europe to the USA and the UK; moving across boundaries thematically, within the texts themselves. While dealing with local socio-historical divides, the texts are equally concerned with crossings of international and transnational borders in political, economic, and cultural terms. *Swedish Crime Fiction* examines the aesthetic, industrial, and cultural traffic of the work: the way the texts, and their characters, embrace, resist, and embody pluralism.[36]

These concerns open out across five chapters. Chapter 1 explores the form's main markers of identity as 'Nation, genre, institution'. It places the works in the historical contexts of Sweden's past, the established generic formulae of the crime fiction, and of the country's entertainment industry. It develops ideas raised in this Introduction, considering Sweden's uneasy situation as a small nation in the global age, disillusioned by the failure of a civic utopia, its isolationist reflexes tested by the ever-increasing encroachment of external influences. As the crime fictions expertly illustrate, beneath the elegant façade of the post-war welfare state lays an all-pervasive murkiness. Such socio-political shadows engulf the form of the crime fiction, and inhabit its rich heritage. The chapter addresses the family history of Swedish crime works, and examines how the nation's output taps into the established sub-genres, tropes, and markers of the police procedural, detective drama, and amateur cop fiction, binding as it does so the conventional elements of melodrama, horror, and the thriller. In turn, the chapter picks up on the specific, industrial history of Sweden's local and global cinematic enterprise, and its small-screen counterpart. It considers the influence of governmental intervention in the formation of bodies promoting Swedish film and television. The crime fictions present a compelling instance of the institution of Sweden's small-nation cinema operating in the global age.

Honing in on a particular preoccupation of Swedish society and the crime fictions, Chapter 2 explores the fundamental importance of collective groupings, as 'Community and the family'. It considers the ways that, following the teachings of the welfare state, the nation adheres to an emphasis on social forms of solidarity and homogenisation. In turn, it explores the impact of such an ideological drive on the individual. The crime dramas are particularly well-placed to examine communities in action, involving themselves in the tight-knit worlds of the police force, press, government, and legal systems. And at the heart of almost all the fictions, there is the family, existing at once as an individual entity – the Salanders, the Wallanders *et al.* – and as representative of the wider nation-state.

Chapter 3 explores another national preoccupation, or element of Swedish life that informs both the dramas and the overarching cultural sensibility: the distinctive landscapes of Scandinavia, as 'Space and place'. The wide open terrains, snowy vistas, and vast forests of Sweden's far Northern hinterlands form an integral, expressive element of the crime fictions. These are much more than impressionistic backdrops adding to the tone and mood of the piece (though that is often an important starting point in the works' development of atmosphere). The natural landscape is at the heart of the texts, directing the narrative, shaping the drama, informing and inflecting the meaning of each piece as it unfolds. The crucial, catalytic criminal acts of murder and subterfuge often take place in the wilds of the Swedish countryside – exposed spaces offering particular iterations of isolation, anonymity, and loneliness to gruesome acts. A body could easily get lost in the middle of a forest that spans for hundreds of miles.

At the same time, the crime dramas are alert to the alternative implications of urban living in Sweden's busy cities. In the third largest country in the European Union with a population of only 9.4 million, crime finds contact in clustered conurbations. The crowded streets of Stockholm are as central to Larsson's *Millennium* trilogy as the retreat to Hedeby Island in *The Girl with the Dragon Tattoo*: the former developing themes around the pressures of public scrutiny and the difficulty of achieving intimacy in the city environment; the latter creating a form of 'locked room' mystery as Blomkvist and Salander are cut off from the mainland (and the rest of the world), left to fend for themselves against the corrupt forces of the Vanger family estate. Regional geographical differences are also important to the crime fictions' distinctive personalities. For example, in *Wallander,* like Oxford for Colin Dexter's *Inspector Morse*, the town of Ystad becomes a fully-fledged character in its own right. Ystad is in the far Southern region of Skåne: 'Historically a Danish-controlled land, Skåne stands out in Sweden for flatness, borderland status, separatist politics and a far-right past.'[37] Geographically and socio-politically, it is a place of extremes. Many of Mankell's novels are equipped with a map of the area, and the filmed versions, particularly the Swedish television series starring Krister Henriksson, make repeated use of distinctive locales in the town including the Hotel Continental: a (real) place of exclusive sanctuary and comfort, constantly breached, in the series, by undercover agents and clandestine killers. Neither the anonymity of Stockholm's crowds nor the solitude of Skåne's vast flatlands and forests can stop the murderer's penetration of privacy.[38]

It is a fascinating and fundamental feature of Sweden that a country so rich in the age-old beauty of the natural environment should be beguiled by all things modern. Chapter 3 closes by exploring this preoccupation, especially in terms of cyberspace. As Lars Trägårdh suggests

> Befitting a nation imagined as 'the people of the future', it was thought that there was little to learn from the past. The celebration of Swedish democracy as a function of 'deep' history gave way to a vaguer, ahistorical and essentialist sense of superiority: Sweden as a 'model' of modernity to be emulated (though rarely equalled). Indeed, the primary function of the past was to serve as a negative counterpoint to the ever-more glorious, modern present.[39]

As with so many facets of Sweden's socio-cultural DNA, this ideological model is rife with complexities and contradictions. Disillusionment with the failings of the past promotes the embracing of modernity in all its forms, with an emphasis on cutting-edge design and the latest innovations in technological development. (Consider, for example, the modern aesthetics and global domination of Swedish home décor brand IKEA, and the country's world-leading status in the telecommunications and pharmaceuticals industries, as illustrated by industrial giants Ericsson and Astra-Zeneca.)

Yet the strive for modernity is accompanied by aspects such as a frenetic pace of life, concomitant pressures of industrial innovation, and a lingering uncertainty of the powers new technologies may possess. These anxieties find acute expression in the crime fictions. As with most detective novels and works of film noir, contemporary modes of communication – letters, telegrams, telephones, the internet – are crucial to the narrative, allowing for plot development and revelatory information. That the present-day objects and trappings of electronic communication are also containers of social anxiety enhances their standing in the Swedish works. The suggestion of modern technology as a harbinger of bad tidings has a history in the country's artistic output beyond crime fiction. As Erik Hedling observes, 'The telephone is also ill-omened in Bergman's films, something that has to do with the negatively charged context of modernity. It starts as early as in *Hets* [1944], and the fact is that not a single telephone conversation in the films leads to anything good.'[40]

In the world of the crime drama, electronic forms of communication also key into prominent social anxieties of surveillance. Again, a related tension exists at the heart of Swedish society: at once holding dear to the preference of the collective over the individual, and yet intrinsically concerned about the powers of these faceless organisations and collective bodies over one's actions. In the *Millennium* trilogy and many of Mankell's *Wallander* mysteries, the spectre-like organisation of SAPO (the Swedish Security Service, better known as the Secret Police) pulls strings in government, the police force, and the law courts. It does so through coercion aided by covert forms of surveillance, using technology to spy on individuals. This is a prime example of fiction representing a fear of 'surveillance society', with the powers of the State misused against the common man. Such anxieties, Chapter 3 argues, are also related to Sweden's unease at technology affording global forms of interconnectedness, again disturbing its entrenched separatist principles. The unlikely heroine of the *Millennium* trilogy, Lisbeth Salander, is a consummate techno-wizard, a hacker extraordinaire, at once embodying and overturning the pre-eminent social anxieties about electronic forms of surveillance.

The final chapter (before the interview transcripts) cuts into the very fibres of the crime drama, exploring the texts' presentations of sex and violence. In almost every Swedish crime fiction committed to paper or film, there is a body, a dead body, at the heart of the narrative. Chapter 4 looks at the form's fascination with the corporeal. As with the works' handling of space and place, there is a key relationship between meditations on the human body – violated by murderers, protected or abused – and national identity. Equally, the move into psychological drama and the various ways in which the killer's motives (for example) are revealed to the reader/viewer opens up further means by which Sweden's fractured state is placed under scrutiny. In particular, the chapter extends thoughts on the texts' handling of sex and sexuality. Sweden is often thought of, from urban myth to sociological fact, as a place of tolerance and the open celebration of sexuality. Addressing related matters of censorship, Chapter 4 looks at how Swedish fictions have engaged with the roles and relationships between the sexes in the contemporary world, and with forms of sexual liberation in a (seemingly) permissive society. Sweden often prides itself on its history of liberalism, and the crime dramas explore the tipping point into taboo and illegal activity, as well as more feral combinations of carnal pleasure and death. As is suggested most vividly in the original Swedish title of *The Girl with the Dragon Tattoo* – *Men Who Hate Women* – many of the crime dramas deal explicitly with forms of gender politics, finding extreme expression in acts of sexual violence. The crimes concocted in the fictions often create opportunities for the works to offer polemic stances on the abuse suffered by women in transgressions of sexual boundaries.

Chapter 5 presents five interview transcripts with leading figures in the world of Swedish crime drama. The first is a full transcript of an interview I undertook in 2011 in Stockholm with Mikael Wallén, Executive Producer of Yellow Bird Productions: the company behind the filmed Swedish versions of the *Millennium* trilogy as well as *Wallander*. This interview provides an essential and exclusive behind-the-scenes look at the workings of the trilogy in production. The second offers an insight into the UK 'arm' of the *Wallander* co-productions, via an interview with the Chief Executive of Left Bank Productions, Andy Harries. The third, fourth and fifth transcripts are of interviews I conducted with Swedish crime novelists Johan Theorin and Mari Jungstedt, and horror writer John Ajvide Lindqvist. In a post-*Millennium* world, Theorin is the writer at the forefront of many critics' minds as the rightful heir to Larsson's throne. His engaging interview provides a very personal insight into the realm of Nordic noir, and the shape of things to come. Originally a journalist for Sweden's ABC News Network, Mari Jungstedt offers an illuminating view of the contemporary fascination with Nordic noir, and the key place of female writers in the genre. John Ajvide Lindqvist's enormously popular and acclaimed novel *Let the Right One In* (*Låt den rätte komma in*, 2007) and its Swedish and US film versions have entered the canon as modern greats (respectively, *Let the Right One In*, dir. Tomas Alfredson, 2008; *Let Me In*, dir. Matt Reeves, 2010). This exclusive interview offers insights into the writer's creative process, cinematic and literary influences, and thoughts on thematic intersections between the horror and crime drama genres.

It is necessary, when focusing on work originally produced in another language, to negotiate the slippery terrain of translation and associated critical and theoretical arguments. Some might indeed argue that without a working knowledge of Swedish, such an undertaking is prone to complication and misreading. While acknowledging that, in the translated versions of the novels, I am at the mercy of the translators' own interpretations, determinations and favoured arrangements of language – more or less faithful to the original writer's words – this does not constitute an impasse to analysis.[41] Rather, I work with what is at hand, and attend to the specific achievements of the artwork in front of me, be it a novel translated into English, or a subtitled film, or an American or British remake of a Swedish television series. If my reading will therefore be different to a German scholar attending to the same source material in German translations and subtitles, then that is to be taken into account, but not perceived as an insurmountable obstacle to work being done. Indeed, linguistic difference is but one of a number of variants at play in any given interpretation, where meanings are inscribed by the reader or viewer's cultural and social distinctions. Dealing with translated material always constitutes a risk. I am happy to follow Gayatri Chakravorty Spivak here, who in 'The Politics of Translation', speaks of fruitful ways in which we might make sense of, and embrace, this risk:

In my view, language may be one of many elements that allow us to make sense of things, of ourselves. I am thinking, of course, of gestures, pauses, but also of chance, of the sub-individual force-fields of being which click into place in different situations, swerve from the straight or true line of language-in-thought. Making sense of ourselves is what produces identity. If one feels that the production of identity as self-meaning, not just meaning, is as pluralized as a drip of water under a microscope, one is not always satisfied, outside of the ethico-political arena as such, with 'generating' thoughts on one's own ... Language is not everything. It is only a vital clue to where the self loses its boundaries. The ways in which rhetoric or figuration disrupt logic themselves point at the possibility of random contingency, beside language, around language. Such a *diss*emination cannot be under our control. Yet in translation, where meaning hops into the spacy emptiness between two named historical languages, we get perilously close to it. By juggling the distruptive rhetoricity that breaks the surface in not necessarily connected ways, we feel the selvedges of the language-textile give way, fray into *frayages* or facilitations. Although every act of reading or communication is a bit of this risky fraying which scrambles together somehow, our stake in the agency keeps the fraying down to a minimum except in the communication and reading and in love. (What is the place of 'love' in the ethical?) The task of the translator is to facilitate this love between the original and its shadow, a love that permits fraying, holds the agency of the translator and the demands of her imagined or actual audience at bay.[42]

This rather romantic, philosophical understanding of translated texts in terms of love and jagged relationships offers an invitation for us to permit the 'fraying' that occurs in the act of translation, and to see language as but one element worthy of consideration, alongside gestures, pauses, and the rhetorical meanings found in the spaces *between* languages. The notion of gesture is crucial to the way in which the book attends to the visual and aural elements of films and television programmes beyond the scope of dialogue as a form of spoken narrative. That is to say, the *mise-en-scène* and performances at play in any given film or series are as instrumental in enacting meaning as the words being spoken and translated. In turn, this approach moves us past notions of 'fidelity' to the original source text (in this instance, the novel) not only in terms of translation, but also adaptation.

There are many illuminating works of Adaptation Studies that favour and contest distinct approaches to the study of filmed versions of written material, offering their own negotiations of associated concepts of fidelity, intertextuality, hypertexts, and hypotexts.[43] An appraisal of one of the most recent contributions at the time of writing reveals some of these debates in action and points up developments in the field. In the *Journal of Adaptation in Film and Performance*, Thomas Leitch offers a striking metaphorical account of adaptations within the sub-genre of vampire fiction, giving rise to discussions of the 'parasitism' of leech (or vampire)-like film adaptations:

> For one of the hoariest clichés in the field is that adaptations act like vampires in sucking the life out of the passive, helpless progenitor texts who enable their existence, often unwittingly or unwillingly, but are powerless to control their excesses. Robert Stam (2005: 7), to take only the most prominent example, has noted the charge of '*parasitism*' levelled against adaptations that 'burrow into the body of the source text and steal its vitality'.[44]

For Leitch, this process of parasitism becomes more complex if considered as a form of symbiotic exchange:

> The communicative nature of adaptation reminds us that just as every adaptation dreams of emulating Shakespeare's ([1600] 2006) *Hamlet* and Disney's *Snow White and the Seven Dwarfs* (1937) in attaining the status of the classic text other adaptations will aim to adapt, 'every successive state of a written text' as Gérard Genette ([1982] 1997: 395) has

ruled, 'functions like a hypertext in relation to the state that precedes it and like a hypotext in relation to the one that follows'.[45]

In turn, Leitch also asserts the influential contribution of the readers or viewers themselves:

> Linda Hutcheon's (2006: 21) assertion that 'adaptation *as adaptation* is unavoidably a kind of intertextuality *if the reader is acquainted with the adapted text.*' The palimpsestuous double consciousness Hutcheon ascribes to readers who experience a given adaptation as an adaptation – they grasp its status as an independent text at the same time they acknowledge its habitation by earlier texts – reminds us of the undead nature of intertexts. And the analogy between adaptation and vampirism allows us to put a new spin on another remark of Hutcheon's – that although 'no text is a fixed thing' that exists in only a single version, the fluidity characteristic of all texts sometimes enters 'in the production process', sometimes 'by reception, by people who "materially alter texts"' (170; cf. Bryant 2002: 7).[46]

Swedish Crime Fiction: Novel, Film, Television is purposefully fluid in its movements between discussions of novels, films, television series, and UK or US remakes of Swedish works. This appears a particularly fitting approach because the status of the filmed Swedish versions of *Wallander*, *Millennium* and *Irene Huss* (to name but a few examples) is one of a merger between works of television and cinema. As the Executive Producer of Yellow Bird Productions Mikael Wallén suggests in his interview in Chapter 5 (and as noted by Niblock), only the first of the three films in the *Millennium* trilogy (*The Girl with the Dragon Tattoo*) was originally conceived as a cinematic release, with the other two scheduled for straight-to-TV broadcast. The immense worldwide popularity of Larsson's novels persuaded him and his colleagues at Yellow Bird to present all three films on the big screen, as abridged versions of a six-part television series. This set of circumstances promotes the idea of flowing transitions from one form to another, and this is echoed in the following analysis's easy shuttling from discussions of written narrative forms and extracts from the novels to an appraisal of film conventions and moments. It is an underlying objective of this book not to restrict the content to studies of adaptation from page to screen, but to allow instead for more fluent comparisons to emerge across and within the chapters.

1

NATION, GENRE, INSTITUTION

What makes these fictions' involvement in the 'borderless world' of the global era most fascinating is their nationality. On a broad level, this relationship often demands attention; as Jonas Frykman notes, 'The more Europe is integrated and the world is globalised, the quicker the dissolution of sedimented practices, routines and traditions proceeds, then all the more national identity is discussed, given a sharper profile and challenged.'[47] As well as existing within the collective group of Europe and Scandinavia, Sweden is also a 'small nation'. Removing apostrophes from the term from here on in, this book follows the definition of small nation offered by the team of researchers – Steve Blandford, Stephen Lacey *et al.* – working in the Centre of the Study of Media and Culture in Small Nations at the University of Glamorgan:

> For the Centre, a small nation is defined, of course, by size in an absolute sense (of population, though not necessarily of landmass) but not only so. Small nations are a phenomenon of both the collapse of the old empires across the world after 1945 and deeper-rooted historical and cultural forces, combined with the assertion of localism within, and against, more established nation states in an increasingly globalised world. Small nations, therefore, are formed out of their often fractious relationship with larger neighbours.[48]

Historically, Sweden's impulsion towards homogeneity and neutrality ends in dissolution through the involvement of other countries. Two examples are of particular importance: transgression from the utopian model of the welfare state, and tentative involvements in war and the European Union. Both instances reveal tensions within the previously, staunchly, homogenous nation, of a country hesitantly opening up to the world. Francis Sejersted offers a concise understanding of the principles of Sweden's welfare state or 'the Scandinavian model':

> In the 1930s, the Social Democratic parties of Sweden and Norway came to power and formed governments in their respective countries. This marked the beginning of a stable period of Social Democratic hegemony. These parties had taken root at the beginning of the twentieth century as revolutionary Marxist parties. They gradually shook off their Marxism, and by the beginning of their period of hegemony they had managed to wrest the great modernization project from the non-Socialist parties and put their own stamp on it. The result is what we might call the Social Democratic order – also called the Scandinavian model, or simply the Swedish or Nordic model ...
>
> The Scandinavian model is marked – to cite just a few of its characteristic traits – by comprehensiveness of social security systems, institutionalized universal social rights, a high level of public support, and a high level of equality, which grew out of a combination of public commitment to the principle of universalism and equality of income distribution, which, in turn, is partly attributable to the strength of the trade unions.[49]

Under this model, Sweden was an export nation. Like the archipelago, it comprised an intricate system of small bodies working together as a homogenous whole. As Sejersted notes, 'Under Social Democracy ... we find the development of a very tight network linking the interests of organizations and the administration.'[50] The emphasis is on countrywide collectivism and protectionism from outside intervention. And yet, with the onset of the Second World War, Sweden struggled to assert its favoured stance of neutrality, with resultant senses of anxiety that resonate into the present day.

In *Sweden, the Swastika and Stalin: The Swedish Experience in the Second World War*, John Gilmour provides an intricate account of the social and political complexities rife at this time in the country's history. Gilmour presents a dual stronghold of separatism as 'the two histories of wartime Sweden. One covers the outward facing struggle to keep Sweden from being drawn into the war while maintaining the welfare and freedom of its citizens. The other covers the immense official and communal effort on the Home Front to mobilise the country's defences, resources and security.'[51] Yet, outside and inside Sweden, protectionist principles are slowly and surely chipped away by the facts of war. Initially, the country's stance appears resolute. Sejersted summarises the historical situation:

> Norway was invaded by Germany on April 9, 1940. The official Swedish reaction to the invasion was expressed in Prime Minister Hansson's radio broadcast three days later. He stressed that Sweden was 'firmly resolved to continue to follow the strict line of neutrality.' This meant that Sweden not only refused to come to the rescue of its former union partner but also, for fear of German reprisal, went a long way toward fulfilling Germany's demands ... [Post-war] it was possible in Sweden to put the traumatic events to rest and establish a national consensus based on the fact that the government's pragmatic policy of compliance with Germany had been reasonable and necessary. It was seen as being to the credit of the coalition government that Sweden had managed to avoid being drawn into the war. Unlike in Norwegian society, no lines of demarcation between innocent and guilty were drawn.[52]

However, as encapsulated by the title of one Gilmour's chapters, there are 'Shades of Neutrality'. As the then Prime Minister Per Albin declared in 1938:

> The Swedish (Social Democrat) Party is not prepared for absolute neutrality. We say instead 'we shall keep ourselves out of the war'. But can we also achieve that? If a situation arises where we cannot keep ourselves out, then we must ensure that we come in on the right side. Even as a neutral, we must have our thinking directed to where our natural position is. We must look further than neutrality. [53]

The complexities of varying social groups' input and undercurrents of feeling would, perhaps inevitably, complicate this official line. Most significantly, there is a notable measure of extremist political views in pre-war Sweden, displayed in fragmentary far right collectives:

> Two main groups evolved, the Swedish National Socialist Party under Birger Furugård and the breakaway National Socialist Workers Party led by Sven-Olof Lindholm. While these failed even to achieve the one per cent of the vote required for *Riksdag* representation, they were more successful in local elections. Other organisations such as the secretive and extreme 'Brown Guard' (who regarded Lindholm as a traitor to Hitler and Germany) were more interested in extra-democratic activities. One estimate of overall membership of Nazi organisations puts it around 30,000 in the mid-1930s.[54]

While small, these groups would affect Sweden's stance on a local level and represent a strand of anti-Semitism also lurking in the country's social psyche. In turn, these factors combined with Sweden's disturbing involvement in forced sterilisation projects:

> In Sweden, Jews – along with Catholics – had traditionally been discriminated against on religious grounds but when nineteenth-century scientific racial studies developed into

full-blown eugenics in the twentieth century, this distinction shifted to racial characteristics. To underline the contemporary respectability of such work, the State Race Biology Institute opened in 1922 with all-party agreement. Their well-meaning focus on the categorisation of people in order to cultivate and safeguard the Swedish 'race' leading to improved lives for all, nevertheless increased the separateness of the Jewish community and of course boosted Swedish interest in Nazi racial theories.

The defensive political mindset that supported the protection of race also led to the discussion of forced sterilisation for the 'mentally deficient' as early as 1922. This practice began in Sweden in 1935 following its earlier introduction in thirty-three American States, as well as Denmark, Norway and Finland. Forced sterilisation in Sweden persisted until 1975, claiming over 60,000 victims and its widespread acceptance can be gauged by only one politician opposing it at the time of introduction. Racial theory had also entered mainstream Swedish opinion facilitating open discussion of 'the Jewish question' but would provide a later unwelcome cultural association with the genocidal policies in Berlin.[55]

The reference to, and 'justification' of action against people via the categorisation of them as 'mentally deficient' recalls the treatment of Lisbeth Salander in the *Millennium* trilogy. Larsson's works form a forensic study of unpalatable truths existing under the surface of Swedish society, not least in the guise of Nazi sympathisers.

The realities of war would also complicate the assertion that Sweden had a 'natural position' to take alongside the 'right side'. Again, an initial stance of resistance and refusal would fall foul of wartime survivalist decision-making. In 1940, Sweden first refused Germany transit through its borders. And yet, as Gilmour sets out, 'Unfortunately, the primary Swedish tactic of refusing transit, on the grounds that the ongoing hostilities between Norwegian and German troops made it unthinkable to support action against fellow Scandinavians, had painted Sweden into a tactical corner. Sweden had relegated its neutrality status argument to a secondary position and the cessation of hostilities in Norway would inevitably bring about a German ultimatum.'[56] Increasingly, desperate to ensure its own supplies, Sweden became caught up in its concessions and encirclement by Germany. The awkwardly close relationship with Germany disrupted Sweden's ties with its Scandinavian neighbours, Norway and Denmark. German reversals on transit in 1943 would ultimately alleviate this uncomfortable position, and restore some sense, for Sweden, of its much-prized belief in national independence and neutrality.

The 'official line' would later be taken up by others, in Establishment portrayals of this difficult period in Sweden's history. As Gilmour illustrates in an astute example, 'the author of "Swedish History" (*Svensk historia*), a text book whose aim was to "ensure that events in our country are correctly understood"'[57] paints this picture of the Second World War:

> Several times, Sweden came into the danger-zone when its peace and freedom were exposed to great risks ... Under pressure from Germany's threatening power-situation, the Swedish Government was forced to concede the demand [for transit] but on conditions that were thought to prevent these transits leading to risks for our country's security or to harm the Norwegian people ... in this case a deviation from strict neutrality ... The great dangers that threatened compelled the Swedish people to national unity ... In the western powers' interests, Swedish exports to Germany were cut back and discontinued completely in autumn 1944.[58]

This portrait remains carefully free of any political blemishes. Yet there still lurked the distasteful encouragements and alliances from Sweden's underground collectives of Nazi sympathisers. In these ways, Stieg Larsson's *The Girl with the Dragon Tattoo* provides an explosively revisionist history of Sweden during and after the Second World War. An investigation into one powerful Swedish family reveals microcosmic social schisms and veiled extremist tendencies.

Are you sitting comfortably? In the luxurious cloisters of the family estate on Hedeby Island, elderly statesman Henrik Vanger takes investigative journalist Mikael Blomkvist on a barbed trip down memory lane, snagging on the branches of his insidious family tree: "'Here's Richard with the veterinarian Birger Furugård, soon to become the leader of the so-called Furugård movement, the big Nazi movement of the early 30s. But Richard did not stay with him. He joined, a few years later, the Swedish Fascist Battle Organisation, the S.F.B.O., and there he got to know Per Engdahl and others who would be the disgrace of the nation.'"[59] Larsson draws out into third-person to present a wider view of the Vangers' fascist involvements across the decades:

> In 1930 Harald and Gregaer had followed Richard's footsteps to Uppsala ... It was quite clear that the brothers all joined Per Engdahl's fascist movement, the New Sweden. Harald had loyally followed Per Engdahl over the years, first to Sweden's National Union, then to the Swedish Opposition Group, and finally the New Swedish Movement after the war. Harald continued to be a member until Engdahl died in the 90s, and for certain periods he was one of the key contributors to the hibernating Swedish fascist movement. Harald Vanger studied medicine in Uppsala and landed almost immediately in circles that were obsessed with race hygiene and race biology. For a time he worked at the Swedish Race Biology Institute, and as a physician he become a prominent campaigner for the sterilisation of undesirable elements in the population.[60]

As explored further in the next chapter, the Vanger clan represents the particularly Swedish stranglehold certain prominent families have on the industrial and economic well-being of the country. As the patriarch of such a powerful group, Harald Vanger's sinister involvement reaches into other areas of the social fabric, including those of the scientific communities. Tracing such ideologically warped interests across one character's lifetime, Larsson suggests the lasting influence of such behaviours on the Swedish sensibility.

In microcosmic form, 'Harald seemed to be an invisible but ever-present spirit who affected life in the village.'[61]

Post-war, the 'model society' of the welfare state would also inevitably suffer, and irreparably fracture in the 1970s. Waves of privatisation, and the new challenges posed by internationalisation and globalisation led Sweden towards a 'third way'.[62] As will be analysed in greater detail in Chapter 2, Sweden's emigration model gave way to an immigration society.[63] A longstanding balancing act had begun between national and international interests.

Paradise lost: the killing of Olof Palme

The assassination of Prime Minister Olof Palme in Stockholm in 1986 was equally fundamental to a shift in the national sensibility, and emblematic of a deep-seated rupturing of Sweden's conception of public and private sanctuary. Walking with his wife from the Riviera cinema on Sveavägen, Palme was gunned down in cold blood and plain view of his public supporters. As was common and ideologically significant for Nordic leaders, he had no security with him. After all, for many, Sweden seemed an 'open house'. Palme's death sent shockwaves through a society unused to political extremism of any kind, and led to a radical rethink of the open-government policy Sweden had pursued for decades.

Andrew Brown summarises the shift in his evocative autobiographical account *Fishing in Utopia: Sweden and the Future that Disappeared*:

> Until he was shot, the country had seemed to be focused on the light-grey modern centre which his cortège wound round on its way from the city hall to the graveyard: a clean region of government buildings, libraries, railway stations, department stores, employment exchanges, insurance companies, hotels and security offices, each very like the other. Now it was apparent that a terrible, disruptive power lurked outside these ordered precincts and held them at its mercy ...

No one knew whether the killer had come from within Sweden or from outside. There was a feeling of foreignness everywhere. It could have come from the outside – Palme's foreign policies had made him enemies practised in assassination. He was the UN's mediator in the Iran-Iraq war. He supported the ANC; some people thought the South Africans had had him killed. There was a theory that the Kurdish terrorists of the PKK had killed him. Croat fascist terrorists had operated in Sweden in the past. His murderer might have been a single Swedish madman – there might even have been a conspiracy of madmen.[64]

As Brown chillingly illustrates, the dream of an open, liberal state died with Palme, replaced by fears of the outsider and paranoid suspicion. It is unsurprising, then, that Swedish crime fiction would pick up on this famous, game-changing murder and mine its allegorical connotations. Moreover, just as terrorist activity in Chuck Palahniuk's 1996 novel and David Fincher's 1999 film of *Fight Club* would foreshadow the terrible events of 9/11 in 2001, the last of the Sjöwall and Wahlöö novels – *The Terrorists* (1975) – would present the then wholly unlikely nightmare scenario of a fictional Swedish Prime Minister's assassination. Brown notes how, perhaps even more alarmingly, this narrative event is presented as an almost cursory strand, secondary to the main storyline:

> Sjöwall and Wahlöö's terrorists are a sinister and ridiculous amalgam of Spectre and global capitalism; their leader is, of course, a white right-wing South African. They are hugely professional and have been hired to assassinate an American politician – a sort of Ronald Reagan figure – when he visits Stockholm. Only the collective genius of Beck and his team defeats them, by working out where they will plant the bomb, which will be detonated by remote control, and then arranging with Sveriges Radio to delay its live coverage by fifteen minutes, so that by the time the terrorists in their hiding place see the cortege go past, the police have cleared the area and damped down the explosion with sandbags.

The contrast of this cold-blooded efficiency with the panicked and incredulous inefficiency of both the police and Sveriges Radio when Palme was assassinated twelve years later could hardly be greater. But there is another, even more unreal element to *The Terrorists*. After the plot against the American senator has been foiled, the book's Swedish prime minister is murdered, almost casually. No one in the novel is greatly affected by the death of the prime minister. There is no suggestion of the convulsion of grief and self-reproach that affected the country when Palme was assassinated. At the precise moment when a sense of irreparable, adult loss overwhelmed the country in real life, the fiction retreated to childish impotence. The fact that it could shows what made the real loss so awful – that an assassination had been something so unthinkable in that it could be played with in daydreams without consequences.[65]

There is a sense that, both within the realist worlds of Swedish crime fiction and the social environment of Sweden in the 1970s, the murder of the Prime Minister is too outlandish an idea to entertain, thus moved to the sidelines of the narrative almost apologetically. This air of disbelief may have accounted in part for the ill-defined, uncertain treatment by the police of Palme's assassination, and the nebulous ambiguity that accompanies the case right to its (lack of) conclusion:

Christer Pettersson was tried and convicted of the Palme murder in 1988, largely on the strength of Lisbet Palme's identification, but later released on appeal – because she had understood from the police that he was guilty before being asked to identify him. The murder weapon was never found.[66]

Palme's murder strips Swedish society of any remaining sense of surety, absoluteness, and fixity. The utopian vision of a truly egalitarian welfare state dissolves, alongside the country's belief in its putatively neutral, protectionist status as a means of creating a free and safely open society. The uncertainty and lack of closure surrounding the identity of Palme's assassin enhances the feeling of threats existing both within and without Sweden's broken borders. Without resolution, the murder inflects and infects the country's sense of itself, caught up in hesitancy and the fear of an uncertain future.[67]

All of these associations hover over Swedish crime fiction, and imbue its narratives with another layer of dread. In offering gruesome scenarios akin to those of Palme's murder, the crime fictions both tap into the anxieties of the collective consciousness and offer therapeutic forms of closure, as their killers most often are caught and get their comeuppance: case closed.

Embracing the new world order?

Pervasive social anxieties about the encroaching presence of foreigners, and bureaucracy in public service, also led to the formation and rise of 'The New Democracy' in Sweden in the early 1990s. A drive towards privatisation only served, however, to increase the distrust in the power of the state. As Brown observes, 'By the end of [the 1990s] the country no longer seemed safe, prosperous or tolerant and even if at its core it still was those things, the progress towards ever-greater safety, prosperity, and tolerance had come to be a pious affirmation, not a historical fact.'[68]

In turn, another 'pious affirmation' – the assertion of neutrality – increasingly, some would say begrudgingly, gives way to tacit forms of interaction with neighbouring countries. Again, lines of demarcation are gradually effaced. Perhaps the most impactful example of Sweden's tentative steps towards international engagement comprises the country's joining the European Union in 1995. The move counters a long-standing opposition to membership, linked to Sweden's long-engrained policy of neutrality. In 'Sweden and the EU: Welfare State Nationalism and the Spectre of "Europe"', Lars Trägårdh sets out pervading national concerns about EU membership and highlights Sweden's stance as a complex combination of nervous hesitancy and vehement opposition:

> Many Europeans view the EU and the move towards an 'ever closer' union with mixed feelings. While security concerns and the 'peace argument' continue to play an important role, it is evident that with the fading memory of the Second World War, the receding threat of a Third World War, and the collapse of the Soviet Union, the process of economic and political integration has increasingly come to be complicated by concerns over 'national identity'. To some extent the emergence of neo-nationalism is an expression of the increasing split between the elites, who tend to be persuaded by integrationist arguments and seduced by the promise of increased economic growth, and the masses, who are both less 'European' in their outlook and more prone to feel threatened by unemployment thought to be linked to 'globalisation'. Thus the political climate has pushed to the fore the latent conflict between the EU 'project' and the *survivance* of the nation, to invoke a Québecois figure of anxiety ...
>
> From this perspective, Sweden has consistently proven to be one of the most Euro-negative of all the current member states. A reluctant late-comer to 'Europe', the Swedes joined the EU only in 1995 and then with only a slim majority of the population voting 'yes' after a heated and divisive debate. In fact, a considerable part of the population continues to oppose EU membership and the discourse on Europe is far more likely to express apprehension over the 'spectre of Europe' than confidence in the 'promise of Europe'.[69]

If Europe becomes a 'spectre' to accompany and increase uncertainties caught in the long shadow of Palme's murder, then the contemporary phenomenon of globalisation haunts Sweden in equal measure. A notoriously slippery, multivalent concept of economic, social, political, industrial, environmental, cultural, and psychological impact, globalisation will 'register aspectually in different parts of the world'.[70] As raised in the opening lines of this chapter, in the case of a small nation like Sweden, globalisation has a 'push-pull' effect. One can understand globalisation to offer an opportunity for parity and symbiotic exchange (cultural, financial) across continents and countries. At the same time, it can be read as an apologia or 'doublespeak' for cultural imperialism, through which the leading large nations can extract, assimilate, and replace the nation-specific values of a given country with its own hegemonic structures and wares. In turn, one reactive result is the bolstering of national identity and a renewed emphasis on regionalism, in face of the collective 'threat' of more anonymous pluralism. And yet, to withdraw from the global marketplace is to risk atrophying in the modern world. While separatist urges may be inspired by globalisation's ever-encroaching reach, the thrust of the global marketplace makes isolation impossible. Perhaps even more so than the impact of Palme's death and the entry into the EU, globalisation has had a profound socio-cultural effect on Sweden, especially in terms of the symbolic value it places as a nation on neutrality. As Allan Pred claims:

> Neutrality is not merely a policy that Sweden has pursued in one way or another since the mid-nineteenth century, but a value-laden term highly charged with taken-for-granted meanings, a term long regarded as unforfeitable, a term deeply sedimented in the collective consciousness of much of the Swedish population. 'Neutrality' has served as a symbol for the nation's freedom, for its position outside of power-bloc alignments, for its consequent ability to take an independent stance on important international issues ... But now the meaning(fulness) and necessity of neutrality had been thrown into question ... would have to be heard and seen differently, if not totally surrendered to hegemonic claims.[71]

Even more subjectively, some scholars see Sweden's small-nation position in an era of global engagement as at absolute odds with the country's collective sensibility of separatism. In his wonderfully outmoded yet lyrically evocative account *On Being Swedish*, Paul Britten Austin gives us a flavour of this 'old Swedish style':

> The cold and distant manner of a Swedish waitress as she takes your order; the icy impersonality of a telephone operator, as if she hated all callers or suspected they were trying to get off with her by the mere act of asking for a number; the usually distant and unsmiling manner of a Swedish hotel porter: all these are part and parcel of this detached and abstract tone of polite intercourse. The old Swedish style was ever: You keep your distance and I'll keep mine.[72]

Contemporary crime dramas like those of Mankell and Larsson explore how 'keeping one's distance' in the global age becomes increasingly problematic. By their generic nature, the texts involve themselves in a pursuit to truth, of getting increasingly close to finding a murderer. In turn, the fictional criminals enact forms of involuntary intimacy: violating the space and bodies of others. After the killing and during the investigation, secrets and scandals involving suspects and victims alike start to emerge, as their personal lives are placed under the microscope. The works' achievement stems from their ability to bind socio-political struggles of separation with those of their human characters' physical location and psychological disposition.

The heritage of a socially conscious cinema

Just as the crime novels of the 1960s to the present day reflect and comment on Sweden's changing status, so too does the country's cinematic output. As with the emergence of a particularly angry artistry in the 1960s via the works of Sjöwall and Wahlöö, the period is central to the formation of a corresponding national aesthetic of film:

> Film-makers in Sweden have been prompted, like everyone, by impulses from either within or beyond their own country. During the 1960s, however, a conspicuous proportion of the

new directors drew their inspiration from social conditions in Sweden – and from political issues prevailing outside the Nordic area. Fantasy took second place to a jarring grainy realism that sought to use film if not quite as agit-prop then certainly as an essay form, a vehicle for comment on injustice and corruption.[73]

As a prime example of Swedish film's intervention into the spreading sense of corruption coming from inside and outside national boundaries, Peter Cowie points to *A Dream of Freedom* (*En dröm om frihet*, dir. Jan Halldoff, 1969), inspired by a police case of the mid-1960s, and *491* (dir. Vilgot Sjöman, 1964), adapted by writer Lars Görling from his novel of the same name. Both examples and Cowie's readings are worth attending to in detail, not least as illustrative of central socio-cultural concerns of the cinema of the period. Of *A Dream of Freedom*, Cowie writes:

> Two young criminals, from different social milieux, join together to rob a bank. During the escape, they are stopped by a police car, and one of the officers is killed. The fugitives reach Copenhagen, where they splurge part of their loot, but are then forced to hide once again in Sweden. Their capture is a grim affair in a snow-shrouded field, with a police helicopter sweeping down and giving the scene the dimensions of a hunt ... The attractions of crime for young people in such a balanced and well-funded society as Sweden remains perplexing to artists and authorities alike.[74]

Immediately, Cowie and the film highlight the correlation in Sweden between criminality and youth. That is to say, crime is seen as a fundamentally modern force, with the implicit suggestion that the contemporary world order, of external influences bearing down on the 'balanced and well-funded' welfare state, is to blame. Then, there is a border crossing, in which the criminals seek refuge in a neighbouring country – here, Denmark. Again, the implication that it is Sweden's permeability, in contrast to its separatist past, that facilitates crime, is centrally posited. Finally, the two images chosen to mark the bank-robbers' capture – 'a grim affair in a snow-shrouded field, with a police helicopter sweeping down and giving the scene the dimensions of a hunt' – are to be seen time and again in Swedish crime fictions in written and filmed form, across the decades. A frozen landscape repeatedly features in the books by Mankell, Marklund, and Theorin, and is brought vividly to life in the screen adaptations. Connotations cluster (or snowball) around the wintry elements: of coldness, distance, neutrality, and concealment. The police helicopter offers a particular vantage point that taps simultaneously into collective anxieties about surveillance and a desire to see the 'bigger picture' clearly in times of uncertainty, picking out the felonious elements from the social fabric. Two notable examples from crime fiction are found in the works of Sjöwall and Wahlöö and their accompanying film versions: *The Abominable Man* (*Den vedervärdige mannen från Säffle*, 1971) and its cinematic counterpart *The Man on the Roof* (*Mannen på taket*, dir. Bo Widerberg, 1976); and *The Laughing Policeman* (dir. Stuart Rosenberg, 1973) of the novel of the same name (*Den skrattande polisen*, 1968).

Cowie textures his analysis by looking back to an earlier film adaptation:

> [In 1964], Vilgot Sjöman had adapted the sensational book, *491*, by Lars Görling, in a clear challenge to the social welfare system. Six youthful delinquents are placed together in an apartment as some kind of obscure 'experiment' by an elderly welfare inspector and a young social worker. The tension among the delinquents reaches a combustible level long before some of them take up with a girl (played by Lena Nyman) and humiliate and exploit her sexual appeal – culminating in a notorious sequence involving her 'rape' by an Alsatian dog. In this quasi-documentary, Sjöman passes a harsh judgement on the supervisors of the Welfare Board, who are seen as more corrupt than the youths they control. Probation becomes a punishment, and boredom a breeding-ground for violence and perversion.[75]

Seen in the 2010s, the allegorical presentation of a microcosmic social experiment (that is either inherently immoral or goes dangerously wrong) recalls other, later film works as varied as *Punishment Park* (dir. Peter Watkins, 1971), *THX1138* (dir. George Lucas, 1971), *Salò or the 120 Days of Sodom* (*Salò o le 120 giornate di Sodoma*, dir. Pier Paolo Pasolini, 1975), and *The Experiment* (*Das experiment*, dir. Oliver Hirschbiegel, 2001). More precisely, Sjöman and Görling give us the first explicit example of a central leitmotif in Swedish crime fiction: of a country championing socialism and social democracy suffering from inherent inequalities coming, inevitably, from its governing bodies. Praising the value of the collective, the country in turn opens itself up to the intrinsic corruption of a state in control of the individual, breeding contempt. Stieg Larsson strikingly revisits and updates this national preoccupation in the *Millennium* trilogy, most notably through the treatment and characterisation of Lisbeth Salander. Effectively orphaned (in typically extreme and politically charged circumstances – setting fire to her father after his repeated abuse of her mother) and placed in the care of the state, Salander is deemed incapable of looking after herself. Her designation as 'mentally unstable' is authorised by the government and she is placed in psychiatric care, against her will, under the abusive watch of Dr Teleborian at St Stephen's Hospital (a state-controlled institution). Upon her release and on the death of a kindly guardian, a new state-appointed Advocat – Nils Bjurman – subjects Salander to sexual degradation. As Sarah E. H. Moore insightfully observes,

> Through all of this the novels ask us to think about the relationship between storytelling, power, and justice. They make plain the special credence given to stories told by social authorities, and the risks of corruption therein; they reveal the degradation in having state officials document the details of one's life; and they show us that the failure of official agents of the state to listen to an individual's version of events can have grievous consequences. Larsson is clearly interested in how and why certain stories are suppressed. Women's untold

stories are of especial significance to him, whether it is that of Harriet Vanger's sexual abuse or Lisbeth Salander's rape. Larsson wishes, of course, to make something of a political point here: the suppression of stories of female embattlement is done in the maintenance of patriarchal social control.[76]

Before opening out these thematic strands and socio-political concerns – delinquency, the state, female embattlement, social authorities – in more detail across the rest of the chapters, it is vital to first provide another contextual scaffold for the works, exploring their generic status as crime fictions.

Identifying crime

John Scaggs' monograph *Crime Fiction* is a touchstone work on the origins, conventions, and sub-genres of the field, and provides a useful starting point. Scaggs' introduction affirms both the popularity of the genre and complications arising from attempts to definitively characterise such a polyvalent form:

> It is worth noting at the outset that while the old adage that crime does not pay might well be true, crime has nevertheless been the foundation for an entire genre of fiction for over one hundred and fifty years. In fact it is the centrality of crime to a genre that otherwise, in its sheer diversity, defies any simple classification that has led me to adopt the title 'Crime Fiction' for this volume. Throughout its history, various titles have been coined to classify and describe the genre. From Edgar Allen Poe's 'tales of ratiocination', to the mystery and detective fiction of the turn of the twentieth century and the whodunit of the period between the First World War and the Second World War, a focus on crime, but only sometimes its investigation, has always been central to the genre. For this reason, the majority of critical studies of the genre over the past twenty years employ the term 'crime fiction' to classify an otherwise unclassifiable genre, and this study will be no different.[77]

In this respect, *Swedish Crime Fiction* is no different, either. But perhaps Scaggs is being too modest here, as his work indeed probes the 'sheer diversity' in exacting detail, the results of which are also particularly useful in helping us identify some of the main figures and features of Swedish work in the genre, across written and filmed forms. In her award-winning book *Talking about Detective Fiction*, celebrated crime writer P. D. James offers equally acute readings of the genre's and subgenres' classifying markers. If one baulks at the inclusion of an interview with the writer of a vampire story – John Ajvide Lindqvist's *Let the Right One In* – in this volume, then James's purposefully attention-grabbing discussion of Jane Austen's *Emma* as a seminal work of detective fiction will also come as a surprise:

> Novels which enshrine a mystery, often involving a crime, and which provide the satisfaction of an ultimate solution are, of course, common in the canon of English literature, and most would never be thought of in terms of detective fiction ... perhaps the most interesting example of a mainstream novel which is also a detective story is the brilliantly structured *Emma* by Jane Austen. Here the secret which is the mainspring of the action is the unrecognised relationships between the limited number of characters. The story is confined to a closed society in a rural setting, which was to become common in detective fiction, and Jane Austen deceives us with cleverly constructed clues (eight immediately come to mind) – some based on action, some on apparently innocuous conversations, some in her authorial voice. At the end, when all becomes plain and the characters are at last united with their right partners, we wonder how we could have been so deceived.[78]

While the example is, of course, positioned to encourage us to question our predetermined understanding of the genre's boundaries, it also proves precisely illustrative of some of the most established conventions of the form. The description picks out key markers including: a closed circle of suspects in a contained setting; clues, concealments, and revelations of the characters' relationships; the governing voice of the author constructing the 'modus operandi' of the plot; the pleasurable deceptions of the reader; the guiding and obscuring of our own deductions; and, ultimately, the provision of solutions to a mystery. To return to the matter of *Let the Right One In* (whether or not it *should* be let into a book on crime fiction), James also offers a cogent affirmation of the essential role of horror tropes in the detective genre:

> One strand of the tangled skein of detective fiction goes back to the eighteenth century and includes the gothic tales of horror written by Ann Radcliffe and Matthew 'Monk' Lewis. Those gothic novelists were chiefly concerned to enthral readers with tales of terror and the horrific plight of the heroine, and although these books embodied puzzles and riddles, they were concerned far more with horror than with mystery.[79]

From Edgar Allan Poe's dovetailing of detection and horror, to the Gothic elements of Sherlock Holmes battling the ghostly hounds of Baskerville, to the ghoulish predilections of Dr Hannibal Lecter, the two forms have always shared strong family resemblances and narrative space. Indeed, as James opines, 'Some critics might argue that horror plays a far greater part than ratiocination in the modern psychological mysteries which deal primarily with atrocious serial murders by psychopaths.'[80] As we shall see, Swedish crime fiction offers its own distinctive, grisly iterations of this generic hybrid.

The reader is encouraged to turn to Scaggs' and James's works for compendious accounts of crime genre's many historical manifestations; for our purposes, it is enough to note several of the most common sub-genres, and their rendering in Swedish form.

Golden Age detectives and hard-boiled PIs

Most helpfully, James provides a concise description of both types of protagonist in a comparative summary:

The differences between the hard-boiled school and such Golden Age writers as Agatha Christie, Dorothy L. Sayers and Michael Innes, are so profound that it seems stretching a definition to describe both groups under the same category. If the British detective story is concerned with bringing order out of disorder, a genre of reconciliation and social healing, restoring the mythical village of Mayhem Parva to prelapsarian tranquility, in the United States [Dashiell] Hammett and [Raymond] Chandler were depicting and exploring the great social upheavals of the 1920s – lawlessness, prohibition, corruption, the power and violence of notorious gangsters who were close to becoming folk heroes, the cycle of boom and depression – and creating detectives who were inured to this world and could confront it on their own terms.[81]

The most pronounced example of the hard-boiled detective in Swedish crime fiction is Martin Beck and, particularly, his on-screen incarnation as Jake Martin as played by Walter Matthau in (fittingly, the American film) *The Laughing Policeman*. Matthau's distinctive style of performance perfectly matches the gruff world-weariness of the PI. Film scholar David Thomson provides an evocative portrait of the screen actor's brow-beaten gumshoe qualities. More precisely, the specific timbre of Thomson's critical sketch and scepticism of Matthau suggests that the actor is caught up in, through performance, a tangled skein of disguise, deception, and derision that is in complete kinship with the same factors so often at play in the world of the hard-boiled detective:

He is a great technician, in terms of movement, response, wisecrack, and exaggerated alarm, even though his sourness usually derides phoniness and self-deception. As a result, it is not easy to gauge Matthau's own nature, for he is fixed in the idiom of smart self-derision and always offers the brilliant spectacle of disguise mocking the need for disguise. The skill of his playing sometimes tends to dispel his assumed misanthropy. And if none of his films is without flaw, that may be because of a final reluctance on Matthau's part to reveal himself. So schooled to the wisecrack, he may be unable to talk straight.[82]

Here, then, is the jaded loner detective, so entrenched in cynicism that he cannot present himself directly to the world, able only to express himself through the sweet, hard-boiled language of Chandler *et al.*

Private eye to public eye: the development of the police procedural

Scaggs offers a lucid account of a different, more recent sub-genre with a long lineage:

> In its emphasis on regulatory authority and social control, there is a sense in which the lineage of the police procedural stretches back as far as the Old Testament stories from the Book of Daniel, or at least to the *Newgate Calendar* stories … the first police procedural is generally acknowledged as being Hillary Waugh's *Last Seen Wearing* (1952) …
>
> In the procedural, it is the police detective as part of the state apparatus of the police force who safeguards society through vigilant and unceasing surveillance, in this way replacing the often questionable vigilante justice of the PI. The transition from hard-boiled fiction to police procedural is, there, a transition from the *private* eye, in the sense of personal, small-scale, and often self-serving investigation, to the *public* eye, in the sense of civic, large-scale policing that serves society as a whole.[83]

Useful as preliminary descriptions, these accounts so far leave out two factors I am particularly keen to emphasise in the readings that follow. First, and as suggested by James's examples from Austen and Gothic horror, is the unstoppable bleeding between generic categories. Correspondingly, in many instances of Swedish crime drama, one work can embody aspects of the Golden Age detective and police procedural *et al.* altogether at the same time. And the combination of different sub-genres can change from novel to film to television series of the same story. For example, in Rosenberg's film of *The Laughing Policeman*, the Beck/Martin character blends PI wisecracks with forensic scrutiny of the police working as an amorphous collective (in procedural duties). As previously noted in this book's Introduction's summary of the *Millennium* trilogy, Stieg Larsson is famously adept at combining the sub-genres of crime drama to striking effect. Secondly, the descriptions do not include references to the appearance, handling, patterns, and variations of visual iconography in the crime drama. Like the Western, the crime fiction offers some of the most vivid imagery and tropes of any genre. The comparison points towards one of the reasons why cinema and television have so readily adopted the form for their own purposes, adding their own unforgettable icons and signifiers in costume, setting, and décor. As Scaggs observes,

> [Mystery and detective fiction] represents the earliest consolidation of various themes, devices and motifs within single texts. [It has] also had more time than later developments of the genre to be appropriated by later fiction but also, more importantly, by other media, most notably film and television. What people remember about characters like Sherlock Holmes, or Hercules Poirot, are strong visual images: Holmes in a deerstalker hat smoking a pipe, Poirot with his waxed moustache and supercilious expression. The vividness of both of these images has more to do with the appropriation of mystery and detective fiction for both the large and small screen than it has to do with the number of people who have read the stories of Arthur Conan Doyle or the novels of Agatha Christie. Similarly, the image of the hard-boiled detective in hat and overcoat with a gun in his hand is largely inherited from cinema and television.[84]

Some films and television series are alert to the immediate impact, associations, and meanings of certain generically established tropes, *and* to the individually expressive possibilities of the filmed image. Bo Widerberg's *The Man on the Roof* (1976) is a good example of a work reflecting key elements of the police procedural and transforming the material through audio-visual style. Widerberg brings an auteurist's sensibility to crime drama, finding artistic freedom within the putative restrictions and parameters of the genre. In the mould of the 1970s US procedural/detective thriller like *Dirty Harry* (dir. Don Siegel, 1971), *The Conversation* (dir. Francis Ford Coppola, 1974), and *The Taking of Pelham One Two Three* (dir. Joseph Sargent, 1974), the film employs many (then radical) strategies of hard-edged realist style.

For example, one particularly striking aspect at work in this mode is the handling of diegetic sound. Dialogue and conversations often overlap in a manner reminiscent of Robert Altman's *M*A*S*H* (1970), with both films using the hectoring sonic mix to convey their characters' and represented community's inability to communicate in a clear and unified way. At the same time, *The Man on the Roof* is infused with more expressionistic elements, recalling strategies employed by Martin Scorsese in his creation of urban and psychological landscapes in *Taxi Driver* that same year (1976). In *A Cinema of Loneliness: Penn, Stone, Kubrick, Scorsese, Spielberg, Altman*, Robert Kolker makes compelling claims for Scorsese's elemental fusion of setting, *mise-en-scène*, and characterisation. In particular, he suggests that the handling of city locales is 'reflective of the energy of the characters ... coloured by the characters' perspective', as indicative of 'a method of integrating the character with the space he occupies so that the two become reflections of each other in a mutually defining mise-en-scène.'[85]

The handling of setting and place as expressive of a character's distorted sensibility carries into *The Man on the Roof* from its opening images onwards. The first scene introduces the killer and is indicative of the film's precise combination of realist and expressionist strategies. Lighting is pronouncedly dramatic (or perhaps, better, Expressionistic), keeping the killer in shadowy silhouette while suggesting a darkly shrouded mind-set. The pockets of light point up the tight confines of the character's living space, opening up an expressive pattern of interest in aspects of restriction across the film. And yet, alongside such poetic techniques, the composition also places the killer's laundry in the back of the frame and apartment: a workaday element familiar from realist film-making. The world is at once one of particularly pointillist detailing of the everyday and a more Expressionist state of (unhinged) being.

This combination carries across into the colours and designs of the street settings: smoky, neon-lit arrangements, its colours simultaneously true to those of real things in the world (red traffic lights, yellow billboards, green cars, blue window frames) *and* evocative of a fevered mind – all shining a little *too* brightly in the night. In turn, the film builds resonance around particular colours and images: there are bursting red blooms of flowers in the first victim's hospital room and in Inspector Beck's house, twinning assailant and captor. For the murder of the first victim – Stefan Nyman (Harald Hamrell) – the film takes things even further. In combining aspects of realist and poetic filmmaking, it also blurs the boundaries between crime drama and horror. While situated firmly, in style and setting, in the realm of our reality (not stepping across into the supernatural), the build-up to Nyman's death in his hospital bed is also reminiscent of Dario Argento's stylistic saturations in horror films. It pre-dates and strikingly resembles Argento's visual orchestrations of the first murder in *Suspiria* by a year. In Argento's film, the glowing eyes of a ghoulish entity emerge from an outside window, before the demon smashes the glass to claim its prey. In *The Man on the Roof*, Nyman (and camera) spot a single shining eyeball of the killer before a knife plunges through the curtain into the victim's body. The voluminous gushes of bright red blood are equal in both works, and take them to the tipping point of narrative film into moments of nightmarish abstraction. As further examples of Widerberg's film and others will show in the chapters to come, the visual signifiers of crime fiction can, dependent on the work's aesthetics, carry deep resonances and surprising, specific complexities.

One final example points up Swedish crime fiction's potentially expressive juxtapositions of characters' physical and psychological condition and those of the country: states and States. Of Inspectors Beck and Wallander, Kerstin Bergman argues that, 'These heroes react both physically and mentally to the problems in society, and they are particularly, and most explicitly, disillusioned by the dissolving welfare state.'[86] In turn, their physical and psychological flaws embody those of their native country. Bergman continues, 'There is a typically Swedish disappointment in these novels, a wounded idealism which would be more difficult to find in countries with a harsher everyday reality and more desperate class differences: the big disappointment requires that there was once a dream which appeared close to being realized.'[87] Disillusionment and disappointment caused by a shattered dream become, in the generic worlds of the crime drama, a variety of internal and external wounds.

Then, in Swedish crime fiction, physical lesions are both combined with and caused by a pervasive, collective sense of disillusionment coming from, variously, the bitterness of the past, and cynicism of the future, caught up in the bleakness of the landscape. We know this as 'Scandinavian gloom'. As many scholars have observed, this 'gloom' infuses many of the great artistic works of Scandinavia, beyond the novel, film, and television, to music (Sibelius, Pettersson), poetry, and the theatre (Strindberg, Ibsen). An entry from London critical review *The Month* from 1866 refers to the phrase in relation to the story of Arne: 'The general tone of this tale is happy and genial, though there are one or two shades of truly Scandinavian gloom ... The manners described are simple and almost patriarchal, though the standard of morality seems hardly to stand at the highest level among the country folk in Norway.'[88] The phrase still has currency. For example, as recently as March 2012, the Ibsen Stage Company organised a talk in London entitled 'Scandinavian Gloom or Room for Something New', stating similar concerns to those of this book: 'the aim of this talk is to understand why there is a growing interest in Scandinavian culture and to reflect on what Scandinavia is currently offering to the cultural life of the UK'.[89] Crime fiction is a particularly apt receptacle for such concerns: offering perfectly morbid conditions for a distillation of disillusionment.

The strength of the weak

Other feelings that run deep through Swedish society take us to the final context to be explored in this chapter – the institutional circumstances of crime fiction in visual form. Sensitivity about local shortcomings and disenchantment with its place in the world both inflect and are engendered by the status of Sweden as a small nation in the global age. At the meeting point of artistic and commercial output, this anxiety is manifest most explicitly in the situation of the country's film industry. As previously delineated, globalisation can be perceived as a tacit form of cultural imperialism. Associated uncertainties are connected to the terms and realities of a small-nation cinema or 'minor cinema', as Mette Hjort explains:

> In the area of film culture, as I have argued elsewhere (Hjort 1996), small-nation status is typically linked to the production of 'minor cinema'. In cultural studies, the term *minor* is associated with Gilles Deleuze and Felix Guattari's insightful work on 'minor literature', a concept anchored in their understanding of Franz Kafka's writings and linked to the idea of subverting a dominant *national* language or culture from within. The term *minor* points, then, to the existence of regimes of cultural power and to the need for strategic resourcefulness on the part of those who are unfavourably situated within the cultural landscape in question, be it a national context or a more properly global one.[90]

While speaking of Denmark, Hjort's qualification of a small nation engaged in the production of minor cinema is equally apposite to our reflections on Sweden. Both countries have a population too small to 'sustain a commercially based, indigenous film industry' without economic assistance from external forces.[91] Both produce work in a language that is by and large only spoken by the nation in question, making it 'difficult to expand the market for film through export and international distribution.'[92] Above all, both have to respond to the 'ongoing influx and dominant presence of American films'.[93]

Hjort goes further afield to develop thoughts on the changing dynamics of globalisation and its impact on Scandinavia's small-nation cinemas (as representative of its commercially driven artistic output in the 2000s). Drawing on comparative quantitative data, Tom O' Regan offers insightful analysis of Australian cinema as reflective of 'foreign language' film in terms of asymmetries of recognition, access, and viability on a global level. Like other small national cinemas, it is seen as marked by unequal cultural exchange due to the pre-eminent role played by imports.[94] For Hjort, 'O' Regan usefully emphasizes the ways in which Australian cinema negotiates "political and cultural weakness", foregrounding the role of cultural transfers in what is to a significant extent an "import culture" ... In many ways O' Regan's important study demonstrates, in detail and in relation to film culture, what Katzenstein earlier referred to as the "traditional paradox in international relations concerning the strength of the weak" (1985, 21).'[95]

Perhaps ironically, as a single player struggling to assert its place on the contemporary world stage, one of the most important strengths of Sweden as a 'weak' minor cinema stems from its entrenched ideological belief in the power of the collective. That is to say, the close (some would say suffocating) relationship between the state and public bodies gives rise, historically, to key initiatives in Swedish film and television. The two most significant developments were those of the Swedish Film Institute (SFI), and the Nordic Film and TV Fund in the 1960s and the 1980s respectively. Both initiatives would put in play determining factors on a local level that would inspire 'new generations' of filmmaking, the likes of which still comprise the majority of Sweden's cinematic output in today's global marketplace. Anders Marklund reflects on industrial and socio-historical factors surrounding the Swedish Film Institute's emergence in 1963:

> The 1960s was an interesting decade in Swedish cinema – just as it was in many other countries around the world – with a number of developments going on simultaneously. Institutional changes included the creation of Svenska filmin-stitutet (Swedish Film Institute) in 1963 with its influential financial support, the removal of the cinema tax, and rapidly falling cinema attendance after the introduction of televi-sion in Sweden in 1956. Among technological changes one should mention the improved documentary-based 16mm equipment, which would now be used in a number of feature films. There were also other changes, ranging from the influ-ential inspiration of the French *Nouvelle vague* (New Wave) to a heightened political awareness in society and among many filmmakers.[96]

Thus as with the given example of the French New Wave, new technological advancements would facilitate a documentary-style aesthetic, in turn informed by a drive of liberal political activism. Pre-eminent film historian Peter Cowie talks of two influential booklets appearing in Sweden in 1962, reflecting these changing affairs and a kindred spirit with Truffaut, Godard, *et al.*:

> One was a diatribe against the quality of Swedish film, *The Vision in the Swedish Cinema* ('Visionen i svensk film'), written by Bo Widerberg the writer and director, who argued that films made in Sweden were divorced from real life, and tended towards escapism and character stereotypes. Widerberg also attacked Ingmar Bergman, the high priest of Swedish cinema during the previous decade: 'Bergman welcomes the coarsest myths about us and ours, emphasises the false notions which foreigners love to have confirmed,' he wrote, going on to reproach the master for his 'vertical cinema' in which man in neither humbled nor exalted. 'The book as a protest,' declared Widerberg with the hindsight of

after years. 'Every new Swedish film was a disaster; it had absolutely no connection with modern society.'

The other key publication was *Can We Afford Culture?* ('Har vi råd med kultur?') by Harry Schein ... His plan of action involved the abandonment of the 25% entertainment tax, and its replacement by a levy of 10% on each cinema ticket sold, the proceeds of which would be funnelled into a new organ altogether – the Swedish Film Institute. 'The Swedish Film Institute expresses in this way,' Schein maintained, 'the status of a free film production in a modern welfare state, in which the government abstains from direct control of production, economically, thematically, or artistically, provided that the film industry recognises its responsibility not only towards its shareholders but towards the art of film as well.'[97]

Important fiscal determinants meet with an acute social agenda. Frustrated by the 'Quality' cinema produced in the past (like the case of the French New Wave), a new generation of filmmakers – led by Bo Widerberg – favour work that is more immediately reflective of contemporary society. The assertion that the government supports such work 'provided that the film industry recognises its responsibility not only towards its shareholders but towards the art of film as well' becomes complicated in the 1970s, during a vast economic downturn. At that time, what is considered 'responsible' filmmaking becomes increasingly bound up with what is considered 'commercially viable', in a way that is strikingly evocative of the UK government's own current position on British cinema in 2012. In both cases, the film industries are urged to make more mainstream work.[98] This leads, inevitably, to a greater emphasis on genre filmmaking:

> The directors who would make most films during the 1970s were closely related to genre production. Mac Ahlberg (aka Bert Torn) and Torgny Wickman, who made most films – twelve and nine respectively – made sex/pornographic films, with titles such as *Porr i skandalskolan/Second Coming*

of Eva (Mac Ahlberg, 1974), and *Kyrkoherden/The Lustful Vicar* (Torgny Wickman, 1970). Olle Hellbom, working closely with the producer Olle Nordemar, made eight features in their series of children's/family films based on works by Astrid Lindgren. Jan Halldoff also made eight films in different genres, for example *Jack/*'Jack' (Jan Halldoff, 1976), based on poet, rock singer and writer Ulf Lundell's successful debut novel. Previously creatively free filmmakers like Bo Widerberg would find significantly fewer possibilities, and would be less productive or be pushed into making genre films. Widerberg made only three features with distribution in cinemas in Sweden during the 1970s, among them the celebrated crime film *Mannen på taket/The Man on the Roof* (Bo Widerberg, 1976).[99]

This book, as a work celebrating, in part, achievements in crime thrillers, is rather less gloomy in its reading of the shift in Sweden's film industry towards genre filmmaking. This is particularly the case in terms of Widerberg's presence as a creatively influential figure and genre filmmaker. As stated earlier, I see Widerberg bringing an authorial signature to his crime film, working within the genre's boundaries in a way reminiscent of Hawks or Hitchcock. This critical stance is, in the chapters that follow, adopted in relation to other, more modern filmmakers and creators of television series. The most important factor to note here is that the socially charged, technologically liberated aesthetic of film in Sweden of the 1960s infuses the genre works that follow.

Whereas the implementation of the Film Institute in the 1960s encouraged the transformation of certain local features of Swedish cinema, the Nordic Film and TV Fund performed equally instrumental changes in the increasingly globalised world of the 1980s. As Hjort explains, 'As an initiative of the Nordic Council, the Nordic Film and TV Fund represents a kind of top-down attempt to change some of the institutional parameters of filmmaking in the North. What we have here is an example of what might be called *reactive* globalization, for the aim was to ensure that Nordic culture would continue to find cinematic expression in a global media culture dominated by Hollywood, that budgets for Nordic film projects would be such that the production values of Nordic films would meet expectations shaped largely by Hollywood products, both in the North and globally.'[100] The Fund was created to inspire a way into the global marketplace that both allows for transnational exchange and reinforces the distinctiveness of local, small-nation output. Accounts point to the concrete example of one film as indicative, in its production and content, of these impulses: *Pelle the Conqueror* (*Pelle Erobreren*, dir. Bille August, 1987). Following Hjort:

> This film seemed to policymakers, administrators, and producers alike to incarnate an ideal mode of Nordic cooperation. The term *natural coproduction* was coined in connection with *Pelle* on account of the way in which the film's story world called for cultural participation that constituted a kind of "natural" invitation for two nations – Denmark and Sweden – to collaborate economically. That is, in the heavily canonized story about peasant migration from Småland in Sweden to the Danish island of Bornholm, the nationality of the central characters clearly identified certain nations as the 'natural' investors. Reflected in August's film as well as in Martin Anderson Nexo's canonized literary work, which the film adapts, is the interconnected history of the Danish and Swedish peoples in the form of patterns of migration and mutually intelligible languages. What we have here is a kind of palimpsest of shared culture, for the literary text, from which the film derives a kind of ready-made appeal, is not simply about a particular period in the history of interaction between Swedes and Danes, but is itself a Nordic rather than merely Danish literary classic.[101]

Crucially, the legislative emphasis on Nordic co-production and content shifts, in the 1990s, towards distribution and exhibition. An audience had to be ensured in at least two Scandinavian countries, and the industry would now be increasingly alert to global strategies of consumption. Thus, the domestic public is satisfied, and the small-nation 'minor cinema' exists increasingly via transnational co-productions. Today, as Sweden is an integral site in increasingly globalised film markets, the traditional borderline demarcation points of cultural-political bodies (such as the SFI and Nordic Fund) become blurred. Rather than the products of a single nation-state, the networks of film production, distribution, and exhibition are transnational. In *Transnational Cinema in a Global North: Nordic Cinema in Transition*, Trevor G. Elkington and Andrew Nestingen offer a positive account of this reality:

> [T]he globalization of cinema should not be implicitly understood as a threat to Nordic national cinemas. One way the role of transnational interconnection can be seen to have stimulated Nordic cinemas is by providing film workers opportunity to influence colleagues and audiences outside the region. Nordic film workers have figured significantly in Hollywood in the past and do so as much as ever today. In the search for marketable cinema, the studio-based industry has increasingly looked outside its own sphere for talent and inspiration, leading to the 'crossing over' of directors like Bille August, Ole Bornedal, Lasse Hallström, Renny Harlin, Harald Zwart, Erik Skjoldbjaerg, and others. Even Lars von Trier, though still independent of the studio system, is largely seen and marketed as an international (not a Danish) director after the success of *Breaking the Waves* (1995) and *Dancer in the Dark*. Similarly, the Hollywood remake of films like Skjoldbaerg's *Insomnia* (1997), Bornedal's *Nattevagten* (1994, remade as *Nightwatch* in 1998 with Bornedal at the helm) and others shows an awareness of the major releases in the Nordic region. Despite a tendency to see Hollywood as monolithic and entirely American, the studio-based industry has moved toward a global model, both in its business practice and in its product, through mergers, partnerships, and the homogenization of product, all based on a global focus, which opens a space for contributions from outside the American sphere.[102]

As the list of case-study texts in the Introduction indicates, Swedish crime fiction is exceptionally active in this process of transnational interconnection. One example is particularly instructive of the ways in which traditional institutional borders are being effaced in this genre. In March 2011, I travelled to Stockholm to interview the Executive Producer of Yellow Bird Productions, Mikael Wallén. Yellow Bird is the company behind *Wallander* in both its Swedish and international incarnations (foremost of original Kurt Wallander stories not based on Mankell's novels, starring Krister Henriksson in the title role), and *Millennium* in both its TV and film versions.[103] During the interview, the distinctions between the British/US models of TV and film production, distribution and broadcast, and those of contemporary Swedish television became clear. In the latter, a more innovative 'outside the box' approach has started to lead to the dissolution of divisions between the different media forms and formats. As Wallén explains:

> The whole [Swedish] *Wallander* concept was based on the investment made by TV broadcasters in Sweden and Germany. The whole project has been designed such that the broadcasters are satisfied, and such that we can produce the movies in decent quality. And we still have a strong DVD market in Scandinavia. So we adapted that concept to the best way of financing the films: that was – giving the German broadcaster rights for Germany, and in Scandinavia the rights to release the first one on cinema to market the new series of films, especially for the DVD sales. So the first film is released at the cinema, setting the way for DVD sales. Then, a month later or so, the second film is released straight-to-DVD. So you release them on DVD about once a month ... That is the marketing tool for the new series on DVD. You have your ordinary cinema-release window of 4 to 6 months, and then the first goes to DVD, and the next month the second one goes to DVD, and so on. And then you have the ordinary window for pay-TV, and then free TV. That is the model for *Wallander*.[104]

This is a radical departure from the more traditional approach still favoured by producers and distributors in Britain and the USA: in most cases, TV drama is to be made for, and broadcast on, television alone. Movie spin-offs of successful series made for the big screen may follow, and may involve crew from the television version, but will be aimed solely, in the first instance, at the cinema audiences. They will also present new stories and scenarios, removed from the serial narrative arc of the television programmes.[105] It is customary for the DVD release of TV series in Britain and the USA to follow the television broadcasts (the opposite way around from the Swedish model). Importantly (and, for this scholar, happily), through the Swedish system, the oft-used catch-all terms 'cinematic' and 'televisual' start to become unfixed. The release of the *Millennium* series followed a similar pattern to *Wallander*; it also further complicated established demarcation lines by receiving cinematic releases in different, truncated forms. Whereas Britain and the USA initially chose to buy and release the made-for-cinema versions of the TV series, other European countries opted instead to show and sell the longer made-for-television films on DVD. It is worth quoting Wallén at length here, as the various intricacies are unpicked:

> The [*Millennium*] series – as with the *Wallander* series – was financed by different sets of broadcasters – German broadcasters, Swedish broadcasters, with the first one set for release at the cinema. The only difference was that because the first book was so extensive, we planned on doing two sets of 90 minutes on each book, so in the end, the series would be six 90 minute films for TV ... When we started financing it, and got closer to the production, we of course realised that the book was selling so fantastically around the world and in Scandinavia, so we asked our main broadcasters at an early stage if it was OK to release all three in cinemas ... It was not until the first one was released on cinema, and was even more successful than we thought, that they changed their minds,

and allowed us to do it. So, it was a really late decision; we had already filmed all three books at that time.

They were broadcast on all Scandinavian channels and in Germany as the 'six times ninety' TV series, and really successfully so, in Germany especially. And in some markets they released the TV series on DVD rather than the feature films, quite successfully ... In Belgium and Luxembourg for example, six months after the initial cinema release, and when they were supposed to release the feature films on DVD, they released the 'two times ninety' versions instead, as a 'deluxe, extra-long version' ... and people were buying even more DVDs than just the feature film. So in some countries, they really played with the options, because there are a lot of options when you have this kind of series ...

In terms of Music Box in the States, and Momentum in the UK, they are doing it in a more traditional way. They are both planning on releasing the 'six times ninety' versions ... The TV series has been sold to the BBC along with the feature films ... it is all a question of what they release first, and a matter of timing schedules with the broadcasters. For BBC Four to schedule it for the same slot as *The Killing* or *Wallander* it should be easier to show the 'six times ninety' versions in that way. Instead of releasing the three 'extra-long' movies, it seems more suitable to show the series in this way.[106]

As alluded to in the above transcript, the roles played by digital television companies and 'niche channels' become increasingly central to the broadcasting of small-nation dramas in the deregulated, globalised, multi-platform world of 'TV3'.[107]

The various versions of *Wallander* provide another compelling case of cross-pollination. The Yellow Bird serial of new stories is based on Mankell's characters but set after the events of the novels, picking up the narrative of the last *Wallander* book, *Before the Frost* (2009; first published as *Innan frosten*, 2004). As indicated in Wallén's comments, the institutional location of these television texts becomes flexible. It is not just the first episodes of a new season that receive a cinema release. The seventh episode of season one – *Mastermind* (original air date 13 December 2005) – was shown, to great acclaim, in Swedish movie theatres. We can also consider the differences between British and Swedish versions in terms of narrative and narration. The UK *Wallander* presents new versions of the Mankell novels. The novels were previously filmed as TV mini-series by Sveriges Television and Tre Vänner Produktion AB, from 1995 to 2007 (pre-Yellow Bird). The UK version concentrates attention on Wallander himself, with colleagues, family, and locales becoming, as it were, cyphers or aspects of his own sensibility.[108] A very different set of filmmaking decisions is in evidence in the Swedish treatments of the *Wallander* novels. The Swedish TV films are shot through with dark humour and an experimental visual style. Often, the Swedish series will punctuate the narrative with hazy dreamscapes floating between diegetic reality and hallucinogenic fantasy, expressing Wallander's internalised anxieties in abstract metaphorical form.

As noted in the Introduction, the most recent incarnation of Swedish crime fiction for the small-screen *Sebastian Bergman* comprises a kind of end-game for the form's convergent behaviours: TV writers adapt self-penned novels for the small screen, calling in film directors to shoot the series. This interlacing of forms cannot help but inspire certain flashes of self-reflexivity. In the first novel, one of the police officers – Haraldsson – is described as being (in the diegetic world) 'wonderfully monosyllabic and firm, just like the detectives in the Martin Beck series'.[109] There is also a set of strong and explicit links to other examples of global crime fiction. The series' set-up is strikingly reminiscent of *Cracker* (another show dealing with a maladjusted psychologist, now in British and US versions) and, like *Wallander* (a series called immediately to mind by Lassgård's presence), there are parallels with *Inspector Morse*. This latter link prompted the *Huffington Post* to ask, 'Have we found the Norse Morse?'[110] The central scenario of the second episode has more than a passing resemblance to the Hannibal Lecter cycle by Thomas Harris: a charismatic serial killer emphasises his similarity to the criminal profiler, and a young female protégée is caught in the crossfire. The film style of John Carpenter also haunts the series, especially through the music and use of POV (point-of-view shots). All of these factors allow for a vigorous re-evaluation of putative divisions – aesthetic, industrial, national – of film and television in the global age. All are expressive of the particular historical, generic, and institutional determinants that inform Swedish crime fiction.

2

COMMUNITY AND THE FAMILY

One principle of the welfare state in particular has worked its way under the flesh of the national body politic, and remains a thorn in Sweden's side: the matter of social equality. Such a strong and singular ideological aspiration has led to a complex of tensions emerging between the perceived and enacted role of the individual in Swedish society, and the wider collective. So intrinsic to the country's political make-up is this dynamic between individual and state that it has become known as the 'Swedish model':

> The 'Swedish model' [is] characterised by an extreme form of statism, built on a social contract between a strong and good state, on the one hand, and the emancipated and autonomous individual, on the other. Through the institutions of the state the individual, so it was thought, was liberated from the institutions of civil society – the family, the neighbourhood, the churches, the charity organisations. The inequalities and dependencies associated with these institutions were to be replaced by an egalitarian social order. In this scheme the state and the people were conceived of as intrinsically linked; the people's home was a *folkstat*, the state was the homely domain of national community, the context in which the ideal of solidarity could be joined to that of equality. At the same time, this Swedish ideology, with its dual emphasis on social equality and individual autonomy,

was understood to be distinctly modern and highly efficient; the *welfare* of the welfare state implied not just solidarity and equality but also prosperity and progress.[111]

For most writers and filmmakers, the interplay between an individual character's psychological and emotional complexity, and the workings of wider social institutions, is fundamental to the creation of a well-rounded fictional world. As already suggested in the Introduction, an established narrative strategy is the development of a central protagonist who is both singular and representative of a wider state. Furthermore, most crime drama concentrates on different communities in the workplace and the impact of those existing outside such solid collectives. The social parameters of the genre allow the writer, filmmaker, and television show-runner the opportunity to explore the institutional intricacies of various 'closed communities' including those of the legal system, the press, the government, the criminal underworld, and, of course, the police force. The relationship of one or a small number of central characters to these social groupings is the prime catalyst in so many of crime fiction's stalwart dramatic scenarios. How many fictional detectives' marriages fail due to the protagonist putting professional duty before personal commitments? Conversely, how many mavericks on the force risk the ire of their superiors by going it alone to get results?

For the socially conscious writer or filmmaker, when there is also a deeply embedded collective anxiety about the self and the state rife in the country under the microscope, there are irresistible possibilities to create new strains of generic DNA. Sweden's long-held belief in the importance of the national community over smaller social institutions makes access behind the curtain in the halls of power, to uncover the more sinister agendas at the top of the social strata, and into the enclosed worlds of professional collectives even more thrilling. Swedish crime fiction is filled with tales involving paranoid conspiracy theories, cover-ups, get-rich-quick schemes and bold acts of autonomy by killer and detective alike. Then, as with the Vangers, the family will also often reassert itself as *the* irrepressible social institution. It will contain specific idiosyncrasies and symbolic currency, standing for a bigger collective, suggestive of a nation's 'family resemblances' across generations. This chapter engages with this constant tussle for control of agency. It looks in detail at works alert to the forceful undercurrents in Sweden's national psyche, at an ideological emphasis on solidarity and homogenisation pulling against a desire for individual betterment, at extremism lurking along the edges of collectives, and some disturbingly adamant assertions of family values.

Crime fiction is particularly adept at exploring the problems inherent in an idealistic national belief (some may say foolhardy or paradoxical) combining the solidarity of the *folkstet* – a sense of collective community built on the workers' movement – and individualist aspirations. Often in these tales, though the encouragement of economic autonomy is meant to be tied to the beneficial power of the state, criminality and capitalist aspiration lead instead to a sort of 'manifest destiny' driven by a desire for individual gain. Both the filmed and written examples, through the distinct aesthetic possibilities of their medium, are able to balance representations of the individual and collective state in striking ways. As Antoine de Baecque suggests of film, for example, 'Through a multiplicity of perspectives cinema, technically speaking, can convey both distance and closeness at the same time, both the singular and the plural.'[112]

For many, the notion of the *folkstet* becomes a 'lost orthodoxy', expressed through the sensibility and disillusionment of the central character. As Andrew Brown observes of (his experience of) the novels of Sjöwall and Wahlöö:

> The strangest thing about Sweden, to an English eye, was always its tremendous conformity. It did not matter what the orthodoxy might be: the point is that everyone knew what was acceptable and proper to believe. In this sense, the Martin Beck stories taught me most when they were most absurd, because they exaggerated what everybody then be-

lieved about progress and the good society. Sjöwall and Wahlöö were communists and in the Seventies there was an assumption that communism, while it might be imperfect, was at least a form of socialism; and socialism then seemed as completely inevitable as global capitalism does now.[113]

Yet there are also contemporary instances that counter this assumption. If, in the early 1970s, Martin Beck stands (on the page) for a form of socialism, then the cinematic protagonists Bonnie and Clyde, of Arthur Penn's film of the same name, complicate such a stance. As Peter Cowie notes, 'In [1967] a saga of doomed outsiders, *Bonnie and Clyde*, entranced audiences in many countries. In Sweden it was perhaps ironic that a society so dedicated to the good of the community as a whole should have embraced a work of art so resolutely on the side of the individual.'[114] Perhaps the popularity of *Bonnie and Clyde* in Sweden is ironic, or perhaps symptomatic of the internal conflict of a modern society struggling to consolidate statist and autonomous impulses. These two iconic figures of the underworld can be seen to represent at one and the same time a fight for the 'common man' – a kind of modern-day Robin Hood double-act – *and* the dangerous end-points of both demonstrating free will regardless of the consequences, and standing up against the brute forces of the state. In the final, blood-drenched moments of Penn's films, the slow-motion pirouettes of Bonnie and Clyde's bullet-riddled bodies perform one last balletic assertion of individual identity while The Man snuffs them out.

Just as the existentialist experimentalism of New Hollywood in the 1970s gives way to a reassertion of the Blockbuster in the 1980s and 1990s of US cinema, so too does the Swedish model move increasingly towards an ideology based on capitalist gain. According to Andrew Brown, 'In some ways, this period [the 1980s and 1990s] looked like Thatcherism: inequality increased as a fact, and was accepted as an ideal. The slogan of the times, launched by the Employers' Federation, was "Bet on Yourself", and while this was meant to encourage self-employment, it also reflected a rising individualism, and a sense that if the Devil did grab the hindmost, this was no longer a problem for the foremost, or even those in the middle.'[115] A good example of the longstanding rift between those seeking self-improvement through personal finance, and those holding dear to communist principles of community, comes in Jens Lapidus's 2006 novel *Snabba Cash*. The title, 'Easy Money', declares a specific interest in this social schism, borne out in the behaviour of its drug dealer protagonist, JW. Originally a poor student, JW lives a double life among the wealthy elite in Stockholm. Using increasingly illicit means to fund his exclusive lifestyle, he hits on a chance to score 'easy money' through selling cocaine. As JW enters the dark world of organised crime his fate entwines with that of Jorge, a drug dealer on the run, and Mrado, a mob hit-man tasked with tracking Jorge down. Here is an early description of JW and his surroundings, the individual and the collective:

> Four guys sat in a living room, pumped to party. JW with a backslick. And yes, he knew a lot of trash resented his hairstyle. Looked hatefully at him and called it a 'jerkoff coif.' But Communists like that were clueless, so why should he care ... The guys in the room were fine, fair kids. Creamy white. Clean features, straight backs, good posture. They knew they were sharp-looking boys. Boys in the know. They knew how to dress, how to carry themselves, how to act appropriately.[116]

There is an irony in the way JW sets himself against the collective uniformity of the communists by a distinctive hairstyle and dismissive attitude, only to align with an alternative group of shared views, the 'boys in the know'. Throughout the novel, displays of conspicuous consumption are met with approval by JW, as a new member of this modern, well-dressed world. It is telling, though, that he uses the phrase 'act appropriately': turning his back on the *folkstet* past while adopting its conformist terminology. Capitalism's attraction, its promise of 'easy money', is always present in the *folkstet* as its shadow-self, its double or doppelganger. As Brown notes of Sjöwall and Wahlöö, 'Not all their villains are millionaires. But there isn't a character in their books who is conspicuously rich who is *not* a murderer, and usually of a particularly blameworthy kind. The successful multinational businessman shot in a Malmö hotel turns out to be a crook whose widow is cheating on him with his trusted assistant. The mysteriously murdered businessman from the pleasant suburbs north of Stockholm makes his money from the sale of pornographic films featuring drugged young women.'[117] In the 1971 novel *The Abominable Man*, Sjöwall and Wahlöö angrily describe a Sweden that is becoming segregated from inside, through the demarcations – the 'haves' and the 'have-nots' – that capitalism proscribes:

> It was Friday evening and Stockholm's cafes should have been full of happy people enjoying themselves after the drudgery of the week. Such, however, was not the case, and it wasn't hard to work out why. In the course of the preceding five years, restaurant prices had as good as doubled, and very few ordinary wage-earners could afford to treat themselves to even one night out a month. The restaurant owners complained and talked crisis, but the ones who had not turned their establishments into pubs or discotheques to attract the easy-spending young managed to keep their heads above water by means of the increasing number of businessmen with credit cards and expense accounts who preferred to conduct their transactions across a laden table.[118]

Quite clearly, the traditional workers – those involved in the true 'drudgery of the week' for the good of the state – are being shut out by the 'easy-spending young': a new generation of business-minded Swedes interested only in themselves, in chasing and making easy money. A sense of collective community is getting lost, a sense perhaps best expressed by the Swedish celebrations of Midsummer:

> At midsummer, all distinctions of wealth just vanished. Everyone queued for the earthen closet. There was a water scoop, a washing-up bowl, and a squirt of soap outside. Everyone drank water from the well, or if they wanted to wash, swam in the river ... Almost everyone slept in tents and no one had any choice about singing.[119]

If only once a year, the utopian values of social equality are enacted at Midsummer. Henning Mankell chooses to open his 1997 Wallander novel *One Step Behind* by describing a group of youngsters on Midsummer's Eve partying in an otherwise deserted woods (or so they believe). Dressed in olden-day finery – the novel describes them embodying 'the age of Bellman, the bacchanalian 18th-century poet'[120]– they are slaughtered by a killer watching their tea-party from close by. In devastating clarity, Mankell suggests how the insular world of a traditional Sweden is threatened by external influences. Autonomous acts of the crazed loner (individualism gone wild) coming from outside can rupture the safety of this inner sanctum. Like Sjöwall and Wahlöö's 'successful multinational businessman shot in a Malmö hotel' who 'turns out to be a crook whose widow is cheating on him with his trusted assistant', to Lapidus's anti-hero obsessed with Italian fashion, certain agents of external influence change the face of Sweden: global capitalism and, as expressed most forcefully time and again from varying political perspectives, the migrant population.

From an emigration society to an immigration society

In the introduction to *Transnational Cinema in a Global North: Nordic Cinema in Transition*, Trevor G. Elkington and Andrew Nestingen set out the figures and effects of this crucial social shift:

> Geographical marginality no longer means homogeneity arising from relative isolation. The economic migrants that came to Sweden and Denmark in the 1950s and 1960s and the political refugees that came from the 1970s to 1990s

make these societies more plural than they've ever been (Pred 2000; Gullestaf 2002). By 2003, approximately 20 per cent of the Swedish population had a background outside the country, as did 10 per cent of the Danish population. Newly emergent hybrid cultural forms contrast with the homogeneity associated with national romantic beliefs about cultural identity, which have dominated in these countries historically. Today, Nordic ethnic nationalism delineates self and other in complicated, sometimes racist ways. Allan Pred and Marianne Gullestad have shown the ways in which assumptions about ethnically homogenous national identity in Sweden and Norway have transformed in multicultural societies. The Danish elections of fall 2001, in which a right-wing coalition including the anti-immigrant Danish People's Party won the parliamentary majority, showed that the seams of Danish society were splitting in its efforts to recast itself as multicultural. All of the Nordic countries have seen extreme-right parties enter the political arena. The Nordic countries have integrated themselves into global networks of migration for more than four decades, with complex social consequences.[121]

Of course, immigration was and is not a solely modern phenomenon. Yet prior to the economic migrations of the 1950s onwards, most human traffic was between Scandinavian nations (Swedes to Norway, sections of the Finnish population to Sweden, for example). More modern market forces dictated a broader set of international movements. As with any migration, the retention of cultural identity becomes of paramount importance and, as Sejested suggests, for Sweden, 'Equality and freedom thus emerged once again as possible contradictions.'[122] In a very short time 80,000 Bosnians emerged in Sweden, and in 1993 Sweden instituted visa requirements that had the effect of trying to redirect the flood toward Norway. The pronounced migration patterns across Swedish borders give rise to (yet) another measure of national insecurity, this time centring around the putative detrimental social impact of 'the foreigner'. According to Brown:

[I]n the elections of 1991 *trygghet* [security] had disappeared and the whole country was on the edge of panic. There had been race riots in some of the smaller towns where employment had stopped. A psychopathic sniper shot eleven dark-skinned men at random (one died) over a period of seven months in Stockholm and Uppsala, using a rifle equipped with laser sights. When he was finally caught, he turned out to be a foreigner by origin, half-German and half-Swiss, who had been teased as a foreigner growing up in a Stockholm suburb because his hair was black, although he was otherwise impeccably Aryan.[123]

The above scenario and its relationship to wider conditions could have been taken from the pages of any one of the fictions explored in this book. Markers of difference, the complex variants of a multicultural population, complicate the homogeneity of Sweden's isolationist past and cause unrest. For some, the dream of equality fuses, all too easily and chillingly, with an extreme need for sameness. This in face of migrant populations coming into Sweden from around the world:

There are about a million people, that is, one in nine of the population, in Sweden today who appear exotic – or just foreign – to the rest. This is a large immigrant population by most European standards, and it seems even larger in a country that was, historically, a place that hungry peasants left. The first and still the largest single group were Finns, throughout the Fifties and Sixties. Then came labour migration from Italy, Turkey, and the former Yugoslavia; that more or less stopped in the Seventies, but increasing waves of refugees poured in, as if to compensate. There were South Americans, fleeing from dictatorships; Kurds, fleeing from wars and oppression; Lebanese; Bosnians; Somalis: the less the rest of the world was willing to take in refugees, the more important Sweden has become to them ... There are now 400,000 Muslims in Sweden, and, among children in Malmö, the most common new boys' name is Mohammed. Of course, anyone born in Malmö is by definition not an immigrant; that doesn't make them welcome, and it need not make them feel at home. It seems to me that one of the distinctive marks of Swedishness is the ability to feel completely excluded from the society around you, precisely because it is so conformist and close.[124]

Exclusion that results through a country's desire for equality-as-equivalence, or uniformity: another essential paradox of modern Swedish life. As its title ironically suggests, Mankell's 1991 Wallander novel *Faceless Killers* explores tensions emerging once the ethnic origins of suspects in a murder case are placed under scrutiny. Fear of 'the foreigner' threatens to infect the community of Ystad, just as some of the townsfolk react against the growing appearance of migrant workers. Shane McCorristine chronicles *Wallander*'s broader, patterned preoccupation with xenophobia as resulting not only from the breaching of geo-political borders, but also a collapse of national solidarity:

> Mankell's novels offer a veritable taxonomy of threats to notions of a secure Swedish identity: sometimes the evil to be combated originates outside the community, sometimes it comes from within, but it is always linked to spectres of the Other (the Other of Swedish injustice towards the subaltern and neglect of the Third World, for example) ... The Other occupies a dominant place in virtually every novel of the Wallander series: the African and Eastern European refugees of *Faceless Killers* (1991); the interaction with Latvia in *The Dogs of Riga* (1992); the presence of South African and post-Soviet killers in Sweden in *The White Lioness* (1993); Swedish-run organ theft in the Third World in *The Man Who Smiled* (1994); the sexual abuse of Third World teenagers in *Sidetracked* (1995); the murder of a Swedish citizen in Algeria and the issue of Swedish mercenaries in the Congo in *The Fifth Woman* (1996); an Angola-based conspiracy to destroy the international financial system in *Firewall* (1998).[125]

If Mankell's novels present us with sets of binary distinctions, asking us to question who is the 'us' and who the 'them', then Stieg Larsson's *Millennium* trilogy goes even further to explore and complicate Sweden's unspoken prejudices. At face value, its over-arching narrative can be seen to indulge in some stark 'Othering' of its own. In a number of ways, Lisbeth Salander is the arche-typal outsider: socially ostracised and awkward, pronouncedly 'Other' in her physical appearance, legal status, and sexual ori-entation. Equally, the main villain of the piece – Lisbeth's father Alexander Zalachenko – is a Soviet turncoat left over from the Cold War. His defection and relocation in Sweden in the 1970s becomes a catastrophic decision by the 'powers that be' in under-hand foreign policy: a most unwelcome breach of the country's borders and national security. Yet at the same time, and particular-ly in terms of the representation of the trilogy's minor characters, potentially xenophobic or isolationist tendencies are overturned. For example, through a brief history of Lisbeth's boss, Dragan Armansky, Larsson provides a wry portrait of the way Sweden deals with difference:

> Dragan Armansky was born in Croatia fifty-six years ago. His father was an Armenian Jew from Belorussia. His mother was a Bosnian Muslim of Greek extraction. She had taken charge of his upbringing and his education, which meant that as an adult he was lumped together with the large, heterogeneous group defined by the media as Muslims. The Swedish immi-gration authorities had registered him, strangely enough, as a Serb. His passport confirmed that he was a Swedish citizen, and his passport photograph showed a squarish face, a strong jaw, five-o clock shadow, and greying temples. He was often referred to as 'The Arab', although he did not have a drop of Arab blood.[126]

In one dense paragraph and in the guise of one character, Larsson compresses variant factors of ethnic and social diversity from across Sweden's history. The description individualises mass migrant shifts from former Yugoslavia with more recent passages of a Middle Eastern populace *and* widespread confusion, presumption, and ignorance surrounding different ethnic groupings judged by appearance alone (Serbian? Bosnian? Muslim? 'although he did not have a drop of Arab blood'). Armansky is an amalgam of modern multicultural identity, and it is most telling that Lisbeth chooses his above all others as the acceptable face of institution – of those closed communities that for so long have forcibly stripped her of her individual rights, and have had her *institutionalised* as an orphan, a mental patient, and a prisoner.

Closed communities in crime fiction

In *Fishing in Utopia*, Andrew Brown reminds us how:

> Detective novelists have always been fond of setting their stories in a closed society, and this has a number of obvious advantages. The stain of suspicion cannot be allowed to spread too far if each suspect is to be a rounded, credible, breathing human being, not a cardboard cut-out to be ritually knocked down in the last chapter. And in a self-contained community – hospital, school, office, publishing house, nuclear power station – where, particularly if the setting is residential, the characters often spend more time with working colleagues than they do with their families, the irritation that can emerge from such cloistered and unsought intimacy can kindle animosity, jealousy and resentment, emotions which, if they are sufficiently strong, can smoulder away and eventually explode into the destructive finality of violence. The isolated community can also be an epitome of the wider world outside and this, for a writer, can be one of the greatest attractions of the closed communal setting, particularly as the characters are being explored under the trauma of an official investigation for murder, a process which can destroy the privacies both of the living and of the dead.[127]

One of the best examples of a Swedish crime novel opening up the 'Russian doll' configuration of an isolated community comes in the first and pivotal set-up of Sjöwall and Wahlöö's *The Laughing Policeman*. In Stockholm, a public bus has been hijacked, with all its occupants killed. As Martin Beck and his colleagues in the police department start to examine evidence and make sense of the crime, tracing the identities of all those aboard the bus, their investigation takes them from this bullet-scarred metal container and into different closed communities within the city: the Chinese quarters, the world of sex workers, the Black community, the underworld of drug gangs, Hippy communes, hang-outs of Hell's Angels, and the gay community. Such exposure brings certain underlying and deep-seated prejudices to the surface. In a similar vein, let's consider Swedish crime fiction's handling of three different isolated societies it most predominantly explores: the press, the police, and the family.

The press

Who guards the guardians? Writing in the time of the Leveson Inquiry, an ongoing public inquest into the culture, practices, and ethics of the British press following the News International hacking scandal, the 'closed community' business of news reporters is at the top of many agendas.[128] More than ever before, as the secretive strategies employed by journalists to expose hidden truths are placed under scrutiny, the ability of the press to mediate and intrude on public and private arenas is highlighted and questioned. While sharing some of the principles and directives of the British press, the coverage and targeting of 'newsworthy' human affairs is measured slightly differently in Sweden:

> If the press spares individuals' private lives (a point on which British and American papers could certainly take lesson from them) it lampoons and is ever ready to criticise all those corporate bodies (*organisationssverige*) of which Sweden, the Model Society, is made up … The popular journalist is never

so happy as when he can nose out a *skandal* from behind of-
ficialdom's bland facades.[129]

So one closed community focuses on breaking into another, ex-
posing its mechanisms and machinations. For the crime writer or
filmmaker, particularly if shades of realism are at stake, then the
investigative manoeuvres of the journalist-as-detective provide
greater access into closed worlds than is afforded by the more
official procedures of the police, the latter often bound up in
bureaucracy and red tape. The journalist, at once a representative of 'the common man' and with professional sanctity, shuttles
between public and private realms, often calling in personal
favours or promising flattering portraits of civic duty for those in
power, to get at the truth. He or she is in a paradoxical position,
an insider getting the scoop, embedded within the collective, yet
also seen as a nosy individual, an unwanted presence, by both the
police and the political figures or public body under scrutiny,
meddling in their affairs and getting in the way. Equally, the journalist can be used by the criminal or turncoat as a middle-man,
being fed information to fox the police, or further the murderer's
schemes. A good, recent example of this relationship is presented
in the Danish-Swedish television drama co-production *The Bridge*
(*Bron/Broen*, dir. various, 2011), as the killer communicates in a
series of phone calls with the journalist Daniel Ferbé (Christian
Hillborg). Fully aware that he is being manipulated by a madman,
Ferbé is led by his own professional ego and vainglorious thirst
for fame to carry out and publish the killer's demands. This sleazy
hack meets a grisly end, his greed for status punished by the venge-
ful killer: another Swedish individual brought down to size by
someone acting autonomously, in his own fevered and murderous
mind, for the 'greater good'.

In contrast, in her 1998 novel *The Bomber*, Liza Marklund
positions her protagonist, crime reporter Annika Bengzton, as a
noble loner standing apart from the pack mentality of the press:

> More journalists were arriving by the minute, a lot of them wandering about with smiles on their faces, greeting colleagues. Annika found this sort of comradely back-slapping difficult, people hanging around accident scenes boasting about which parties they'd been to. She shrank away, pulling the photographer with her.[130]

Later in the novel, Marklund has Bengzton and killer use the same metaphor to describe the collected masses of the press as insects, 'The radio reporters looked like big insects with their broadcast equipment strapped to their backs.'[131] The shared language complicates Bengzton's position. While taking the ethical high ground, looking down on the way the news-hungry hounds of the press act in unsympathetic unity at crime scenes, her individualist stance places her alongside the killer as an outsider, looking in from a distance.

The 2003 film of the novel develops these tensions between Bengzton as individual and member of the press in its composition of characters in the workplace. It presents the news editorial boardroom in the much-favoured modern style of a roving shaky-cam, suggesting the team's constant anxiety or unpreparedness for the next big news story, and senses of immediacy and immersion in this high-pressure world. While apparently unprepared itself in terms of a carefully composed *mise-en-scène*, the film keeps Bengzton separate from her colleagues in the frame. The free camera provides an intimate feel but keeps Bengzton at a distance. The film does the same with the killer, holding us with the news reporters, presenting nothing from the murderer's perspective. Our sense of the fictional world is filtered through a 'press-eye view', and Bengzton's separateness again aligns her with the killer's outsider status.

A more recent and celebrated instance offers a corrective for the collective. Stieg Larsson's Mikael Blomkvist is an individual investigative reporter fighting for the common man, against corrupt autocrats of industry, and as part of the worthy, Left-leaning team of *Millennium* magazine. Here is how he is first described (by other characters) in the 2005 novel *The Girl with the Dragon Tattoo*:

> 'He had become known for his job as a political and finan-
> cial reporter. He has primarily been a freelancer, with one
> full-time position at an evening paper in the late 80s. He
> left in 1990 when he helped start the monthly magazine
> *Millennium*. The magazine began as a real outsider, without
> any big publishing company to hold its hand. Its circulation
> has grown and today is 21,000 copies monthly. The editorial
> office is on Götgatan only a few blocks from here.'
> 'A left-wing magazine.'
> 'That depends on how you define the concept "left-wing".
> *Millennium* is generally viewed as critical of society, but
> I'm guessing the anarchists think it's a wimpy bourgeois
> crap magazine along the lines of *Arena* or *Ordfront*, while
> the Moderate Students Association probably thinks that
> the editors are Bolsheviks. There is nothing to indicate that
> Blomkvist has ever been active politically, even during the
> left-wing wave when he was going to secondary school ... He
> has done some devastating individual portraits of captains
> of industry and politicians – which were most likely well
> deserved – and caused a number of resignations and legal
> repercussions.'[132]

In 'Journalism and Compassion: Rewriting an On-Screen Crusader for the Digital Age', Sarah Niblock argues that the character of Blomkvist as conceived on page and screen adds 'a new ethical dimension' to fictional depictions of reporters.[133] Niblock continues to note how, 'By displaying vulnerability and humanity, Blomkvist challenges the traditional representation of the journalist in dramatic fashion ... His interaction with his counterpart Lisbeth Salander forces him to reconsider his journalistic approach from one of a professionalised, objective model to a position of compassionate advocacy.'[134] While operating for the 'greater good', according to Niblock's reading, Blomkvist has achieved an ethically attractive objectivity, yet in order to develop as a person and gain compassion, he must place more of himself in his profession-al role, recognising his stance as an individual supporting others. This is the antithesis of the complex intertwining of self and state that dictates Ferbé's behaviour and undoing in *The Bridge*, driven by egotism, money, and hatred. In Blomkvist, Larsson posits an alternative route through the capitalist-led world of journalism in the 2000s, affording a form of selfhood that balances autonomy with solidarity: in short, a modern version of the utopian model of social equality set out at the beginning of this chapter.

In comparing cinematic versions of the character in the Swedish and US films of *The Girl with the Dragon Tattoo*, Niblock finds the relationship between markers of individual and collec-tive responsibility differently poised:

> Mikael Blomkvist is portrayed as, and believes himself to be, an ethical and professional journalist of the highest calibre, set apart from his peers in the mainstream. In both the US and Swedish films he is introduced to the viewer as he leaves court, after being convicted of libel, to face the waiting press. In the Swedish version, however, his casual, leather-jacketed representation is quite distinct from the besuited news re-porters who swoop and encircle him at the start of *The Girl with the Dragon Tattoo*. In the US version, his image resembles that of the slick on-screen newsreader presenting the latest details on the scandal. Daniel Craig's Blomkvist is an ideal-ised figure physically, sexually and professionally. Far from being socially outcast, he has a positive relationship with his daughter, is presentable, displays physical desirability and, as time passes, enjoys a conventional sexual relationship with Lisbeth Salander. He is portrayed as a typical hero figure, in control of his life, relationships, and even his destiny.
>
> The Swedish Blomkvist is instantly established as an outsider, a luminal, maverick journalist set apart from the mainstream, while in the US version he is coded as a profes-sional but fallen, once part of the journalistic establishment but now excommunicated. The US approach coheres closely with the idea of journalism as a profession or semi-profession,

as opposed to an occupation or vocation. There has been an ongoing process towards professionalisation over the past 30–40 years, which suggests it can no longer claim to be a trade or a craft. Key signs of this include the emergence of a professional journalistic ideology (such as attention to objectivity), the growth of professional institutions and codes of practice.[135]

In both, Blomkvist is the maverick, and crime fiction on page and screen likes nothing more than the go-it-alone protagonist getting results *their* way. In the Swedish film, as he is connected to a vision and values of the past, he moves more awkwardly with his capitalist contemporaries, who look more like suited and booted businessmen than news reporters. In the US movie, Niblock's interpretation presents us with a more socially integrated individual, marked by and at ease with Anglo-American facets of 'professionalism' (read – the commercial turn of the professions into industries led by brands and market shares) rather than embodying the welfare state. Yet this is not to suggest that Larsson presents us with a wistful vision of a broken utopia. As Erika Vanger notes to Blomkvist of her family's control of the national press: "'We owned six daily newspapers in Norrland. That was back in the 50s and 60s. It was my father's idea – he thought it might be politically advantageous to have a section of the media behind us. We're actually still the owners of the *Hedestad Courier*.'"[136] Larsson fuses the insidious propagandist agenda of neo-Nazism with the close-knit, tight-lipped worlds of the family and the press, suggesting the depth and density of containment at play in Sweden's closed communities.

The police

Given the peculiar Scandinavian bond of self and state, and the genre's favouring of a lone detective locked in a love-hate relationship with his colleagues and superiors, it is unsurprising that the closed community of the police has great dramatic and expressive force in Swedish crime fiction. Describing the place and purpose of 'the force' in the police procedural, Scaggs contributes to our thesis on 'the oscillation between the private and collective':

> [T]he variety of individual characters in the team of police officers is significant for the sub-genre as a whole. It is the skills that they bring to the team as individuals which allow the team to work collectively to investigate crime, and, furthermore, it is this individualism which gives a face to collective police agency in the procedural, which 'mediates the public's fears of an overextended and inhumane police power' (Winston and Mellerski 1992: 6). It is also an example of the oscillation between the private and the collective that is evident in other areas of the procedural, such as the setting and the frequent alienation or marginalisation of central characters within the team in general.[137]

Production designer of the British television series *Wallander* Jacqueline Abrahams picks up on the importance of setting in expressing the dynamic of the collective, in her DVD commentary for the documentary film *Wallander Country* (2010):

> So this is the police station, the idea being that it's open plan, so you emphasise that people police together ... they discuss like a police family ... In the middle of a case, they will go up and get coffee, they will get *kanelbullar* [cinnamon buns], and they will come back and sit down, you know, I think there's the sense of not having a hierarchy.[138]

Yet interestingly, the 'Swedish' equation of architectural openness and professional equality is complicated by thoughts expressed by Helene Tursten's main character Detective Inspector Irene Huss in the 2000 novel *Torso* (*Tatuerad torso*). Where Abrahams realises an open-plan British televisual equivalent of a Swedish police station to capture particularly Scandinavian inflections of teamwork, Huss contrasts her experience of a meticulously compartmentalised Sweden with the ranging spaces of a Hollywood US workplace:

The police movie was over just after midnight. Irene turned off the TV, stretched, and yawned. Goodness, how confused and messy it seemed to be at police stations in the USA. Large open office spaces where the desks stood close together, and every attempt at creating a close relationship was doomed to fail. Collared whores, drug dealers, and murderers walked past each other between the desks. In the middle of it all, cops stood and quarrelled and fussed about their work problems. And everyone went around indoors armed. It would seem to be too easy for a suspect to pull a gun out of a holster amidst the general confusion.[139]

Again, and as we shall explore further in Chapter 3 on 'Space and place', there are particular measures of closeness and distance at work in the Swedish sensibility, so crucial to the enforced intimacies of the crime drama. For Huss, the American workspace places people (too) closely together in a way that will only defeat the building of close relationships (not least by the presence of the gun!) This, when considered with the 'frequent alienation or marginalisation of central characters within the team' raised by Scaggs makes for a fascinatingly complex dynamic played out by the central detective protagonist.

For some, the crime drama provides an ideal space for polemic commentary on the impact social change has on the police in Sweden, at any given time. The chief instigators of this strategy are Maj Sjöwall and Per Wahlöö. Throughout their Martin Beck novels (1965–1975), they criticise the broken promises of the Social Democratic Party particularly in terms of the state's treatment of the police force. As Daniel Brodén describes in 'The Criminal and Society in *Mannen på taket*':

According to Sjöwall and Wahlöö, the capitalistic class society permitted criminal exploitation of its citizens. The worst perpetrators were not ordinary criminals, but profiteers who acted within the boundaries of the law and made living conditions worse for everyday citizens. In the dissertation *Roman om en forbrydelse* (1976), literary historian Ejgil

Soholm emphasises how the two authors' bitter criticism of the police force reflected the hostile debate surrounding the nationalisation of the Swedish police force in 1965. The national organisation, which had been divided into smaller police districts, was then reorganised into a modern state bureaucracy with the National Police Board as executive authority. The book series by Sjöwall and Wahlöö, which began the same year as the nationalisation of the police force, shows how the social responsibility of the police is abandoned in favour of dangerous militarisation and cold-hearted crime fighting.[140]

The novels are adept at conveying the effects that a wrangling of control from the smaller collective of the police station by the state has on the individual officer. In some instances, nationalisation leads to local divisions, both geographical and social. Here are two descriptions taken from the novel of *The Laughing Policeman*:

While they were still serving as ordinary beat officers on the beat in Malmo, he [Kvant] had many a time seen Kristiansson lead drunks along the street and even across bridges in order to get them into the next precinct.[141]

Kvant was incorruptible. He never compromised over things he saw, but on the other hand he was an expert at seeing as little as possible.[142]

For Sjöwall and Wahlöö, there is a bitter irony in the real impact of the state's 'liberation' of the individual from the institution. This Sweden becomes a place of bureaucratic borderlines. In turn, a wider sense of collective camaraderie breaks down through the individual's refusal of personal responsibility. Bo Widerberg's 1976 film *The Man on the Roof*, made a year after the publication of the last Martin Beck novel, carries on the authors' overarching thematic exploration (or political project): mapping the vectors of separateness of the police amongst their own and the public. Here are some fleeting moments from across the film, apparently inconsequential in their relationship to the plot, but that build into a meaningful inquiry about the meeting points of individual and collective. As Officer Rönn (Håkan Serner) is introduced in the film, his first words, in talking to a member of the public (victim? perp?) are 'I don't give a damn; up since 8am'. The addressee is passed from one officer to the next, manhandled without care. Yet later, when visiting the film's first crime scene, Rönn carefully hands an accompanying rookie cop his handkerchief to wipe away vomit from his mouth, concerned for the young officer's inexperienced reaction to the sight of a mangled corpse. Then, this passing gesture of solidarity contrasts with Martin Beck's awkward connections with his colleagues, often bumping into them, jostling for space, and in one brief instant banging his head on the rookie's car door – too close for comfort.

Henning Mankell addresses the flipside of this relationship, suggesting the public's growing distance from the police. Tellingly, such thoughts are voiced by his loner protagonist, as Kurt Wallander mourns a past of broken promises, echoing Sjöwall and Wahlöö's disillusionment:

> Wallander walked back to Mariagatan with his bags. He was back at the station at a quarter past two. Everything still seemed deserted. Wallander continued to work through his pile of paper. After the assault in Skurup came a burglary in central Ystad, on Pilgrimsgatan. Someone had broken a window in the middle of the day and emptied the house of various valuables. Wallander shook his head as he read through Svedberg's report. It was unbelievable that none of the neighbours had seen anything. Is this fear starting to spread even in Sweden? he wondered. The fear of assisting the police with the most elementary observations. If this is the case then the situation is far worse than I have wanted to believe.[143]

Particularly elaborate expressions of a policeman's precarious connections with colleagues and the public come in the 1973 American film *The Laughing Policeman*. The film is especially sensitive in its handling of the agents of human presence – voices and bodies – to convey measures of intimacy and conflict between one person, Jake Martin, and the greater collective. From the outset, it explores the tensions emerging from Martin's gruff and singular attendance, his need to rely on other people, and his difficulty in being heard, in making his presence felt. The film begins in silence, that is to say, without dialogue. After a beat, the first words are given to Martin, and it is telling that they are immediately shaped as a need for answers from others: 'What've we got, Lou?' As the crime scene unfolds around him, police sirens blanket all other sounds, and Martin's commands get lost in the mix. The film tapers the sirens' wails away upon the arrival of the Chief of Police. Yet, while we might expect (from his arrival, from the soundtrack) this man's physical presence to inspire a focused directive, bringing the team together 'in one voice', his appearance heralds instead an avalanche of swearwords and overlapping dialogue. As Robert Altman pioneered three years before, in the hectic overlay of different wartime characters speaking all at once in *M*A*S*H* (1970), and Spielberg would repeat four years later in *Close Encounters of the Third Kind* (1977), a collision of human voices adds a sense of verisimilitude and a route through which to explore the problems emerging from a social group's inability to communicate decisively. Martin's single simple question, 'What've we got, Lou?' – a call for clarity, purpose, and teamwork – is now drowned out.

The casting and persona of Walter Matthau contribute directly to these complicated frictions. Alongside our memories of his screen performances filled with comic grumpiness and savvy, sad, frowns, we can recall how Thomson characterises the actor as 'a great technician, in terms of movement, response [and] wisecrack ... so schooled to the wisecrack, he may be unable to talk straight'. Matthau's responsiveness to movement informs a moment early on in *The Laughing Policeman* (it's hard to imagine him laughing) which reveals the character's ability to inspire passing instants of unity in the police force. The scene opens on a team, his team, stood and slouched by the station's entrance. It is only a transitional shot, establishing the location before we move inside, with no 'key' dialogue or action (just a mumble and jostle here and there) but it speaks volumes. Before Martin's arrival, the images of collected officers appear as a still tableau. Martin's movement through the vertical axis of the frame, right through the middle of the gathered team and across the station's threshold, calls them to action. They move with him, as one, into the station. Yet this is not a clean and cohesive 'snap to' of the ensemble following the leader, seen to such effect in more modern American works like *The West Wing* (dir. various, 1999–2006). Rather, the rag-tag team slumps through the entrance after Martin, caught (reluctantly, involuntarily) in his gravitational tug towards duty. Their demeanour matches Martin's, and Matthau's jaded loping action, but it matches it, and, for a while at least, they walk together.

The actor's technical understanding of response and wisecrack can be sensed in moments when Martin pauses for a beat before entering the fray. In these little instances of fleeting introspection, Matthau-as-Martin allows himself a brief second of detached observation, a private moment of scepticism. But he must push on, his duty dictating that he ploughs into the crowd, makes connections, asks questions, finds clues, tracks one person through the many. His individual cynicism carries into the crowds with him, infusing the tone of the scene and the film. At the same time, 'unable to talk straight', to say what he means, he is denied true closeness to other people.

In sequences when Martin becomes one of the team, the film sets up a new tension, between the police and the public. Again, it does so through attention to, and variations of, bodily movement. In the aftermath of the first attack, the police work together to push observers back, mob against mob. They cordon off roads and rooms, setting up divisions between the public and the now private, commandeered space of the crime scene. The film places the victims, too, in a separate aesthetic realm, shot in black-and-white as a series of still photographs. Whereas the police find ways to divide themselves from the public, they draw nearer to the victims. There is a close corporeal relationship at work when the team handles the dead bodies. The film emphasises the physicality and necessarily intrusive intimacy of such procedures. The officers jerk the stiffs around, pulling off socks for toe-tags, dragging out body bags, all the while smelling, smoking, spitting, chewing, coughing. We could celebrate the film's handling of these moments in terms of no-holds-barred realism, but there is also something more. The earthiness of the instant breaks through all the cordons, official lines, and red tape of a murder scene, all the flimflam of an institution, to show man's bodily commitment to others. Words don't get in the way here.

The final, strange shot of the film unsettles the dynamic again, leaves it open and anxious. After the killer is caught and the crime is solved, the scene is set for full narrative (dis)closure. The usual panoply of cop team farewells – the begrudging approbation of the Chief to Martin, the 'see ya arounds' – and increasingly long shots, pulling us from the world of the film, is assembled. Yet out of nowhere, the camera chooses to finally land and stay, in freeze-frame, on the exasperated face of one of Martin's colleagues, another officer, previously unseen and seemingly secondary to the story now ending. What are we to make of this decision? If taken in relation to the above remarks on the tussle between the one and the many, then the shot is a little less shocking. The scene's shape suggests that this irked colleague is frowning at Martin, the central character still causing friction in the collective, even while the man of the hour. Equally, it could hint at how Martin's embittered attitude is not only seeping into the force, but also now passing from one man to the next, like a baton (or a truncheon). Above all, it leaves the film's close appropriately jarring, like a symphony ending in a sorrowful minor key. An unresolved sense of frustration at the state of the world lingers on, and the camera could catch any one of the marginalised faces in the street, and see it.

The family

Despite the Swedish model promising the emancipation of the individual from the institutions of civil society, the family, above all else, refuses to relinquish its hold, constantly resurfacing in Swedish crime fiction as the narrative glue, the key to society's crimes. As many characters in British soap operas consistently remind us, 'it's all about the family (faaaamily)'. From Shakespeare to *The Godfather* (dir. Francis Ford Coppola, 1972) to *Mad Men* (dir. various, 2007–ongoing), families in narrative fiction are presented as both corporeally and psychologically specific, and as representative of nationhood. The same is true in Swedish crime fiction, perhaps best exemplified by the operatic tragedy at the heart of the *Millennium* trilogy, as Lisbeth Salander battles against her father Zalachenko: a Soviet turncoat, crossing geographical and political boundaries to come in from the cold, latterly operating under the secret protection of the Swedish state. This creation of national/familial sin connects with the appearance of family units as corrupt industrial entities in the *Millennium* trilogy. *The Girl with the Dragon Tattoo* begins with Blomkvist's downfall in the Wennerström affair: our 'hero' suffers the consequences of taking on a corrupt family-led corporate empire. Soon after, he is embroiled in the murky affairs of the Vanger family, with secret histories of Nazi-sympathisers and serial killers. Such melodramatic tropes serve as suitably heightened signifiers of the dangers of close-knit families leading a nation's business in the world. The situation becomes even more tightly localised in the *Wallander* mystery *The Man Who Smiled*, through the concentration on an all-influential Swedish family at the heart of such corrupt global operations: the Harderbergs (whose gruesome practices we shall learn more about later). Sejersted sets out the historical antecedents of the contemporary situation:

> The period between 1950 and 1975 represents the golden age of industrialism in Sweden ... Characteristic for Sweden, the ownership structure of large industrial firms was

concentrated in a few groups, sometimes referred to as the 'fifteen families'. Typically these ownership groups held close relationships to the largest Swedish banks. The Wallenbergs were the dominant group, having a controlling interest in [amongst others] SAAB, Scania-Vabis, L. M. Ericsson, and SKF. An important feature in the structure was their bank, the Stockholms Enskilda Private Bank. The group members typically held ownership positions in their bank, which was simultaneously their most important source of loans.[144]

Karsten Wind Meyhoff makes the links between fact and fiction in her article 'Digging into the Secrets of the Past: Rewriting History in the Modern Scandinavian Police Procedural':

> During his investigation Blomkvist maps out a family history that goes back several hundred years and tells a classic tale of how many of the large family owned companies in Sweden were built ... The privately controlled Swedish company Vanger represents the many Swedish companies controlled and owned by powerful families. It is no secret that these family owned, mega-corporations dominate a large part of Swedish corporate life and society. The families have typically been very secretive about their internal affairs and fortunes, and one of the attractions of Larsson's story is that he gives us access to the hidden world of these dynasties.[145]

Even before the film starts, the 2012 DVD release of David Fincher's *The Girl with the Dragon Tattoo* prioritises the idea of allowing 'access to the hidden world' of the Vanger family as an all-powerful Swedish dynasty. The DVD menu screen presents a looping series of still photographs of the Vangers, concentrating on shots of a much younger Henrik and his grand-daughter, Harriet, enjoying happier times together. The faded, weather-worn images contrast with the pin-sharp quality of the DVD. We are being coaxed into the story by candid pictures, an intimate portrait of one family. But it is not until we enter the world of the film proper, pressing Play, that we discover how misleading these nostalgic images are, when presented with, in time and as Henrik Vanger puts it to Blomvist, the 'most detestable collection of people you will ever meet: my family'. Just as Blomkvist and Salander use modern-day technology – the internet, photographic software, surveillance recordings – to reveal the secrets of the past, so too does the film ask us to call upon the machinery of the digital image to gain access to this hidden world. We will explore this idea further in the next chapter. For now, we can note that the idea of a collision of past and present forms, breaking the veneer of a surface presented to us, is inextricably connected in Fincher's film to that of dynasty. Viewers and characters move beyond the sepia-tinted photographs of yesteryear into the true history of the Vangers, using the trappings of the modern to reclaim the past, just as the Vangers, as a commanding Swedish family, will use the same forms to hide it.

Fincher's film develops the idea in its textures. A good example is the form taken by Henrik Vanger's flashbacks to moments spent with Harriet. They occur when he recounts the terrible tale of Harriet's last days on the island to Blomkvist, when an accident on the bridge leads to her disappearance. The film presents these memories in a hyper-real aesthetic, bleaching the image while picking out details on the edge of the frame in saturated colours (including, for example, children's bright red toy windmills, turning in the breeze). The effect hints at the importance of things flickering on the periphery, a clue to the killer's position, present but just out of sight (on the day of the accident, in the photographs, in the world of the film). Moreover, events of the past are being presented in a thoroughly modern form of filmmaking: the slick stylisation presents another veneer that Blomkvist must negotiate and move past in order to get at the truth (the real instead of the hyper-real).[146]

Much later, in an almost silent scene, Blomkvist creeps into Martin Vanger's ultra-modern house to uncover (and stumble into) the murderer's underground lair. The money from an unseemly past and immensely influential family business – now a contemporary Swedish 'mega-corporation' – has created, for Martin, a modernist palace. Blomkvist's stealthy passage through the house reveals the extent of its glass and steel surfaces, its metallic sheen. Glass dividers are slid open and chrome buttresses criss-cross into a kind of luxurious cage. Drugged and dragged to the basement, where Martin conducts his grisly torture and killing of young girls, Blomkvist finds himself being filmed on a digital camera. His misery is being memorialised for Martin's later enjoyment, in cutting-edge celluloid form, just as Blomkvist's image will, presumably, join the other head-shots of murder victims displayed as Polaroid photos across the basement walls. Here, then, is a collection of wipe-clean surfaces containing the truth of terrible past actions. The parade of victims' head-shots recalls the array of framed flowers sent to Henrik by Harriet: contrastingly oblique types of family galleries, one a dreadful 'assumed family' of victims; the other a coded message of intimacy from granddaughter to grandfather. Further, the plastics of the photographic images chime with the texture of the plastic bag placed over Blomkvist's head by Martin. Crucially, there is a hermetic seal to the bag, the photographs, the modernist glass house, all suffocating, keeping past and present encased. The aesthetics of Fincher's film present a family dynasty keen to preserve a superficial facade of wealth and respectability through luxury and the impenetrable textures of modern living. It is only when these hard edges and smooth surfaces are broken that the bloody messiness of the Vanger history oozes out.

In Swedish crime fiction, a grubby past will breach present-day veneers, splintering influential family lines. Another revealing example comes in the 2007 small-screen adaptation of the prequel *Wallander* mystery, *The Pyramid*. In an apparently unremarkable scene (designed to establish the characters and their relationships), the drug king-pin's extended family sits around the dinner table. The arrangements of linen, china, music, and occasion suggest a desire, perhaps a little forced, to epitomise the fine rituals of upper middle-class social etiquette. Yet, as the sequence proceeds, cracks begin to show. A supercilious aunt corrects the youngest member of this decidedly nasty dynasty – a chattering prim girl – for mis-pronouncing 'him' as ''im'. Upon delivering her rebuke, the aunt breaks form too, hilariously oblivious, shovelling food into her mouth in a most unbecoming manner. The scene recalls the grotesquery of *Greed* (dir. Erich von Stroheim, 1924), when a well-heeled family gorges on luxurious meats in a disgusting display of consumption. This is new money, made from drug deals, and the little scene conveys the dark flip-side and ugly standing of one of Sweden's all-powerful national families.

Bringing the closed networks of press, police, and family together, Nordic noir, like any noir, most often presents the loner protagonist, reporter or detective, in an unhappy marriage. In this respect, Robert B. Pippin goes even further, painting the genre a deeper shade of black:

> The noir representation of bourgeois domestic life – the peaceful, secure, commercial and domestic activity many heroes in Hollywood Westerns were desperately trying to establish – portrayed it as so stultifying and banal that even crime began to look attractive to those trapped in it. The most powerful and effective human passions seemed to be greed, revenge, lust, and craven fear. The state of modern marriage seemed absolutely horrific, either some sort of stupefied self-satisfaction or a seething, barely controlled state of mutual loathing.[147]

Swedish crime fiction presents a measured, tempered variation on this theme, again most often through descriptions or arrangements of bodies in space. In Colin Nutley's *The Bomber*, Annika Bengzton's family is repeatedly presented in images of play, yet they are always in a rush, caught in the frictions of bodily activity: tumbling in bed and on sofas, running to appointments, rubbing each other the wrong way. In Bo Widerberg's *The Man on the Roof*, a dynamic of physical proximity and emotional separation is conveyed in the very first images of Martin Beck at home with his wife and daughter. Beck stoops at the kitchen table absorbed in work on his model boat. His daughter stands over him holding a cold cloth to his brow: a little pressure gently applied from offspring to father. Meanwhile, his wife is tucked away in the kitchen, swaddled (comfortably cocooned?) in her fluffy dressing gown. Later, the film frames wife and husband in different rooms and doorways of the house, like figurines on a clock mechanically emerging in an hourly ritual from separate compartments, as Beck collects piles of blankets from the cupboard: padding around the home.

The *Wallander* films are especially adept at expressing the graded distance of the eponymous detective from familial intimacies. A striking example occurs in *The Pyramid*. The split connection between Wallander (Lassgård) and his god-daughter Eva (Moa Gammel) is conveyed in the frame through geometric meeting points of horizontal and vertical lines, designs, and coloured stripes. Eva has died from a drug overdose. When Wallander goes to visit her, to see the body, the scene begins in long shot: the dead girl stretched out horizontally on the hospital bed, draped in white sheets, the only colour coming from a single red rose set upright in a stem glass. Wallander stands stock still above the girl, his fixed position accentuated by the vertical red stripe of his long scarf dangling down his body, its colouring matching that of the pert rose. Stark horizontal and vertical lines suggest how Wallander and his goddaughter have always been at cross purposes. Wallander is upstanding, but perhaps too rigid, when it comes to his family, in his stance. Yet as he looks down on the girl, the lighting adds a soft red tint to his face, a spreading of emotional involvement.

The most complex, and moving, account comes in the textual and contextual histories of *Before the Frost* (novel 2001 *Innan Frosten*; translated 2005 Laurie Thompson; tele-film 2005). It is the only episode of the Henriksson series to be adapted from a Mankell novel (all the others are new stories and tele-plays, sanctioned by the author). *Before the Frost* presents us with a particularly interesting case as the novel was to mark a shift of emphasis from

Kurt Wallander to his daughter Linda. As the back-cover blurb of the Vintage book declares, 'Linda Wallander, in preparation to join the police force, arrives at Ystad. Exhibiting some of the hallmarks of her father – the maverick approach, the flaring temper – she becomes entangled in a case involving a group of religious extremists who are bent on punishing the world's sinners. Following on from the enormous success of the Kurt Wallander mysteries, Henning Mankell has begun an outstanding new chapter in crime writing.'[148] The novel was to be the first in a trilogy centring on the young female police officer. Yet, the suicide in 2007 of the actor playing Linda – Johanna Sällström – led to a devastated Mankell shelving the book series.[149] There are also shifts in the film, made before Sällström's death, as if uncomfortable with fully redirecting the attention from father to daughter.[150] And, within the diegesis, there is a tussle for control between the Wallanders.

More than in any other episode or version of Kurt Wallander on screen, this is the most eloquent expression of his dynamic with his daughter. The novel opens the way for meditations on this subject, as 'Linda Caroline Wallander wondered if there were any traits that she and her father had in common which yet remained to be discovered, even though she was almost 30 years old and ought to know who she was by this time.'[151] It is the television episode that best reveals the nuances of this relationship. Consider, for example, the sequence when Kurt and Linda Wallander visit, on official business, the home of a missing woman's family (the Medbergs). The episode is acutely alert to the expressive potential of composition here, in terms of costume, colour, and framing. Its style reveals the complex of roles and feelings, personal and professional, binding, entangling, restricting father and daughter. Wallander is dressed in a white shirt, light chinos and a pale yellow tie flapping in the wind behind him (tugging him back), scurrying behind his daughter. Linda, in contrast, is dressed in a stark dark blue police uniform, with bold yellow trim and lettering: POLIS. Yet it is too big, too baggy, held together by an oversized belt. Linda holds tight to the belt as she walks, seeking support, whereas Wallander has his hands in his pockets.

The weight of the moment falls with Linda. She approaches the house, taking her first steps as an officer on duty. The sound of her footfall up the path, her knock on the front window, is a little unnatural in its over-amplification. Here, the film conveys the purposeful, slightly forced way Linda goes about making her mark. She is new to this as well as aware that her father is watching her every move, and so are we. These actions might be clunky but they are leading; Kurt follows silently behind. An awkward dynamic between generations is echoed in the first sight of the family being questioned. A little boy emerges from the front door, his mother following behind, nudging him out of the way – a little too heavily, like everything else here. Something's wrong. The usually eloquent and steadfast Wallander struggles to find his place in this situation, cast adrift by his daughter's presence in the role of policewoman. He is out of uniform, out of his comfort zone as the roles become complicated. He stands on the edge of the frame and room, his flimsy reflection held in the glass where the child previously stood: a trace of his former self.

3

SPACE AND PLACE

As the example from *Before the Frost* illustrates, Swedish crime fiction emphasises the powerful connection between closed communities and spatial arrangements. This chapter concentrates on the latter factor, exploring how characters and texts negotiate the architecture of social control, disorganisation, and conflict, the neighbourhoods of collective action and communal unrest. At the heart of the chapter, and many works of Swedish crime fiction, is a question about 'what occurs in settings where the idea of a public or common good has been lost'.[152]

Once the application of terms 'space' and 'place' in crime fiction is established, the chapter addresses how Sweden's settings are handled in the works. For example, Swedish crime fiction makes frequent expressive use of the country's wide open terrain, and its crowded cities, dotted amidst vast woodlands. The chapter then details the texts' interest in border crossings: national, transnational, in views from outside (foreign filmmakers looking 'in'), and from outsiders, inhabiting marginal spaces of society. After considering the different spaces and places' respective associations of exposure, containment, and entrapment, the recurrence of particular locations is scrutinised: the city (so central to noir), the country house and locked rooms (both established sub-genres of the form). Finally, the chapter turns from the works' engagement with physically concrete or naturally established spaces and places, to consider their interest in the more modern, virtual setting of cyberspace. Swedish crime fiction, alert to and sharing the country's fascination for all things cutting-edge, explores the internet's capabilities for anonymous surveillance, personal intrusion, and global connections.

I'm taking 'space' to mean those areas we encounter that do not have a fixed geographical denomination, zones existing outside of clearly categorised and delimited physical regions. So, Stockholm, the police station, and a dining room are all places, whereas the site people use at the edge of the city limits to gather and make their criminal plans is a space, as is a shaded spot in a seemingly boundless forest, or a swirl of eddies in the sea. In his essay 'The Place of Pessimism in Henning Mankell's Kurt Wallander Series', Shane McCorristine stresses the meeting points of location and sensibility, the way the novels evoke both Wallander's and Sweden's outlook in descriptions of the landscape. In turn, he provides a useful definition of 'place' in this context: '"Place" is understood here in the broad sense of a category that can be equally thought of in terms of location, locale and an individual's own sense of place or emotional ties with the world.'[153] As Tytti Soila notes, such poetic associations have long been a mainstay of Swedish art, especially film: 'The Swedish silent film was characterised during the "golden age" by realism expressed in films where man was described as an integral part of nature, linked to the environment of his childhood. Changes in weather and seasons, views of mountains and plains, images of roaring rivers and swaying birch groves were actively linked to the descriptions of characters and associated with their fate.'[154] And, for Scaggs, the rendering of localised setting in crime fiction is indicative of the genre's entrenched realist aspirations across time and countries:

> [An] identification of how detective stories very quickly suggest or depict a scene in an implied space in the contemporary world significantly relates the fiction of the Golden

Age, and its variants, to the realist tradition, and the central importance of realist spatial setting is evident in the almost obligatory presence of maps in Golden Age fiction. *The Mysterious Affair at Styles* features a map of the murdered Mrs Inglethorp's bedroom, and most of Christie's subsequent novels also feature maps, whether or not they are helpful to the reader. The use of maps, along with the use of titles that fix a particular event in spatial terms, can be seen throughout Christie's *oeuvre* ... Similarly, maps of various kinds, including those of a topographical, meteorological, and geological nature, are central to the twenty-first-century investigations of *C.S.I.*[155]

Many of Mankell's *Wallander* mysteries feature maps that move ever closer to the protagonist's stomping grounds: of the Southern region Skåne, of the town Ystad, of streets and places frequented by the detective (Istvan's Pizzeria, Fridolf's Cafe, Österleden and Stortorget). Stieg Larsson is at pains to describe the shops, bridges, and homes of Hedeby Island in *The Girl with the Dragon Tattoo*, paying as much attention to mapping the contours of this isolated (fictitious) locale as he is to setting out the complex webs of deceit spun there by its occupants. While Scaggs' description draws a through-line from Agatha Christie to *C.S.I: Crime Scene Investigation* (dir. various, 2000–ongoing), there may also be particularly modern reasons for heightening senses of space and place in Swedish crime fiction. For example, Slavoj Žižek uses Mankell's novels to explain how a particularly emboldened national locale has become the norm for modern crime fiction in the global age:

> The main effect of globalisation on the detective fiction is discernible in its dialectic counterpart: the powerful re-emergence of a specific locale as the story's setting – a particular environment ... The specific colour that the locale of his novels brings is the Scandinavian one with all existentialist-depressive connotations ... [156]

Žižek's claim raises two crucial and interconnected aspects of space and place in Swedish crime fiction. First, there is the aura of a Scandinavian mood traced through the relationship between landscape, characters, and national sensibility (the bleakness so often emphasised in reviews of, say, the country's TV detective dramas). Second, Žižek hints at Sweden's anxiety about its tentative place on the globalised world stage, constantly asserting and questioning its own spatial markers of national identity, even while such fixed signposts dissolve in transnational patterns of convergence. Both speak to crime fiction's awareness and use of Sweden's 'specific colour' in geographical form.

Sweden's geographical identity

Sweden's geography, as with so many other facets of its national identity, is informed by an isolationism complicated by borderline closeness to others. The country shares boundaries with Norway, Denmark, and Finland. Yet, as Austin observes:

> Not lying, like Norway, along the ocean routes, or, like Denmark, facing the continent, Sweden in many ways was for centuries more of an island than Britain. At the beginning of the nineteenth century even the small villages were broken up, the better to till the available soil ... Half a century ago, almost the whole nation lived in such solitudes. Now two-thirds have suddenly moved into town. They have brought with them, one feels, their isolation. Distances, more physical, have been introjected, swallowed.[157]

The topography of its capital, Stockholm, offers a particularly concentrated example of this interplay between separation and connectivity. It is built on fourteen islands, with the archipelago comprising 24,000 islets. Water surrounds the city, and each small land mass retains an individual identity. The bridges between islets and countries carry cargo and a meaningful charge, as Brown eloquently suggests:

The Öresund bridge smelled of sea and wet concrete when I drove across it to Sweden in a blue-gray dazzle of fog. It traverses the fifteen kilometres of strait between Copenhagen and Malmö. Only half of it is airborne: the rest runs through a tunnel and across an artificial island, Pepparholmen, which was built at the same time as the bridge, a little south of the existing, natural island Saltholmen, so as not to disturb the nature reserve there. You could not have a more dramatic, nor beautiful, symbol of the power and prosperity of Sweden at the end of the twentieth century; nor could you have a clearer statement that the century has ended: the bridge fixes Sweden to the uncontrolled world outside, when through all the years of social democracy the ideal of the country was of a psychological autarky which could deal with the outer world entirely on its own terms.[158]

As intermediary spaces, the bridges suspend Sweden's situation between division and communion. One particular, contemporary example encapsulates this suggestion more than most. The Öresundbro Bridge was completed on 1 June 2000, connecting Sweden with Denmark, or more precisely, the Southern province of Skåne and its capital city Malmö (previously Danish territories) with the Danish capital Copenhagen. According to Bo Tao Michaëlis:

The bridge to Malmö has not only stirred a renaissance for [a] 'freedom movement' [of Skåne reclaiming its historic Danish character]; it has also connected Southern Sweden more closely to Copenhagen than to the country's actual capital, beautiful Stockholm. Nowadays, Swedes/Skånings work in Copenhagen and Danes live in Malmö. The bridge has transformed Malmö into a large suburb of Copenhagen; generally speaking, our capital could be seen as a Manhattan to a Malmö that, via one of Europe's longest bridges, has become a northern European Brooklyn![159]

It follows that such an imposing super-structure would also make an impression on fictions exploring meeting points of Sweden and

Denmark. In Michaëlis's collection of short stories, *Copenhagen Noir*, Kristin Lundberg creates an impressionistic portrait of Malmö, a view from the bridge. In the story 'Savage City, Cruel City', Lundberg connects the bridge's associations of suspension and fluid exchange with the social and psychological states of his characters. His criminal has 'offered to transport goods from Poland to Sweden' while his detective – Nils Forberg – 'has crossed several boundaries in the course of his life … Now he was in a gray zone, neither alive nor dead, and yet – a bit of both'.[160] While Lundberg extends into overt social commentary – calling Malmö 'one of the larger suburbs of Copenhagen' – the Öresundbro Bridge's impact also registers in even starker terms in the Swedish-Danish television crime drama *The Bridge*. Just as Lundberg suggests violence at work in the commuter train that 'shoots out between Malmo and Copenhagen, penetrating the morning like a flaming arrow',[161] the pivotal crime in the TV series revolves around a body found lying across the exact mid-point of the bridge, comprising two different corpse halves: half in Sweden, half in Denmark. The investigation that ensues causes old divisions between the two countries to surface, as both police forces and sets of politicians try to control the story. In both fictions, while the bridge speeds up a dual process of diffusion and compression – as borders dissolve and people mingle shoulder to shoulder in busy city spaces – the 'traditional' Swedish sensation of loneliness lingers.

A sense of individual remoteness, found even in built-up urban settings, may well stem from, paradoxically, the wide open (shared, public) nature of huge parts of Sweden. Two short remarks from Richard Hill and David Haworth capture the connections of land and sensibility, and the inherent contradiction between openness and emotional detachment. While, 'Foreigners are impressed by the freedom of movement and right of access the country offers: no "private property: keep out" signs … Swedes find it difficult to console, for example, a workmate who has lost a close relative. Instead, "consideration" is shown by keeping a distance or by acting as if nothing had happened.'[162] Further, once more, Brown perfectly evokes the extent of Sweden's widely accessible, instantly isolating spaces, their profound physical and psychological *reach*:

> I don't want to overestimate the wildness of these woods: they were logged regularly and broken by frequent small-holdings. None the less, it would have been possible to travel from Lilla Edet to Lapland without ever leaving the forest except to cross roads; and, a couple of years later, a pack of six wolves was tracked from Russia, through Finland and Swedish Lapland, and then for a further 1,600 kilometres down the spine where Sweden and Norway are joined until one of them broke off, header further south, and killed a sheep in a field just outside of town.[163]

The possibilities for Swedish crime fiction, in using the vast open spaces of the country and countryside as voids into which people can vanish, are equally endless. In the *Van Veeteren* mystery *Borkmann's Point*, Håkan Nesser, in multiple ways, sets the scene:

> When Simmel flicked his cigarette end into the water and set off in the direction of the municipal woods, the murderer knew that tonight was the night. True, there were only about three hundred yards of trees here between the Esplanade and Rikken, the yuppie part of the town where Simmel lived, and there were plenty of lights along the paths; but not all were working and three hundred yards could prove to be rather a long way. In any case, when Simmel heard a faint footstep behind him, he was barely fifty yards into the woods and the darkness was dense on all sides.[164]

The link to the murderer – who knew that 'tonight was the night' – enacts the genre's age-old technique and thematic of realising the dangerous element that lurks at the edges of 'safe' urban spaces, playing on middle-class fears of their respectable cocooned dwellings suddenly being penetrated by ne'er-do-wells and criminals. A comparable scenario plays out in British writer Ian McEwan's thriller *Saturday*.[165] There, in contemporary London, Henry Perowne, a moneyed neurosurgeon is brought into conflict with a young working-class man, Baxter. Baxter's aggressive threats culminate in his breaking and entering Perowne's plush home. Chiming with concerns central to our discussions, the narrative takes place, following an introductory quotation from Saul Bellow's 1964 novel *Herzog*, 'In a city. In a century. In a mass. Transformed by science. Under organised power. Subject to tremendous controls. In a condition caused by mechanisation. After the late failure of radical hopes. In a society that was no community and devalued the person. Owing to the multiplied power of numbers which made the self negligible. Which spent military billions against foreign enemies but would not pay for order at home. Which permitted savagery and barbarism in its own great cities.'[166] At the same time, *Borkmann's Point* taps into something more locally specific. As Simmel plunges into the woods' dense darkness, Nesser uncovers national anxieties attached to Sweden's geography. The country's peculiar landscape means that there is an enduring widespread closeness between such 'well-to-do' urban environments, and wild open terrain. Such is the elemental force of Sweden's historical, pre-industrial pull, that it only takes a couple of steps into the woods for the all-encompassing darkness to envelop you, strip you of your yuppie trappings and out of your comfort zone. Again, shadows of the past shroud the present in fatal, fatalistic ways. A similar scenario is described in the first novel of the *Sebastian Bergman* cycle. The reporting of a missing boy – Roger Eriksson – is worded thus by his mother, Lena, to policewoman Klara:

> 'And you have no idea where he might have gone? Could he have stayed over with friends, something like that?'
> 'No, he would have called me.'
> Lena Eriksson paused briefly and Klara assumed that her voice was breaking, but when she heard the sucking intake of breath on the other end she realised that the woman was taking a long drag on a cigarette. She heard Lena blow out the smoke.
> 'He's just disappeared.'[167]

The mother's words are chilling in their resignation. Her acceptance of her son's desertion may, of course, come from knowledge of previous similar vanishing acts and misdemeanours. But it also suggests a broader, more haunting aspect: as if it were an inescapable fact that in this country, people have always just disappeared.

In contrast, no matter how hard the detective protagonists in Swedish crime fiction try to disappear, to find solitude in the countryside and at the ocean's edge, their commitments to the community keep pulling them back into the city. In *Borkmann's Point*, Nesser (over)emphasises the distance that Van Veeteren's chosen holiday destination places between himself and others, as 'The sands went on forever. Went on forever, the same as ever. A calm, grey sea under a pale sky ... Alongside a drier grayish-white expanse where beach grass and windswept bushes took over ... In the hazy distance he could just make out the church steeple in s'Greijvin, but it was a long way away.'[168] Yet, in the compression of many miles over a few pages, he is soon called back to headquarters. Across Mankell's novels, Wallander dreams of escape to the countryside and even to far-off lands. He achieves a trip to Egypt with his father in *The Pyramid*, but is unimpressed and quickly returns to the station in Ystad. Similarly, in *The Man Who Smiled*, during a year of sick leave that only sends him further into spiralling depression and bouts of heavy drinking, he repeatedly tries to head away from home and himself:

> During that time a sense of powerlessness had come to dominate his life and affected his actions. Time and time again, when he could not bear to stay in Ystad and had some money to spare, he had gone off on pointless journeys in the vain hope of feeling better, perhaps even of recovering his zest for life, if only he were somewhere other than Skåne. He had taken a package holiday to the Caribbean, but had drunk himself silly on the outward flight and had not been entirely sober for any of the fortnight he spent in Barbados. His general state of mind was one of increasing panic, a sense of being totally alienated. He had skulked in the shade of

palm trees, and some days had not even set foot outside his hotel room, unable to overcome a primitive need to avoid the company of others.[169]

Closer to home he fares no better. He takes an isolated guesthouse by the sea in the wilds of Skagen, a remote region which projects into the waters between the North Sea and the straits of Denmark. Walking along the barren beach, he is stopped and found by an old friend, Sten Torstensson, asking for his help in a family matter. The 'primitive need to avoid the company of others' is again overturned as intimates suddenly pop up out of nowhere to draw Wallander towards personal and professional duty. He can't escape his life in Skåne; as the bearing of region and character fuse, they reveal a particular quality of Mankell's work:

> Wallander makes sense of his place through a habitually pessimistic turn of phrase: one of the most common words he employs to describe Skåne is 'desolation' ... also a word Wallander uses to describe his personal life ... and it is this exaggerated interlinking of landscape and psychology, personhood and place, that marks out Mankell from other recent Scandinavian crime writers such as Åke Edwardson and Stieg Larsson.[170]

Mankell, *Wallander* and Wallander are thoughtful about the striving of a person, region, and nation to preserve particular aspects of selfhood in an environment of constant, often violent flux and exchange. In Mankell's mysteries, from a forensic concentration on one place, Skåne, Sweden's hidden secrets are unearthed, its schisms magnified. As Wallander ponders in *The Pyramid*, 'An underground fissure had suddenly surfaced in Swedish society. Radical seismographers had registered it. But where had it come from?'[171]

The tele-film of *The Pyramid* responds to this question by shaping visually arresting examples of 'pure cinema' to suggest splits in the social fabric, blots on the landscape. It opens with archetypal shots of sea and fields: the oft-seen windswept natural features of Sweden on film. Yet it quickly complicates more conventional associations of all-immersing bleakness as a bi-plane cuts into the frame, like a fly buzzing around a (national) portrait, spoiling the canvas and blanket mood. A small dot getting bigger as it grows nearer to the camera and ground, the aircraft's passage recalls the celebrated arrival of the deadly crop-spreader in *North by Northwest* (dir. Alfred Hitchcock, 1959), suddenly zooming and looming over Roger O. Thornhill (Cary Grant). Like Wallander, no matter how many times he tries to hide under and in the big skies, bad-lands and dustbowls of America, Thornhill will be found. *The Pyramid* and the landscape are both instantly inflected by Hitchcockian design: something wicked this way comes ('But where had it come from?') We later learn that the plane is carrying drugs over the border: crack(s) across national lines creating fissures in Swedish society.

Border crossings

The fact that the plane is flying consignments of heroin into Sweden from Denmark undetected and under the radar opens up thoughts on border crossings. A recurrent concern for Mankell, the theme becomes particularly redolent in *The Pyramid*, from the very first lines, describing the plane's trajectory:

> The aeroplane flew in over Sweden at a low altitude just west of Mossby Beach. The fog was thick out at sea but growing lighter closer to shore. Contours of the shoreline and the first few houses rushed towards the pilot. But he had already made this trip many times. He was flying by instruments alone. As soon as he crossed the Swedish border and identified Mossby Beach and the lights along the road to Trelleborg, he made a sharp turn north-east and then another turn east. The plane, a Piper Cherokee, was obedient. He positioned himself along a route that had been carefully planned. An air corridor cut an invisible path over an area in Skåne where the houses were few and far between.[172]

This intricate description recalls aspects brought to the fore in Bellow's words cited earlier, of a place and time falling foul of 'a condition caused by mechanisation. After the late failure of radical hopes.' In this 'society with no community', the economic betterment of the self becomes more important than collective responsibility. As a consequence, the self is mechanised, 'flying by instruments alone'. The flight-path is second nature, the illegal trafficking so frequent that it is enacted without feeling or moral concern, and becomes *automatic*. It is telling that Mankell withholds any description of the criminal's physiognomy; he's not fleshed out. Further, detached from the earth (and so becoming unearthly) in aeronautic technology, the individual steers an invisible path, beyond the reach of law, 'somewhere between the spotlights'.[173]

Mankell deepens the exploration of this theme by linking Sweden's post-welfare state strive for global capital gain to conditions of national and personal insecurity. As the character Blomell remarks in *The Pyramid*, "'There is nothing in this world that is absolutely secure ... Nor will there ever be. Those who have enough money and motivation can always find their way across a border, and back again, without interception."'[174] For Mankell, here and elsewhere, the transnational impulse of global capitalist exchange *as enacted by the Swedish individual* is the single greatest threat to the state of the nation's soul. Through the matter-of-fact expressive register of colleagues at work on a police procedure, the author is able to set out the dangers in stark form. A good example comes when Officer Rydberg explains the criminal activities of the seemingly harmless Eberhardsson sisters, in detail:

> 'According to the Swedish securities register centre, the Eberhardsson sisters had stocks and bonds totalling close to ten million kronor. How they managed to keep this from being subject to the wealth tax is a mystery. Nor do they appear to have paid income tax on their dividends. But I've alerted the tax authorities. It actually appears that Anna Eberhardsson was registered as a resident of Spain. But I'm

not clear on the details of this yet. In any case, they had a large portfolio of investments both in Sweden and abroad. The Swedish securities register centre's ability to check international investments is of course minimal; this is not their job. But the sisters invested heavily in the British weapons and aviation industries. And in this they appear to have shown great skill and daring.'[175]

As Rydberg asserts, nothing is clear except a growing pattern of uncertainty. The sisters' global transactions are as spectral as the earlier description of the airborne drug-smuggler. Again, 'invisible paths' are taken to cross borders, between Britain, Spain, and Sweden. Again, individual criminals are mechanised: through investments 'in the British weapons and aviation industries'. Insult is added to injury in their tax evasions, a complete betrayal of schemes central to the welfare state. This, according to Rydberg, is the 'tip of the proverbial iceberg', or the peak of the pyramid, rot spreading from the automaton individual's circumnavigation of old principles of social democracy throughout Swedish society. Mankell reconnects with the idea of border crossing and the diffuse spread of a social malaise via a more succinct metaphor a little later in the novel, when Rydberg says, in total exasperation, '"Nothing surprises me any longer. Greed knows no bounds when it sinks its claws into people."'[176]

In another exchange between Wallander and his colleague, Rydberg, Mankell develops the connection further still, linking a method of murder to the effacement of national and regional borders. Both are presented as longstanding forms of violence growing from capitalist desires, which, in turn, threaten Swedish identity:

> Wallander stood up. 'I'll see you at one,' he said. 'For now, let Martinsson focus on the plane ... Have we ever had anything like this?'
> Rydberg considered. 'Not that I can remember. There was a lunatic who planted an axe in a waiter's head about twenty

years ago. The motive was an unpaid debt of thirty kronor. But I can't think of anything else.'

Wallander lingered at the table.

'Execution-style,' he said. 'Not particularly Swedish.'

'And what is Swedish, exactly?' Rydberg asked. 'There are no longer any borders. Not for aeroplanes nor serious criminals. Once Ystad lay on the outskirts of something. What happened in Stockholm did not happen here. Not even things that occurred in Malmö were typical in a small town like Ystad. But that time is over.'[177]

Once the axe falls, it cuts the ribbon between regions, countries, chaos, and control. Ystad is no longer on the outskirts of something, because everywhere is now part of a global hinterland. In *The Girl with the Dragon Tattoo*, Stieg Larsson adds his own flourish to this pattern through the framed flowers sent to Henrik Vanger every year on his birthday: 'Most often the parcel was posted in Stockholm, but three times from London, twice from Paris, twice from Copenhagen, once from Madrid, once from Bonn, and once from Pensacola, Florida. The detective superintendent had to look it up in an atlas.'[178] As Vanger believes the well-travelled gifts to be a cruel annual reminder from Harriet's killer, the connection between criminality and global consumerism is sealed. Equally, the Wennerström affair is presented by Lindberg (standing in for Larsson?) as a striking polemic of the impact of transnational capitalism borne of the 1980s and 1990s:

'You remember those days: everyone was so optimistic when the Berlin Wall came down. Democracy was going to be introduced, the threat of nuclear war was over, and the Bolsheviks would turn into regular little capitalists overnight. The government wanted to nail down democracy in the East. Every capitalist wanted to jump on the bandwagon and help build the new Europe ... It was a capitalist's wet dream. Russia and Eastern Europe may be the world's biggest untapped markets after China. Industry had no problem joining hands with the government, especially when the companies were required to put up only a token investment. In all, the A.I.A. [Agency for Industrial Assistance] swallowed about thirty billion kronor of the taxpayer's money.'[179]

Greed knows no bounds when it sinks its claws into people. Similarly angled descriptions are found in Lapidus's *Snabba Cash*, as JW appraises the appearance of his new gang:

> Button-down shirts from Paul Smith and Dior, and one specially made by a tailor on Jermyn Street in London. One from the brand A.P.C. – French – with an American collar and double cuffs. Two of the guys wore Acne jeans. Gucci on another: intricate designs on the back pockets. One wore black cotton slacks. The blazers were elegant. One from Balenciaga's spring collection: double-breasted, brown; a somewhat short model with double pockets on one side. One was ordered from a tailor on Savile Row in London: visible seams at the cuffs and with a red silk lining. The wool was super 150s, no higher quality anywhere. The telltale sign of a nice suit: the fluidity of the lining, that it didn't sag. This particular jacket's lining was softer, more fluid, and had a better fit than anything that could be found in the stores in Sweden.[180]

Consumer goods flow across national borders to refashion Sweden, perfectly suiting the progressive criminal. The meticulous listing of couture labels by the novel's underworld protagonist calls to mind Brett Easton-Ellis' *American Psycho* (1991), in which serial killer Patrick Bateman is as maniacal about the pedigree of his cuff-links as he is blasé about the choice of his victims. The act of chic cataloguing folds a disturbing banality into obsessive behaviour, insidious by design. In Lapidus's example, the international patch-work stitches back together Sweden's torn social fabric as a more modern model, while the anti-hero admires the cut's *fluidity*.

The view from outside

Just as modern Sweden becomes a product of international consumption, so too is Swedish crime fiction, with its strong tradition of remakes and co-productions, increasingly globalised. Another way of responding to Rydberg's question – 'what is "Swedish" exactly' (any more)? – is to consider the picture from the other end of the telescope, from the perspective of those looking in from outside, at how foreign filmmakers conceive the spaces and places of this country. The idea that national sensibility might, in fact, be best captured in art by an outsider, is not novel. Examples in cinema abound, from (as noted earlier) Alfred Hitchcock's treks across the American landscape via Warner Bros., Paramount and Universal, to, say, Alfonso Cuarón's adaptation of P. D. James' dystopian view of future Britain in *Children of Men* (2006).

At first, perhaps as self-conscious of its place as both an adaptation and a Hollywood remake, David Fincher's 2011 film *The Girl with the Dragon Tattoo* opens *outside* of time and space, with a bravura title sequence separated from the diegetic world of the narrative and, thus, from Sweden.[181] The sequence is at once unexpected and strangely familiar. Trent Reznor and Atticus Ross's electronic soundtrack bleeps and crackles across the entire film, and their take on Led Zeppelin's 'Immigrant Song' (a telling title) kicks proceedings off in arresting style. Whereas the credits introduce music to weave its way alongside the visual fabric of the rest of the film, the visuals of this opening sequence stand completely alone.

Nothing in the long-running trailer campaign or poster design prepares you for this sudden assault of impressionistic detail, melding CGI bodies with close-up shots of computer hardware, thorns, insects, tyres, wires, and fire, all dipped in a monochromatic wash of dead-of-night black. Abstract chunks of trappings associated with the film's world – keyboards and motorcycle components – are glued together by a gloopy rain of black liquid (oil? Molten rubber? Tattoo ink?) Spiky textures play against the gelatinous mess out of which springs a naked human couple (male? Female?) It is uncertain whether the pair seeks to rend free from each other's sticky embraces, or blend more firmly together as one. Their forms slip, slide, and sink in goo, before a beginning and ending are announced in quick cryptic images: a phoenix rises from the flames, and the entire screen is swallowed up by one of the morphing figures. In more ways than one, the start to the film is slick.

As well as quickening the pulse, the opening sequence declares its difference to the Swedish film version of *The Girl with the Dragon Tattoo* (dir. Niels Arden Oplev, 2009, opening more traditionally, inside the narrative world, on one of the main characters), while alluding to another lineage entirely: the James Bond films. In style and design, the title sequence explicitly recalls the famous work of Maurice Binder on fourteen Bond openings, from *Dr. No* (dir. Terence Young, 1962) to *Licence to Kill* (dir. John Glen, 1989). As Charles Taylor notes:

> His title designs – swirling neon fogs of colour set against enveloping backgrounds of velvety black – are all about freedom, not only the freedom of a filmmaker to work abstractly instead of narratively, but a metaphor for the sexy and liberating physical exhilaration of watching James Bond's adventures. You could say that Binder was to Isaac Newton what Blofeld was to Bond. His title sequences are three-minute refutations of the laws of gravity: figures jump and bounce and run through the colourful voids, or simply luxuriate in mid-air as if the atmosphere itself had become the most inviting bed in the universe. The sequences are a distillation of the films to colour and movement and sex.[182]

If we follow Taylor's interpretation, then a more precise description of Fincher's opening titles would be 'Anti-Bond'. Colour is immediately stripped away, and the emphasis is equally on restrictions to bodily movement as it is to a sense of free expression: the couple are ensnared by wires and each other. Further, the erotic aspect of Binder's work is made complex. The sensorial quality of the sequence, emphasising texture, has a sensual edge, but is bound up in the sadomasochistic pleasures of bondage as much as those of Bond. This is not a portrait of 'the most inviting bed in the universe'; the thorns, straps, and watery depths look sinister, painful, suffocating. Equally, the celebrated and fixed iconography of Binder's Bond sequences – guns and girls – becomes less clear here. Polymorphous forms and androgynous bodies hint at *The Girl with the Dragon Tattoo*'s explorations of unfixed identities. Expressions of ambiguity – the blurring of forms and lines – are at the heart of Larsson's trilogy: physical, political, institutional, and sexual. The textures of the opening are also in synch with the film's narrative and thematic threads. The elastic plastics and supercharged blast of the opening sequence prepare us at an instinctual level for a tale of emotional pliability and the act of being taken to breaking point. And, in emphasising the intermingling of forms and allusions, the opening speaks of its mixed heritage: the novels, the Swedish films, a Led Zeppelin song transformed into Electronica, of James Bond the cinematic phenomenon, and, indeed of Daniel Craig's appearance in the film. All gets tangled together in a two-minute fix of pure adrenalin.

When the film moves inside its story world and into a cinematic shaping of Sweden, we are presented with a landscape that emphasises the mythic, dark fairytale qualities of Larsson's book. Consider the way the film moves us to the scene of the crime, the estate on Hedeby Island. Mikael Blomkvist (Daniel Craig) and lawyer Dirch Frode (Steven Berkoff) are carried to the Vanger lair in their car, cutting through crisp and even snow. I'm reminded of the arrival of the satanic hearse in Jean Cocteau's *Orpheus* (1950), and the steady passage of the limousine taking Bill (Tom Cruise) towards the lusty dread of the manor house, down the masonic rabbit-hole, in Stanley Kubrick's *Eyes Wide Shut* (1999). Like mechanical ferrymen, all three automobiles slowly chug the protagonists to their underworld fates with an automatic sense of certainty. Fincher's camera glides as easily as the vehicle, in long unbroken strokes on the vertical plane. Camera and characters drift towards Henrik Vanger's country seat and he appears to greet them, as if by magic. The frontal camera angle and forward momentum slide the house into view, presenting something very similar to the proscenium aspect of a stage setting: *A Doll's House*, perhaps. Everything floats towards us as if part of a passing dream, but the presence of car and declamatory camerawork also suggest a well-oiled engine, the cinematic dream-machine cranking out its fantasies. Greased by the slick gloss of the pre-credit sequence, the scene's mechanics smoothly drive the journalist to his fate. As Henrik beckons Blomkvist into his drawing room, to sit by a welcome fire, sip a fine red wine and hear a tale of mystery, the bolt slides snug into its fixing.

Whereas Fincher creates a self-consciously trancelike image of snowbound Sweden, a far and otherworldly land of myth and magic locked inside a music-box, the British (BBC) version of *Wallander* creates a more grounded, nationally specific landscape. While the use of readily recognisable and authentic settings shores up the series' realist agenda, the filmmakers were also keen to embed a sense of Swedish identity in the colours and arrangements of its locales. In her article 'BBC *Wallander*: Sweden seen through British Eyes', Anne Marit Waade argues that '[A] specific view of "Swedishness" is present in the diegetic world and in the Swedish words and references visible on screen (e.g. street signs and newspapers). It is also there in the way everyday places are displayed and performed in the series: the specific soundscape, the rural landscapes, the flowers, the forest, the beach, the farms and the twilight.' [183] This thesis chimes with remarks made to me by the Executive Producer of the series, Andy Harries (with the full interview transcript appearing in Chapter 5). Discussing the handling of space and place in *Wallander*, Harries articulates the clear vision that informed his decisions to produce and shape the series in a particular way. Three extracts from the interview encapsulate three connected principles in action:

I was only interested, though, in making the series if it was set and filmed in Sweden – I didn't want to relocate the setting to, say, East Anglia ...

The idea was for the series to be like a translated novel. We found a visual equivalence: when a character picks up a newspaper, it is in Swedish. When they turn on the television, it is in Swedish. The signposting will be in Swedish, but the characters will talk English to each other. You have to decide, in television, what the rules of your narrative world are. You have to believe you are in Sweden ...

If you look at the first shot of the first episode [*Sidetracked*] – it is of Ken [Kenneth Branagh] as Wallander in the field – it was Ken's idea to open with this image: a brilliant analogy of the rape field and the young girl's assault, and also in terms of the impact of the yellow and blue colours – those of the Swedish flag. You are announcing, through the composition of the very first image of the series, that you are in Sweden, coupling this with the colours of the credit sequence and the use of Swedish typography.[184]

These are the coordinates that map out of the British *Wallander*'s narrative world, in terms of space and place. The use of English dialogue allows British/American viewers to quickly find their way into the world, while the diegetic presence of Swedish language signposts its national specificity. Typically Swedish landscapes (the rape fields) affirm this effect while, at the same time (and, here, in a demonstrably literal sense), adding local colour. Waade picks out another example from the same episode to suggest further layering at work: 'In *Sidetracked*, a Scandinavian symbol is used quite explicitly in a long shot of five swans flying over the water. The five swans is a familiar symbol within Scandinavian culture representing the five countries of which Scandinavia is comprised. In other words, national Swedish landscapes and symbols emerge pragmatically along with Scandinavian ones.'[185]

Exposure and entrapment in local settings

As in the above British/Scandinavian example, the texts shape their landscapes to reveal aspects local to character, plot, and particular space or place, while simultaneously conveying broader resonances of Sweden's status. In many instances, the handling of location reflects the relationship (as per the previous chapter) between the individual and the many – the lone (often loner) protagonist, and the national population or community as agents of social machinery. Most often, this is achieved through a play of tensions between physical, social, and psychological measurements of exposure and entrapment. An eloquent description of the prison in *Snabba Cash* provides a good starting point:

> Österåker was a close-security prison, a correctional facility of the second degree. Speciality: those condemned for drug-related crimes. Heavily guarded from both directions. No one and nothing got in that wasn't supposed to … And still they didn't succeed. The place used to be clean – during the previous warden's days. Now bags of weed were catapulted over the walls with slingshots. Dads got drawings from their daughters that were actually smeared with LSD. The shit was hidden above the inner roof in the common areas, where the dogs couldn't smell it, or was dug down in the lawn in the rec yard. Everyone and no one could be blamed.[186]

Conventionally taken as the archetypal social emblem of containment, prison becomes, in Lapidus's novel, a place of chaotic permeability. At once microcosmic and site-specific, contraband goods cross its borders, as ethical, physical, and legal boundaries start to blur. Similarly, the character of Lisbeth Salander in Stieg Larsson's *Millennium* trilogy appears at first sight an uncomplicated archetype, only for such assumptions to muddy as her story unfolds. She is, undoubtedly, positioned as an outsider: socially awkward, sexually ambiguous, sporting counter-cultural punk garb, spiked hair and an equally thorny fuck-you attitude. Yet, she is also, quite forcibly, trapped within and by society, institutionalised. The powers-that-be conspire to keep her strapped down and locked up:

> When she turned thirteen, the court had decided, under laws governing the guardianship of minors, that she should be entrusted to the locked ward at St. Stefan's Psychiatric Clinic for Children in Uppsala. The decision was primarily based on the fact that she was deemed to be emotionally disturbed and dangerously violent towards her classmates and possibly towards herself. All attempts made by a teacher or any authority figure to initiate a conversation with the girl about her feelings, emotional life, or the state of her health were met, to their great frustration, with a sullen silence and a great deal of intense staring at the floor, ceiling, and walls. She would fold her arms and refuse to participate in any psychological tests.[187]

Larsson feathers such nightmarish images with examples of his protagonist's attempts at flight from incarceration. (As Bo Tao Michaëlis reminds us, 'Noir loves flight, ill-fated love, the cold avenger').[188] Through the trilogy, Salander flees Hedeby Island, to become airborne, jetting from Sweden to stand triumphantly atop the Rock of Gibraltar. Lisbeth's various chosen venues of exile also reveal the text's transnational impulses: sharing time between Stockholm, the Caribbean, and Spain. When in the homeland, she escapes the horrendous treatment of the closed psychiatric ward to live in a luxury apartment overlooking Stockholm's sweeping cityscape. Notably, the spacious apartment remains unfurnished: no trappings.

Perhaps the richest example of space reflecting tensions between the many and the individual, exposure and entrapment, is found in the central scenario of *The Man on the Roof*. As the title suggests, book and film act as metonymic explorations of a society under fire. Widerberg's directorial skill in creating a politically charged aesthetic extends to his handling of locale. Daniel Brodén gauges the film's balance of realist detail and expansive spectacle:

Mannen på taket was an unusual film. It was both a dense action film and social-political film, and the combination of subtle acting, authentic locations, and bit parts played by drug addicts increased the film's credibility. Also, the film had a special atmosphere engendered largely by the unstable camera and the restless music characterised by the use of a flute. But the really unique feature for Swedish cinema was the large-scale action scenes: a killer makes his stand on a rooftop in central Stockholm and shoots down a police heli-copter that crashes onto the crowd below. The filming of this sensational helicopter crash, with thousands of extras, got considerable attention in the media. *Mannen på taket* was a Swedish film which had scenes that could compete with the mass panic scenes of the Hollywood thriller *Jaws* (Steven Spielberg, 1975), the hectic chase scenes of *The French Connection* (William Friedkin, 1971), and the spectacu-lar roof-climbing in the French *Peur sur la ville/The Night Caller* (Henri Verneuil, 1975).[189]

Widerberg's *The Man on the Roof* is particularly alert to the tropes and meanings of surveillance associated with the police procedur-al. The emphatic sound and presence of one man on a roof, open to the elements, training his gun on the crowds exposed below, are set against glancing acts of concealment. The film's first victim glimpses his killer's shrouded face through the hospital window, only to be stabbed through the eye. A pattern of visual composition develops around slivers of light in closed curtains and doors. The film plays out a scenario in which the divisions keeping criminal tendencies at bay, already cracking up, suddenly snap. Previously repressed anger bursts out, through the broken thin blue line, spraying onlookers with bullets. A state of seized freedom leads Stockholm into paralysis.

The city

Across time and countries, works of noir have naturally gravitated towards the city. While Swedish crime fiction is as interested in the isolation and exposure afforded by the country's ample forests, it too is attracted to aspects of urban realism, to the grime, crime, and disillusionment of the big city. Cynicism and disappointment collect like dust around city blocks. According to Scaggs, this matter is tied to another American literary tradition:

> What is significant about the fiction of [Dashiell] Hammett, [Raymond] Chandler, and Ross Macdonald is that the urban environment they depict is similar to that of T. S. Eliot's *The Waste Land* (1922) and the earlier 'The Love Song of J. Alfred Prufrock' (1915). In *The Waste Land*, the modern industrial city is depicted as a hell whose inhabitants have been 'undone' by a kind of death that is not physical, but spiritual and emotional. They are 'human engines' leading empty lives without meaning or significance, trapped in a city that is both London in 1922, and all modern cities ... Chandler's Los Angeles, in particular, is a city character-ised, above all else, by its 'unreality', and Marlowe's sustained commentary on, and analysis of, the details of architectural décor spring from his probing the surface of this unreality. The frontier myth of California as a place of abundance and opportunity has created 'an empire built on a spurious foundation, decked in tinsel, and beguiled by its own illu-sory promise' (Babener 1995: 128), and this vision of Los Angeles is central to Chandler's novels. His Los Angeles has been described as a 'metropolis of lies' (Babener 1995: 128), and the description is equally appropriate for both the city's architecture and its denizens, who gravitate there in response to the city's gilded promise of forging a new identity, and leaving the past, and past identities, far behind. Marlowe's Los Angeles is a city of facades, of stucco and fake marble. It is the home of Hollywood, 'the kingdom of illusion' (Babener 1995: 127).[190]

The description of 'human engines' joins hands with Mankell's pilot in *The Pyramid* flying by instruments alone. And, of course, there is a pronouncedly American history of the city appearing as a character in its own right, in film noir. The idea of artifice ('gilded promises') masking and cracking to reveal an ugly urban reality echoes Travis Bickle's thoughts on New York in *Taxi Driver* (dir. Martin Scorsese, 1976):

> 'Whatever it is, you should clean up this city here, because this city here is like an open sewer, you know? It's full of filth and scum. And sometimes I can hardly take it. Whatever – whoever becomes the president should just really clean it up. You know what I mean? Sometimes I go out and I smell it, I get headaches it's so bad, you know ... They just never go away you know ... It's like ... I think that the president should just clean up this whole mess here. You should just flush it right down the fuckin' toilet.'

Now compare Bickle's desperate disenchantment of life in New York with Beck's take on 1960s Stockholm:

> Nothing in town was very attractive just now, especially not this street with its bare trees and large, shabby blocks of flats. A bleak esplanade, misdirected and wrongly planned from the outset. It led nowhere in particular and never had, it was just there, a dreary reminder of some grandiose city plan, begun long ago but never finished. There were no well-lit shop windows and no people on the pavements. Only big, leafless trees and street lamps, whose cold white light was reflected by puddles and wet car roofs.[191]

According to our protagonists, whereas New York decays from within, shifting from Big Apple to rotten mess, Stockholm is a half-finished idea going nowhere, a gilded promise that was never kept. As in *Taxi Driver*, the film of *The Laughing Policeman* uses saturated colours and the neon lights of the rain-drenched city to reflect a sense of sickness. Dirty greens, bleached blues, and sudden woozy blasts of yellow (especially in advertising hoardings, for Al's burgers or Cutty Sark whisky) fill the frame. In many of the works, there is also an emphasis, like in *Taxi Driver*, of the city seen from a moving car. This is most striking in *Snabba Cash*. Cars take the characters, and us, to the police station, the woods, and through the city at night, curb-crawling by seedy nightspots. A constant queue of cars spewing out exhaust fumes adds to the city's fug, and keeps people moving along: pressed together yet locked apart in their separate tin boxes. The car allows a close view of the city, but also a sense of detachment, holding the driver behind glass and metal. And then, as if from nowhere:

> The men from the van grabbed hold of her. Put something over her mouth. She tried to scream, scratch, strike. She gulped for air and became dizzy. There was something in the rag they were holding over her mouth. She threw her body around, yanked at their arms. It didn't help. They were too big. Built. Brutal. The men pulled her into the van. Her last thought was that she regretted ever moving to Stockholm. A shit city.[192]

The car and the city can suddenly swallow you up. Both provide the writer and filmmaker with the perfect vehicle for exploring modernism's seamy side.

Country houses, locked rooms and snow-bound mysteries

The hermetic seal of the car is also the prevailing quality in works that move away from the city and into the sub-genres of 'the country house' and 'locked room' mysteries. Setting the action – and murders – in a self-contained environment creates a useful microcosm and neat narrative parameters. The implications of both sub-genres limit the number of suspects to a small group of guests or occupants within the restricted settings. Tightly confined spaces also assist in building senses of pressure and tension. A particular strand of work shores up the constrictions even further under banks of snow, in the 'snow-bound mystery' of which Agatha Christie's 1949 play *The Mousetrap* is the most famous example. The best-known modern incarnation of this sub-genre is *The Girl with the Dragon Tattoo*, as Blomkvist and Salander find themselves trapped with the suspects on Hedeby Island. As Larsson describes, 'High banks of snow presented a picturesque contrast to Stockholm. The town seemed almost like another planet, yet he was only a little more than three hours from Sergels Torg in downtown Stockholm.'[193]

One of the most extreme instances of the sub-genre in Swedish crime fiction takes us much further away, to a remote church in Kiruna. Leaving Stockholm, heading North beyond Östersund, Storuman, into the frozen lands and national parks of Jokkmokk, Pieljekaise, Muddus, towards the Arctic Circle, to the northern-most city in Sweden – Kiruna – in the province of Lapland. Further North there is only roadless, uninhabited land. To the East, boreal forests stretch for hundreds of miles into Finland and Russia. Snow falls all year round. This is the setting for Åsa Larsson's novel and subsequent film *Sun Storm* (*Solstorm*; the novel was re-titled *The Savage Altar* in the UK). The novel's main protagonist is Rebecka Martinsson, an attorney living in Stockholm, who is called back to her childhood roots in the far North. Out of the blue, she receives a call from a childhood friend who tells her that her brother has been murdered inside a church in the village of Kurravaara outside Kiruna. Martinsson has to return to her hometown in Kiruna and get involved in the search for the killer.

As well as luxuriating in the age-old atmospherics afforded by the setting's icy landscapes, Larsson immediately marks the territory out in modern terms: 'The plane to Kiruna was almost full. Hordes of foreign tourists off to drive a dog team and spend the night on reindeer skins in the ice hotel at Jukkasjarvi jostled for space with rumpled businessmen returning home clutching their free fruit and newspapers.'[194] While geographically remote and climactically hostile, modern resources of travel and life-style mean that Kiruna can cater to those in search of accessibly exotic isolation, and the corporate commuter. Yet, as we move nearer to the features of the landscape, Kiruna reveals itself as a cold and insular place, housing a particularly close-knit commu-nity. Larsson first evokes a sense of physical closeness through descriptions of a cramped family home: 'The accommodation on the upper floor consisted of the big kitchen with the alcove for the sofa bed, and another room. This had been the children's bedroom. Grandmother and Grandfather had slept in the alcove in the kitchen. Sanna was lying on her side on one of the beds, her knees drawn up so that they were almost touching her chin.'[195] Then, as a consequence of outside interference, the whole population decides to 'shut up like a giant clam'.[196]

While keeping hold of the novel's interest in Kurravaara's locked-room likenesses, the visual possibilities of cinema also lead the 2007 film of *Sun Storm* towards the region's distinctive wider landscape. In the opening images, the camera turns immediately to the skies, to the majesty of the Northern Lights. The lights' ethereal stripes fill the night sky with colour, in perfect contrast to the monochrome frost underfoot. However, like the novel's descriptions of aircraft passengers, the film quickly complicates suggestions of exotic natural splendour by adding an unexpectedly modern element. As the camera pans right to left, it brings into view the sight of a modern church building, all metallic struts and plastic sheeting. This building, this church, forms the shell under which the clammed-up community gathers. Its modern fabric accentuates both its artifice and flimsiness, especially when placed in front of the spectacular natural backdrop of the Northern Lights. Something unnatural is going on, truths hastily manufactured and glossed, not so far removed from earlier words about 'an empire built on a spurious foundation, decked in tinsel, and beguiled by its own illusory promise'. As the story of *Sun Storm* unfolds, the murder of the charismatic church leader is discovered, and a horrendous tale of child abuse revealed. The church's flimsy shell and gilded promises cannot protect its body of worshippers. The Northern Lights take on an ominous quality, too, as the character Sven-Erik gloomily observes, '"It looks fantastic, but any day now they're bound to decide it causes cancer. We should probably be walking around with a silver parasol to protect us from the radiation."'[197] Even in the far North, the inhabitants of modern Sweden are unhealthily exposed.

Cyberspace

As with the car, the city, air-flight (and even the ozone layer), modernity is seen in Swedish crime fiction to rupture man's relationship with the natural world. The apex of this condition removes us entirely from the earth-based geography of Sweden's forests and conurbations into the virtual realm of cyberspace. The texts engage with the possibilities and dangers of digital technology: of hiding behind anonymity or creating multiple identities, blurring public and private boundaries, penetrating people's lives in covert acts of surveillance. In doing so, they also point up Sweden's vehement fascination with the shock of the new. This, as Lars Trägårdh suggests, is a longstanding fixation:

> The great symbol of Sweden's love affair with all things rational, utilitarian and modern has become the famous Stockholm Exhibition of 1930. Much more than a showcase for functionalism in modern architecture and design, it has come to represent a more general turn towards rational planning, functionality and engineering in its broadest sense, including, of course, very much the idea that society, too, could be properly designed so as to maximise the welfare of its population.[198]

Yet, as Sjöwall and Wahlöö have demonstrated, functionalism in modern design can only work if complete (rather than remaining a half-realised 'bleak esplanade, misdirected and wrongly planned'). Andrew Brown develops the idea of Sweden's architectural drive for modernity becoming both a passion and a draining neurosis:

> The capitalist prosperity of social democratic Sweden seemed to have come at the expense of all sorts of human kindnesses. Everything old and wooden and ramshackle had been remade in concrete as the country grew richer. It was all more practical, more sensible, and more hygienic, but at the same time dreadfully dispiriting. Central Stockholm had been almost entirely rebuilt and dehumanised in the Sixties. The process culminated with the whole country changing to

driving on the right in 1967. In the years before the night when everything changed, all new roads, and even cars, had been built for the future, when people would drive on the other side of the road, so in the years immediately preceding the change-over, you had the unnerving feeling of being at fault simply for not living in the future.[199]

An explosive example comes early on in the Liza Marklund mystery *The Bomber*. A terrorist group blows up the Victoria Stadium in Stockholm, an Olympic venue:

> [Bengzton] didn't hear the angry shouts behind her as she stared up at the immense construction in front of her. She had driven past often and each time had been fascinated by the scale of the job. The Victoria Stadium was being built into the rock itself, excavated from the old Hammarby ski-slope. The environmentalists had made a fuss, of course; they always did whenever a few trees were cut down. The southern bypass carried on right through the rock and beneath the stadium itself, but the opening had been shut off with concrete blocks and emergency vehicles. The flashing lights on the roofs of the vehicles reflected off the wet tarmac. The north side of the stadium leaned out above the opening of the tunnel like a great chanterelle mushroom, but now it was torn in two.[200]

Rather than weight the description of the event solely as an attack on Sweden's home territory and global interests, Marklund suggests that the bomber's act of destructive violence equates with that necessary for the new structure to embed into Stockholm's natural landscape.

A sense of loss caused by entrenchment of the new is particularly strong in descriptions of communication technology. There is at once a celebration and fear of electronic devices. *Sun Storm* reveals the village inhabitants' distrust of Martinsson's tape recorder. In *The Laughing Policeman*, Beck bemoans having to constantly talk to his colleagues on the radio. The texts move beyond a simple rehearsal of traditional ways 'versus' modernity. Computer technology, in particular, is seen as vital to the process of tracking the killer. Yet, in turn, the intimate connection afforded by technology between criminal and detective is presented as troubling. In *The Bomber*, Bengzton's proficiency with computers leads to a close relationship with a woman receiving death threats. Then, the computer binds Bengzton and the killer in online and real worlds. When a later bomb goes off in Sätra Hall and kills off the character Stefan Bjurling, the title 'serial killer' appears on *Bengzton's* computer screen.

Hacking is at the heart of Stieg Larsson's *Millennium* trilogy. In Lisbeth Salander, we are presented with a heroine not only consummately skilled in navigating cyberspace, but who has all but withdrawn entirely from the real world. In her article 'Salander in Cyberspace', Sarah Casey Benyahia explores the *Millennium* films as a meditation on the shifting, uneasy relationship between the state and the individual in the era of new technology. The narration of the trilogy is perceived as functioning as a discourse on the policing of society in the virtual world. Just as crime fiction can be read as representing anxieties about the future of cities in a time of rapid change, the *Millennium* trilogy explores similar disquiet about cyberspace. Salander is seen as a product of society's fear of, and attraction to, the digital world. As Casey Benyahia remarks:

> For the individual, the possibilities of ambiguity and deception created by cyberspace can alter the nature of social exchange, introducing a precondition of uncertainty or anxiety into all virtual contacts. The inherent necessity of questioning the declared identity of participants is part of a persistent anxiety about the effects of new technology, where issues around privacy and unwanted revelation are cause for concern. In *The Girl with the Dragon Tattoo*, Salander's introduction is similarly ambiguous; it isn't clear if she is criminal or victim or why she is spying on Blomkvist. As the narrative develops it is apparent that it is Salander who is in control of the investigation, who has access to all the information,

but who remains hidden, carrying out her surveillance in secret. This is the paradox of the virtual world, threatening because of the simultaneous possibility of concealment and revelation.[201]

If *Millennium* presents us with the most elaborate exploration of cyberspace in the form, then Fincher's 2011 film develops the theme to a sophisticated degree. It binds form and content to express the anxieties of virtual contact. The film's slick aesthetic – (too) easily dismissed as superficial stylisation – echoes the sleek design of digital software, and the sheen of a computer interface. The look of the film suggests how the shiny objects that allow us entry into the digital world are both superficially attractive and, in their hard surfaces, alienating. Thus, cyberspace and electronic forms of communication are not just plot devices, themes to be addressed via the narrative, in dialogue, or items of tech-y decor scattered throughout to make the film feel up to date and cutting-edge. They are intrinsic to the film's workings, with a deep investment in thinking through effects of technology on the individual.

Examples can be found across the film. We have already discussed the glossy designs of the pre-credit sequence: an arresting clash of plastic fragments, oily pools and fire. Then, in early scenes following Blomkvist as news of the Wenneström case breaks, television screens in cafés and shops hang heavily over the journalist's head. Re-viewing the film a second time, these images can be seen as a foreshadowing of Blomkvist's ultimate fate: caught on camera (literally) strung-up in Martin's basement lair, ready for slaughter. Consider also the way the film brings the Vanger affair into Blomkvist's life. As the journalist prepares Christmas Eve festivities with his wife and daughter, Dirch Frode calls his mobile with an invitation to come to Hedeby Island. Listen carefully to the way Blomkvist's phone rings, the precise layering of sound so that its shrill notes echo around the family home: an electronic spectre wailing a warning signal, only to spirit the journalist away. Later, after sex with his lover Erika Berger (Robin Wright), Blomkvist sits hunched over his laptop. Fincher breaks up the frame with the hard diagonal lines of angle-lamps and furnishings, splintering the space between man and woman. Blomkvist's physical closeness to technology – touching the phone to his ear, tapping on the computer keyboard – leads only to increasingly fractured intimacy with other people. At the same time, the film suggests how Lisbeth negotiates the dividing lines of real and virtual world with more ease, turning aspects of detachment, anonymity and alienation into an extreme form of individualism. The notion of cyberspace as an open frontier, frightening to some, proves liberating to Salander. The speed and dexterity of her movements through cyberspace find tangible 'real-world' expression in the shots of her riding on her motorcycle – navigating the webs of roads and bridges on the streets of Stockholm and out on Hedeby Island. Cyberspace offers her a position of immunity, a site from which she can map her experiences in the geographical spaces of the real world:

> The periods of freedom which Salander experiences are created through her ability to outsmart her opponents, through technological and cerebral expertise demonstrated in hacking and surveillance. Her escape at the end of the first [Swedish] film – which is revisited at the beginning of the second – is into an impossibly perfect, fantasy world of blue skies, dramatic scenery and an elegant beach apartment. Salander enters into this fantasy *mise en scène* in the guise of a new persona, that of the glamorous and sophisticated woman. The incongruity of this persona in comparison to the androgynous, gothic Salander of the physical world makes sense in the context of the limitless world of cyberspace – the elegant Salander is an avatar, the tropical paradise a symbol of the virtual world and its role as a sanctuary.[202]

4

BODIES

'And why murder? The central mystery of a detective story need not indeed involve a violent death, but murder remains the unique crime and it carries an atavistic weight of repugnance, fascination and fear.'[203]

Swedish crime fiction is a showcase for murder's bloody allure. Corpses pile up, despatched in a huge variety of surreptitious, inventive, and frenzied ways. The killing of another human being represents the crossing of a final set of boundaries: moral, legal, psychological, and physical, as the knife drives home. As the novels, films, and television programmes present these acts of mutilation and execution, drawing back the shroud and feeding our rubbernecker's curiosity for carnage they also take us into the minds of the killers and their pursuers. And, just as the nation-state can be seen as a body to be breached and protected, so too, in crime fiction, is it often represented in corporeal form, by the physical being of the protagonists. Swedish crime fiction investigates its lead characters' desire for separation and self-preservation against the intervention of other bodies (familial, governmental, and homicidal). Physical attacks by serial killers and murderers are bound to the bleeding of socio-political issues across Sweden's borders. Many of the texts are particularly concerned with the violation and enclosure of the female body, *Millennium* being the best-known example. Across the trilogy, we learn (and are shown in horrific detail) how Salander is brutally raped by her guardian, strapped down in a psychiatric hospital, and buried alive. Such violent transgressions are coupled with stories of human trafficking, forming one of the central narrative threads of *The Girl Who Played with Fire*. As we have seen, notions of entrapment are set against those of freedom and self-expression for the central character.

Having considered the spatial arrangements of characters in settings, we can now turn further inwards, to look at their bodies and minds. Most pronouncedly, the physical health of the lead characters often gains metaphorical significance. Take Kurt Wallander, for instance, in all his various manifestations: overweight, drinking too much, exercising too little. Diabetes hounds him in the books and films, reflecting as it does a lack of national well-being. In his Foreword to *The Pyramid*, Mankell confides that he feels 'confirmed in [his] impression that Wallander has in a way served as a kind of mouthpiece for growing insecurity, anger and healthy insights about the relationship between the welfare state and democracy'.[204] Such 'healthy insights' are reached through an unhealthy state, with Wallander falling foul to the sickness of modern times. The first chapter of *The Pyramid* begins with a description that neatly encapsulates this motif:

> Wallander woke up shortly after six o'clock on the morning of the eleventh of December. At the same moment that he opened his eyes, his alarm clock went off. He turned it off and lay staring into the dark. Stretched his arms and legs, spread his fingers and toes. That had become a habit, to feel if the night had left him with any aches. He swallowed in order to check if any infection had sneaked into his respiratory system.[205]

As the new day dawns, Wallander is called to consciousness. Methodically, he tests the conditions of the self against any infection that might have seeped into his sleeping system, when at the unconscious mercy of the wider world. Like the fog that often hangs over Skåne in Mankell's novels, in Wallander's world, there is a sense of drifting sickness, shadowy and diffuse. The idea of an ungraspable malaise suggests the qualities of trauma, as Nestingen observes:

> The introduction to Inspector Wallander in *Faceless Killers* establishes that Wallander's story is one of trauma. Because the traumatic experience by definition can never be completely integrated into consciousness, and hence is impossible to narrate, Wallander's traumatic past obstructs the understanding of his character. The reader can never know the meaning of the traumatic event, for Wallander himself cannot make conscious sense of it. As a result, Wallander's figure is built on an absent cause. This traumatic narrative structure also deflects our attention onto Wallander's body, for his ongoing struggle to cope with trauma is represented through his body, which is central to the attribution of a fatigued affect to him.[206]

A kind of transference is at work, as a metaphysical strain of being in the world finds form in bodily impairment. We can read the pain as sociological as well as existential, as psychosomatic angst about the conditions of modern living. A similar diagnosis can be reached for the characters in *The Man on the Roof*. Most of its characters suffer from a form of sickness. Nyman is killed in hospital. Beck's daughter is first introduced holding her head, with a migraine. Upon seeing Nyman's bloody body, one young officer retches in the corner. Beck's face constantly glistens with sweat. Even baby Johan can't escape, his bottom covered in excrement. Something in the air, in the world, is causing an abject reaction.

At other times, the works suggest the fragmentation of self and society by cutting up body parts. Such acts of dismemberment can take literal form, as the victims are hacked to bits. Equally, through the magnification of close description in the novels, and visual composition in the films, the presence of certain body parts of the protagonists can be amplified or separated in the frame. An archetypal mode of introducing the killer on-screen in crime films and programmes is to show their bodies in darkness, and their hands in close-up. This is the case in *The Man on the Roof*, as we are presented with a shadowy figure and gloved hands cleaning a knife blade. In *The Bomber*, Colin Nutley quickly establishes a pattern of editing shots of body parts into abstract collages. Footage of Olympic participants is presented in this way, and connected to the close-up shots of a mangled corpse in the opening scene. Both are violently cut, chopped up to be made pointedly anonymous.

Alfred Harderberg, the villain of the *Wallander* mystery *The Man Who Smiled*, is an evil entrepreneur involved in the global trafficking of human body parts from (dependent upon which version is considered) Africa or Brazil, sold to Westerners. The television incarnations of Harderberg (played, respectively, by Claes Månsson and Rupert Graves), point up his particularly disturbing and aloof standing, as a global entrepreneur, by audio-visual means: sidling him quietly into a scene; marking his considerable on-screen presence through long silences and an impenetrable, ever-present grin; connecting him at one remove to Wallander through phone messages and emails sent from around the world.

Mankell's novels, on the other hand, make Harderberg's transnational situation more explicit by name-checking countries touched by his influential activities: he has property in Barcelona, a bank account in Macao '"wherever that is"', businesses in Zimbabwe, and a Brazilian wife with interests in companies exporting coffee. As Mankell has Wallander muse, he is everywhere and nowhere at the same time: 'his life is one long absence'.[207] All forms play on Harderberg as representing a modern (and unsettling) paradox of simultaneous presence and distance. He is globally connected (commercially, technologically), but at one and the same time, exists as an ethereal 'brand name', manifest only in the silence and remoteness of the corporate rich. There is a gutsy irony, worthy of the Gothic genre, in the fact that this powerful position of detachment comes from dealing in the disembodied. For Mankell, as for many, the fact that Sweden's welfare state was replaced by a business-led model of international enterprise encouraged unwelcome forms of hierarchy and anonymity. As national collectivism gives way to a small number of autocratic collectives, people become segregated. Little companies with an eye for world commerce violently (and here, literally) cut the workforce to pieces.

Acts of dismemberment in the Irene Huss mystery *Torso* create a striking commentary on gender politics. *Torso* displays a particularly lusty fascination with grisly deaths and bodily mutilation. Indeed, so much so that the DVD menu features the gleeful design of a bloodied circular saw. The torso of the title is found abandoned without head or limbs, anonymous and freakish. In the film, it is first shown, in close-up, cut off from the world, stuffed into a plastic bag. Later, it is displayed in all its gory glory on the mortician's slab, in a scene reminiscent of *The Silence of the Lambs* (dir. Jonathan Demme, 1991). As with the character FBI agent Clarice Starling (Jodie Foster) in Demme's film, *Torso* presents a strong female protagonist struggling with the ostracising elements of a predominantly male working environment. Alienation is suggested in literal acts of division. The film couples victim and lead character by introducing Irene Huss in similarly fragmented form. In the credit sequence and opening scene, close-ups isolate parts of her body, concentrating on each strike of the fist or foot as she demonstrates Judo moves.

A comparable strategy is found in the novel *Sun Storm*, as the opening description of female lead Anna-Maria, through the eyes of a male colleague, performs a leering appraisal of her physique:

> Carl von Post clamped his teeth together so hard that his jaws ached. He'd always had a problem with this midget of a policewoman. She seemed to have her male colleagues on the Investigation squad by the balls, and he couldn't figure out why. And just look at her. One meter fifty at the most in her stocking feet, with a long horse's face which more or less covered half her body. At the moment she was ready for a circus freak show with her enormous belly. Like a grotesque

cube, she was as broad as she was tall. It just had to be the
inevitable result of generations of inbreeding in those little
isolated Lapp villages.[208]

The diatribe accentuates aspects of physiognomy: aching jaws, by
the balls, horse's face, and enormous belly. By honing in and ex-
aggerating certain of Anna-Maria's body parts, this contemptuous
male colleague estranges her, pulls her apart in an act of violent
separation. The first description of Lisbeth Salander is similarly
shaped, picking out different body parts and connecting their isolation to a state of alienation:

> Armansky's star researcher was a pale, anorexic young woman
> who had hair as short as a fuse, and a pierced nose and eye-
> brows. She had a wasp tattoo about two centimetres long on
> her neck, a tattooed loop around the biceps of her left arm
> and another around her left ankle. On those occasions when
> she had been wearing a tank top, Armansky also saw that she
> had a dragon tattoo on her left shoulder blade.
>
> She had a wide mouth, a small nose, and high cheek-
> bones that gave her an almost Asian look. Her movements
> were quick and spidery, and when she was working at the
> computer her fingers flew over the keys.[209]

Even through the supposedly sympathetic viewpoint of her supervi-
sor Armansky, Salander is objectified as a series of separate, curious
parts, each marked out by their otherness, their removal from 'the
norm': anorexia, piercings, tattoos. The alignment of Salander's
body to wild and unpredictable beasts – wasp and dragon tattoos,
quick and spidery finger movements – makes her seem all the more
alien. Whereas the novel quickly reveals Salander's dragon tattoo
in the middle of this description, the films – both Swedish and
American – keep it concealed until moments of physical intimacy
between Lisbeth and her lovers (Blomkvist and Miriam Wu) and
attackers (Bjurman and Zalachenko). An emblem of carnal power
appears when she is at her most exposed. Etched on her back, the
dragon only unfurls to full glory when Salander is facing away

from the camera, from us. Paradoxically, the sight of the tattoo marks an act of asserted identity even as, especially when, the character withdraws from us, remaining unknown and unknowable.

Sex and sexuality

The body in Swedish crime fiction is also the site onto which treatises about sex and sexuality are written, often in blood. Historically, Sweden has a stereotypical image as a place of advanced sexual liberation. It is imagined as a permissive society, a liberal utopia with free love for all. As Brown recalls, tongue firmly wedged in his cheek, in recounting his first acquaintance with some Swedish friends on his home turf, 'I was probably the first man they had met in Wales who didn't expect all Scandinavians to be imaginatively compliant nymphomaniacs.'[210] In *Death in a Cold Climate*, Barry Forshaw develops this notion, and links it to Swedish cinema of the 'sexual revolution':

> A constant source of annoyance – or wry acceptance – among Swedes visiting Great Britain is the fondly-held, slightly envious British notion (also nurtured by Americans) of Sweden as a fount of sexual liberation and erotic adventure; a land without inhibitions where all forms of erotic behaviour are tolerated, and saunas are used more creatively than simply to open the pores of the skin. Much of this perception stems from the sexual revolution of the 1960s, which was by no means a solely Swedish phenomenon. The writer Håkan Nesser is fond of nailing one particular culprit in this identification of unbuttoned sexuality with the Swedes: the great international success of the 1967 film *I am Curious Yellow* (directed by Vilgot Sjöman), which, though largely a dispiriting (and would-be humorous) leftwing political tract, famously featured a deal of nudity and one groundbreaking scene in which the plump actress Lena Nyman fondled the penis of actor Börje Ahlstedt. According to Nesser, the massive international success and censorship furore surrounding this film (largely because of its relatively minimal erotic content)

established a template in the minds of non-Swedes for the country; a template, what's more, which hardly told the whole story. Swedes, according to Nesser, have been living with this lazy cliché ever since.[211]

The sexual overture of *I am Curious – Yellow* joins a chorus of similar works in the 1960s, including Henning Carlsen's *The Cats* (*Kattorna*, 1965), Mai Zetterling's *Loving Couples* (*Älskande par*, 1964) and *Night Games* (*Nattlek*, 1966). A wildly successful glut of Swedish 'sexploitation' films also appears in this period, as Peter Cowie illustrates:

> Films like *Dear John* (dir. Lars-Magnus Lindgren from a novel by Olle Länsberg, 'Käre John', 1964) and its predecessor, Lindgren's *Do You Believe In Angels?* ('Änglar, finns dom?' 1961), emerged in a bizarre symbiosis with a stream of films on the mechanics of sexual relationships. Among the best of these exploitation movies was *I – a Woman* ('Jag – en kvinna', 1965), featuring Essy Persson as an innocent young nurse whose intercourse with a hospital patient opens a vivid world of lust and its techniques. Among the worst was *The Language of Love* ('Kärlekens språk', 1969), a kind of staged documentary on the numerous positions and erogenous zones that provoke sexual satisfaction. *The Language of Love* was made for 700,000 kronor, and brought in more than 6.5 million kronor in its first full season of release. Not surprisingly, such an economic miracle spawned a series of cloned imitations, all of which furthered Sweden's reputation for mechanised, unemotional sexual habits.[212]

The 'golden age' of such output came in the 1970s, the time of *Deep Throat* (dir. Gerard Damiano, 1972), and in which, 'approximately one-fifth of the Swedish film production for cinema release would be more or less pornographic'.[213] According to Mariah Larsson, the supercharged sexuality of Swedish cinema reflected, and grew out of, wider debates held in the 1960s on sexuality, censorship, and freedom of expression: 'These debates had been characterised by liberalism, tolerance, a certain kind of reasonable argument and by what might be described as a sex-positive standpoint in opposition to a supposed ideal of chastity within established institutions.'[214] Thus strongly influential and conflicting factors emerge: a 'lazy' on-screen cliché borne out of the sexual revolution; a sense of Sweden's 'mechanised, unemotional sexual habits' fed by film; and intersections with pornography and sexploitation reflecting the country's 'sex-positive' standpoint. Combinations of these determinants feature across Swedish crime fiction, also gaining ground, as we have discovered, from the 1960s onwards. Two recurrent strands of interest emerge, on occasion troublingly intertwined: homosexuality and sexual violence.

A tolerant form?

Coming from under the banner of Sweden's tolerant society, crime fiction displays a complicated dynamic in terms of homosexuality. In implicit and explicit ways, the crime narratives often suggest links between deviant criminal behaviour and gay practices. A strident set of examples is found in the film of *The Laughing Policeman*. Warning signs appear early on in the narrative. The fact that a suspect's roommate is gay is revealed in order to enhance a sense of mistrust and to detract from an officer's misogynist meddling. Then, as the investigation develops and various urban communities are questioned, more and more gay spaces are intruded upon by the police, displayed to the viewer from the outsider's perspective of the heterosexual officer. The Ramrod – a club for gay male clones; The Frolic Room – a biker bar; a transvestite strip club – all are presented as places filled with grotesques, their openness a cause of the officers' contempt: 'Things are looser now. Just a couple of years ago, this would be enough to put you away.'

Comparable instances occur in *Torso*. The plot – searching for the tattooist who worked on the dismembered body – takes our protagonists to Copenhagen. Denmark is perceived in the novel (and in Sweden) as a more relaxed and permissive society, yet with a suspicious tendency towards excessive hedonism and immoral indulgence. A less restrictive attitude towards alcohol consumption appeals to the visiting Swedes: 'When they got back to the hotel, the bar was overflowing. A big group of Swedes filled the room, making noise. There was a sign on the wall announcing that it was a "Jell-O shot evening."'[215] A greater sense of liberation is also enjoyed by gay Danes, much to the consternation of otherwise sympathetic Swedish character Jonny Blom, who observes a notification for, '"A wedding. But, damn, it's two guys."'[216] As in *The Laughing Policeman*, settings marked out as gay spaces in the film of *Torso* are presented as 'Other'. When Irene Huss enters a gay sex shop to question the owner about a murder, pornographic products and sex toys clutter the frame in colourful abundance. Throughout the conversation between Huss and the owner, the *mise-en-scène* is composed such that rows of dildos and butt-plugs are pushed to prominence in the foreground. There is an uncomfortable aggression at work in the film's presentation of gay lifestyles. When the products are linked – by their spatial proximity – to a samurai sword hanging overhead on the shop wall, the threat of violence becomes explicit. That the plot revolves around sadomasochistic behaviour may justify such a tone and connections, but by associating all gay practices as vicious, the film sensationalises its subject matter, and enacts a queasy conflation.

Two further examples can be seen to offer partial correctives to this unpleasant tendency. *The Bomber* presents one of its main characters – Christian – as having an affair with her secretary, without fuss. Yet soon enough, another jilted gay lover – the 'demonic dyke' – emerges in the narrative as a threat. Then, there is the polygamous bisexual character of Lisbeth Salander in the *Millennium* trilogy. Throughout the trilogy, Larsson sets descriptions of Salander's consensual sexual acts with men and women alongside passages detailing her horrendous history of sexual abuse. Yet he is distinctive in never allowing or suggesting a causal connection between sexual violence and homosexuality.

Sexual violence

The jury is out on Larsson's feminist credentials. Forshaw offers an intricate reading of Salander's case. First, he describes a prevalent argument proffered by those defending Larsson's detailing of Salander's sexuality and sexual abuse:

> Larsson allows the consensual sexual encounters to be described in a non-judgemental fashion, notably the lesbian encounters involving the bisexual Salander ... The feminist writer Andrea Dworkin's ineluctable linking of male desire with rape is echoed by all the violent brutalisation which is to be found within the pages of the trilogy, and her assertion that sexual intercourse is the pure, sterile, formal expression of men's contempt for women has a Larssonian ring. But such apparent misandry – on Larsson's part – is undercut (as if in exoneration of the male sex) by Mikael Blomkvist's formidable series of positively-described amorous conquests. What's more, the trilogy's crucial episode involving heterosexual, consensual sex (as opposed to similar positively described lesbian encounters) takes place between Lisbeth Salander and Mikael Blomkvist, and is conducted exclusively on her own no-nonsense terms rather than his.[217]

Yet, as Forshaw goes on to note, there is a sizeable critical community equally suspicious of Larsson's handling of sex and sexual violence in the trilogy:

> While the various sexual assaults described in the novels could hardly be described as titillating – except perhaps in terms of a very specialist reading of the books – their extremely graphic nature has nevertheless been characterised as gloating and exploitative. What's more, the sheer number of assaults endured by the luckless heroine (not to mention other female members of the dramatis personae) stretches credulity. The syndrome has been described as inviting in even the most enlightened reader something akin to a kind of remark famously made by antediluvian judges to the

effect that Salander must be – in some unconscious fashion – 'asking for it'. Certainly, the author presents his heroine as a serial victim (although of course, those who rape or brutalise Salander inevitably play a very heavy price, often inviting far worse violence on their own persons than they inflicted on their seemingly helpless victim).[218]

That readers would assign blame to Salander for her repeated, brutal victimisation strikes me as astonishing, a scenario almost as upsetting as the descriptions themselves. The act of committing Salander's treatment at the hands of rapist Bjurman to film, without falling foul of sensationalism, is tackled with aplomb by director David Fincher. In the rape sequence, the film walks razor edges of suggestion and visualisation, melodrama and realism, stylisation and straightforwardness. Once the violence begins, the camera pulls back and out of the closed bedroom door. The flourish seems designed to call the bluff of naysayers, to *appear* to shy away and shield the viewer from an awkwardly extreme example of on-screen sexual violence. But this is a film about alienation and sexually charged sadism, and Fincher's portfolio – especially *Se7en* (1995) and *Fight Club* (1999) – puts pay to any doubts about the director's squeamishness. (And after a beat, a cut takes us back into the room, to witness the full dread of Salander's encounter.) The particular way in which the camera slides assuredly back from the bedroom, as if on a mechanical track expresses two connected states. First, there is the suggestion that its removal associates with Bjurman's selfish, hate-filled lust: all other factors are immediately expelled from the instant of sexual fulfilment; only his cruel pleasure counts. Then, the move recalls that of the car taking Blomkvist to Hedeby Island and Cowie's remarks about 'mechanised, unemotional sexual habits'. The camera's smooth and steady movement suggests both how Bjurman is caught up in an unfeeling, automatic reflex for sexual violence, and how Salander is now locked irreversibly into her fate. There is little here to suggest 'titillation'. Rather, the mechanical eye of Fincher's camera, previously the subject of widespread criticism for lustily filming bloodied bodies in *Fight Club*, captures and represents the inhuman indifference of the attacker and of wider society, allowing such violence against women to go *overlooked*.

The violence of the gaze is a recurring factor in Swedish crime fiction, more often attacked than justified within the texts. Sometimes though, the line blurs. *The Laughing Policeman* explores the obsession of Beck's (now murdered) partner with sex crimes. The fact that a police officer (and close colleague of Beck) harbours such insidious desires complicates audience alignment and more habitual processes of emotional engagement. The film makes the terrain even more treacherous by including numerous acts of violence, linked to sex, by policemen. Beck (or Jake Martin in the American film) slaps his dead partner's wife around to get to the truth of her involvement in sets of sexually explicit photographs. Martin's new partner becomes complicit in repeated POV shots of him ogling women through keyholes, on posters, in strip joints. In the end, all three male protagonists are culpable of sexual aggression, and the moral ground remains decidedly muddied. We may look again at the strange, final image of the film, as the camera captures the exasperated face of one of Martin's colleagues, another officer, previously unseen. We can do better. What went so wrong? Such melodramatic projections on my part fit with the timbre of *The Laughing Policeman*, and Swedish crime fiction's fascination with bodies as conveying the characters' moral status. As Andrew Nestingen remarks:

> In Sjowall and Wahloo's novels, the lazy beat cop figures a moral distinction, which also helps us to see the legacy of melodrama in later Scandinavian crime fiction ... Mankell's Wallander epitomizes this melodrama. The beleaguered, physically suffering figure continually asks, 'What is happening in Sweden?', linking the crimes and his experiences to the state ... Wallander is also a melodramatic victim. His isolation and fatigue convey his moral status by suggesting that his fidelity to his convictions has caused alienation and bodily suffering.[219]

Nestingen offers two possible future directions for Swedish crime fiction. First, he sees the melodramatic mode as increasing, because 'melodramatic narration well suits the project of contesting the morality of the welfare state's transformation under neoliberalism'.[220] The mode also appeals to a readership now attuned to the extreme body horror of Salander's treatment in the *Millennium* trilogy (and, a little further afield, in Jo Nesbo's Norwegian *Harry Hole* mysteries). In turn, when the police are as susceptible to alienation and bodily suffering as many of the victims, Nestingen questions whether they can 'remain a symbolic agent capable of reassuring readers about the immutability of the dominant social and moral order.'[221] Their replacement, it appears, emerges in the form of 'entrepreneurial investigators' like Liza Marklund's journalist Annika Bengzton, and Stieg Larsson's Lisbeth Salander and Mikael Blomkvist. These protagonists' entrepreneurialism befits the global state of modern Sweden, but provides only a flimsy carapace against attacks on the body, both individual and national.

5

INTERVIEW TRANSCRIPTS

All interviews were conducted by the author (SP).

Interview A: Yellow Bird Productions

Interviewees: Mikael Wallén (Executive Producer, Yellow Bird Productions) (MW) and Erik Hultkvist (Business Development, Yellow Bird Productions) (EH). Conducted at Yellow Bird Productions, Stockholm, Sweden, 30 March 2011.

SP: Yellow Bird is now part of one of the biggest global media conglomerations [in the world]; could you tell me about the connections to different companies?

EH: Yellow Bird was acquired in 2007 by Zodiak Television, which was a listed Swedish production group and, alongside Yellow Bird, Zodiak bought a lot of other media companies from other countries, including the Netherlands, Belgium, Russia, the UK – so expanded from being a Scandinavian group into a pan-European group. In 2008, Zodiak Television was acquired by De Agostini, which is an Italian media conglomerate, and we merged with two other production groups called Marathon and Magnolia (from France and Italy). So those three organisations – Zodiak, Marathon, and Magnolia – merged into one big media production group, and then last year [2010] De Agostini also bought RDF media group which was quite a big UK/US media production group and merged all together, becoming what is now called Zodiak media group, with the headquarters in London. There is also the connection to UK-based production company Touch Paper, which was part of RDF previously.

MW: Depending on how you are counting it, it is part of the third largest group in the world, in TV.

SP: Looking at your website, the tagline is 'We turn bestsellers into blockbusters'. So there is a niche market for adaptation – is that right?

MW: Absolutely. The company started in that way, as a joint venture between the writer Henning Mankell and the producer Ole Sondberg. They started the company in that way, and also started to acquire some rights, to make the first thirteen Swedish *Wallander* movies and we've kept doing that; even if we look into doing other things, about ninety-five per cent is books, and about eighty per cent is bestsellers. As most bestsellers [in Sweden] are crime, that means we predominantly produce crime drama. It doesn't have to be crime, but it is easiest with crime ... we are also working with Henning Mankell's other books; the most recent example is *Italian Shoes* that we are trying to develop into a feature film ... together with Left Bank [Productions] in the UK.

SP: You mention the importance of Henning Mankell in setting up the company. Was there a determination, then, from the beginning, in terms of adapting *Wallander*?

MW: Yes, that was the whole idea behind the company.

EH: I think it was started with the sole focus of one project, which was to turn the Wallander character into a franchise, making films based on the character.

MW: At that time, they had already produced [for television] all the novels in the Swedish language.

EH: So the idea was to make a series of films based on the Wallander character, and to finance that internationally ... The company has grown organically from there.

MW: Ole [Sondberg] was a producer of these sorts of films before *Wallander*; he made *Beck* – that was a franchise too; he took the Beck character and made more films out of that.

SP: The *Millennium* and *Wallander* series are extraordinarily successful across the world; before we talk about the global success of your productions, could you tell me about the Scandinavian success – was that in place before the interest from Europe and America? How popular were the *Wallander* series and *Millennium* series in Scandinavia?

MW: The *Wallander* films have been around since 2005–2006 in terms of the franchise, and even before that as the first films based on the books were out in the nineties. Wallander has always been a well-known character and a successful character on film and TV. But of course in Sweden, *Wallander* has been more aimed at DVD/TV, not feature films, and is very strong on DVD/TV. Sixty to seventy per cent of the Swedish population know about the Wallander character and a lot have read the books. But they are not successful in the same way as the *Millennium* series. When we put a *Wallander* movie out as a cinema release as we do from time to time, maybe we will get 150–200,000 admissions in Sweden, and there is not a market for it in the rest of Scandinavia on cinema, but when we launched *Millennium*, it was a totally different thing. Of course, it was a different kind of success. In such a short time, [Larsson] sold so many books in Scandinavia – he sold close to 10 million books in Scandinavia in two or three years.

EH: *Wallander* has been very strong on TV and DVD ever since we started making them. Every time we [or previously, our co-producing partner] put up a *Wallander*, even if it is pay-TV and DVD before going to free-to-air TV, they have a 50 per cent share [of the audience]; it's a habit to watch a

Wallander or *Beck* movie on a Saturday or Sunday night on TV4 in the 'crime slot'.

SP: Was Yellow Bird involved in the original *Wallander* films?

MW: No, it was before Yellow Bird's time.

EH: But Ole [Sondberg] was involved in the *Beck* series.

MW: At that time, *Wallander* was sold to SVT and the first film was actually an in-house production.

SP: Were you surprised by the enormous success of the *Millennium* trilogy?

MW: We hoped for Swedish success, even if the numbers were more than we had thought, and the Scandinavian success was a surprise to us because Swedish films are not usually that successful here or in Denmark; even the Scandinavian success was beyond our expectation. And of course, the success outside Scandinavia was just unbelievable. We would have been satisfied had we sold the TV series and movies to twenty countries around the world, and if one or two of the countries gave them a cinema release, we would have been glad. And then suddenly we sold them to sixty countries, with many giving all three films cinema releases: well beyond our expectations ... On cinema and DVD it is a different sort of exposure when it is three movies instead of one. Of course, a lot of it is based not only on the quality of the films but also on the success of the books ... It is clear that people outside Scandinavia see these films in a different way to us – they are considered more like art-films, and we see them more as traditional thrillers.

EH: We received better critical acclaim abroad, than in Sweden. This goes for the *Wallander* films as well.

MW: For example, the Swedish *Wallander* films are considered only as 'industrial TV' in Sweden, but when shown on the BBC, we got hundreds of emails from British viewers saying how fantastic they are.

EH: It seems that a lot of Swedes view the BBC versions of *Wallander* as better, whereas it almost seems to the opposite in the UK. It seems harder to win your 'own' audience.

SP: Why do you think that the *Millennium* and *Wallander* series are so popular?

MW: Of course people start watching them, or buying them on DVD, or go to the cinema because they know about them beforehand; otherwise it is difficult to market Swedish films abroad … I guess part of it is because of the Swedish 'touch' to the films in some way, or the Scandinavian 'touch'.

EH: I think as well it has a lot to do with the main characters; the Wallander character is very compelling, and the Salander character is equally compelling – I think it has a lot to do with that, that there is something about them and their qualities that differentiate the films from a lot of other crime drama.

MW: Sometimes the stories are quite dark, and they offer some criticism of Swedish society and the Swedish way of living – elements you don't see that often in other crime dramas.

SP: There seems to be this real sense of excitement, internationally, about Nordic noir right now – could you say why it is happening?

MW: In Germany it has been there for many years.

EH: They have always been very interested in Sweden and Swedish culture.

MW: In the English-language countries it has always been a problem with subtitles. In Germany you don't have that problem as they dub everything, and still they are, have always been, close to our Swedish culture – they have always been close to us as people. With the dubbing, they don't have the problem of subtitles like in the UK. In other 'dubbing' countries like Spain and Italy and France, they have previously perceived Swedish programmes as 'something strange'; it is only recently that they have started to become interested in them.

SP: Can we talk a little bit about the relationship between film and DVD, and television and film because, especially with Yellow Bird's productions (and this may be a wider production pattern in terms of Sweden), you release some *Wallander* films to the cinema, some to DVD, and then to television. Then there is also the question about the cinema/television releases of the *Millennium* trilogy.

MW: The whole *Wallander* concept was based on the investment made by TV broadcasters in Sweden and Germany. The whole project has been designed such that the broadcasters are satisfied, and such that we can produce the movies in decent quality. And we still have a strong DVD market in Scandinavia. So we adapted that concept to the best way of financing the films: that was – giving the German broadcaster rights for Germany, and in Scandinavia the rights to release the first one on cinema to market the new series of films, especially for the DVD sales. So: the first film is released at the cinema, setting the way for DVD sales. Then, a month later or so, the second film is released straight-to-DVD. So you release them on DVD about once a month.

SP: So you would show the first episode in the new TV series at the cinema, and that would be directly related to DVD sales?

MW: Yes, that is the marketing tool for the new series on DVD. You have your ordinary cinema-release window of 4 to 6 months, and then the first goes to DVD, and the next month the second one goes to DVD, and so on. And then you have the ordinary window for pay-TV, and then free TV. That is the model for *Wallander*.

EH: It's easier to look at the productions as a TV series, rather than as feature films. But they are ninety-minute films.

MW: So twelve out of the thirteen in a series are direct-to-DVD movies, but in Sweden you don't have only direct-to-DVD movies, you will first start with the cinema release as the first point of financing. This is the model for well-known characters like Wallander and Beck.

SP: It's a different model to Britain, for example for a series like *A Touch of Frost* [dir. various, 1992–ongoing] or *Lewis* [dir. various, 2007–2012], you don't show the first episode on the big screen, in the cinemas ...

MW: And you don't release them on DVD before showing them on TV ...

SP: Exactly, so that's very different. With that in mind, do you put more money into the production of the first episode?

MW: Yes, usually it has around fifty per cent more money, the first one, at least; sometimes it has one hundred per cent more money, actually.

SP: And do you frontload the marketing campaign towards that?

MW: Yes, of course when you have a feature film, you have a feature film marketing campaign; when you have it on DVD, it is just some ads in some papers. But, when it's a feature film, it will mean posters around the towns, that sort of thing. Absolutely – [there is] a lot more money in marketing the feature films.

EH: In the first *Wallander* series, more than one film was released at the cinemas.

MW: Three out of thirteen ... partly because of the success of the first one, and also it was the first series when they launched the *Wallander* franchise – the first movies without being based on any books – so they thought it needed more than one feature film release.

SP: In the case of [the *Wallander* episode] *Mastermind*, it has a cinematic quality.

MW: We put more money in *Mastermind*, and *Before the Frost* was the first one. And we used other directors – people who usually do feature films.

SP: Is it correct that only the first film of the *Millennium* trilogy was produced for a cinema release?

MW: Yes, because the series – as with the *Wallander* series – was financed by different sets of broadcasters – German broadcasters, Swedish broadcasters, with the first one set for release at the cinema. The only difference was that because the first book was so extensive, we planned on doing two sets of ninety minutes on each book, so in the end, the series would be six ninety-minute films for TV. That was the plan.

EH: With the first film released at the cinema as a shorter version of the 'two times ninety'.

SP: So, did the 'two times ninety minute' shooting schedule happen?

MW: Yes, they were filmed in that way, and they were broadcast on all Scandinavian channels and in Germany as the 'six times ninety' TV series, and really successfully so, in Germany especially. And in some markets they released the TV series on DVD rather than the feature films, quite successfully ... But in the UK and US they are more traditional [in their models]. In Belgium and Luxembourg for example, six months after the initial cinema release, and when they were supposed to release the feature films on DVD, they actually released the 'two times ninety' versions instead, as a 'deluxe, extra-long version' ... and people were buying even more DVDs than just the feature film. So in some countries, they really played with the options, because there are a lot of options when you have this kind of series. But, most countries are traditional; distributors in this business are traditional. So usually they keep the TV series, maybe to sell it to a TV channel or maybe release it as an extended version a year or two after. That's the most common way of doing it.

SP: So the longer series is available on DVD in some countries, and was shown on TV in Sweden ...

MW: And in Norway, and Denmark, and Finland, and Germany. France – Canal Plus – bought the TV series in the very early stages, even before we knew it was going to be three feature films, and it was released on Canal Plus before it was on the cinema.

SP: Are Britain and America interested in taking the DVD of the longer series?

MW: In most other countries, it's a 'distributor thing', because the distributor buys all the rights and can use them as they please. And in terms of Music Box in the States, and Momentum in the UK, they are doing it in a more traditional way. They are both planning on releasing the 'six times ninety' versions … The TV series has been sold to the BBC along with the feature films … it is all a question of what they release first, and a matter of timing schedules with the broadcasters. For BBC Four to schedule it for the same slot as *The Killing* or *Wallander* it should be easier to show the 'six times ninety' versions in that way. Instead of releasing the three 'extra-long' movies, it seems more suitable to show the series in this way.

SP: What about the relationship with the BBC, when you made the co-production of *Wallander*? How did that work?

MW: It was in a way a three-part co-production [of six films] between Left Bank, Kenneth Branagh, and Yellow Bird … We are in pre-production of three more films this Fall. In Germany, they were able to put the British/Swedish films on a different time slot [due to Kenneth Branagh's star status], because they could market it as an 'American movie' or something like that. They put it on primetime, whereas our Swedish ones are on late primetime. Around the world, of course it's easier to sell the British one to English-speaking countries – they've been sold directly to Australia, Canada, the US, South Africa, and other English-speaking countries. But in other countries the Swedish one has been easier to sell. From the beginning, it was easier to sell them to Southern Europe – in some ways, perhaps the British version has suffered as a result, because certain channels have already bought the Swedish one. For a broadcaster, it can be complicated to have a series with the same name: a bit strange! The British version has been sold to the US by BBC Worldwide; BBC Worldwide have made it a co-production. They have a special slot – Masterpiece – on all the PBS channels in the States, so they were in it from the beginning, buying from the BBC ... The Swedish one is sold to a small broadcaster in Washington ... We are doing a deal with Music Box – the same distributor as for the *Millennium* series – so they will probably buy all the *Wallander* mysteries – including the Swedish ones, and then they will sell it to TV and release it on DVD. It's not until the *Millennium* series that there has been any interest from the States.

SP: One of the things I notice about the British/Swedish version of *Wallander* is that it was one of the first series screened in Britain in HD.

MW: When we made the first thirteen *Wallander* films in 2003–2004–2005, they were produced using old-style cameras: 16 mm. Then when we were starting work on the later thirteen Swedish films and these three [the first three British/Swedish films], it was in the middle of that shift from analogue to digital. We were quite lucky with some of the DPs [Directors of Photography] on the first series – including Anthony Dod Mantle who has won an Oscar for *Slumdog Millionaire* [dir. Danny Boyle, 2008].

SP: What current or future productions are you working on?

MW: We are filming Liza Marklund – another Swedish crime writer – six of her books.

EH: We recently finished a feature film in Norway, based on Jo Nesbo's book *Headhunters*. It's a stand-alone thriller that Jo Nesbo has written. We produced that together with a Norwegian production company. This is the first Scandinavian production for us not in the Swedish language. This is not part of the *Harry Hole* series ...

EH: And then we shoot six times ninety films in Gothenburg based on the *Irene Huss* books by Helene Tursten, together with a Gothenburg production company. We have already produced six.

SP: There is quite a close relationship between Yellow Bird and certain authors.

MW: Yes, and we are encouraging them to have more influence than they may have been used to in the past, in most cases. We give them approval, we give them insight and access into all the rushes, if they want to. We listen to them and their views.

SP: Is there an interest in Sweden in British crime drama?

MW: Yes, for a long time. In the beginning, they were running on SVT, and then TV4 started to show some of them. Now they don't receive the same ratings as before, though. It used to be that they would receive enormous ratings, as there were not that many of them. Now they have started to show more, and to show them on niche channels: Channel 9 is the niche channel for Channel 5; TV4 has TV4 Plus, TV3 has TV6, so they are putting British crime drama on their smaller channels. There is still an interest, but before it used always to be an event: a *Morse* would receive 1.5 million Swedish viewers.

Interview B: Left Bank Productions

Interviewee Andy Harries (Chief Executive of Left Bank Productions) (AH). Interview conducted at Left Bank Productions, London, 8 December 2011.

SP: First of all, could you tell me about the ethos and origins of Left Bank Productions?

AH: Left Bank was set up four and a half years ago, although I've been in television for a long time, starting at Granada TV in the late Seventies. The ethos of Granada is firmly engrained in my work. The culture at that time was very distinct and very clear: to make programmes that made a difference – coming from a journalistic background this had a particular appeal for me. I've always been interested in doing real-life stories dramatically – this was the drive behind my work on *Longford* [dir. Tom Hooper, 2006], *The Deal* [dir. Stephen Frears, 2003], and *The Queen* [dir. Stephen Frears, 2006] – to tell a story dramatically in a way that you couldn't in factual terms. The roots of this culture of filmmaking stem from Granada. After, I was driven by a desire to make 'my' sort of programmes through my own company. So Left Bank was set up with a very clear intent on making quality, top-end television with an international dimension. In this way, *Wallander* was a natural project for us. It came about because Ole Sondberg [Executive Producer, Yellow Bird Productions] approached me with the English rights to the Henning Mankell novels. At that time [2006] Mankell was not so well known in the UK. I'd read a couple of the Mankell novels, and liked that as well as telling good stories, the books were intrinsically about Sweden and Swedish society. I'd always been interested politically in Sweden, as a post-sixties state culture. I was only interested, though, in making the series if it was set and filmed in Sweden – I didn't want to relocate the setting to, say, East Anglia. I then went to the BBC, and Jane Tranter – who was then running BBC Drama – showed interest in the project. Very shortly afterwards, I heard that Kenneth Branagh was a fan of the books, and rang his agent. We then visited Ystad together, and the project started from there.

SP: It sounds like there are certain aspects of the work you did with Granada and Left Bank that helped guide your interest in *Wallander* as well as Ole Sondberg's call.

AH: Yes, I came to the meeting with a fundamental interest in Sweden and appreciated the political dimension of the novels – the opportunity was there to make more than 'just another' crime drama. And all of my work in television comes from a huge love of film – something Ole shares, having gone on to make *The Girl with the Dragon Tattoo*. So I've always been interested in making series with filmic frameworks.

SP: And that is the case with the British/Scandinavian co-productions of *Wallander* which has a particular cinematic quality. How did the project work as a tri-partite production, between Yellow Bird, Left Bank/BBC, and Kenneth Branagh's company? It might also be helpful here to explain the relationship between Left Bank and the BBC.

AH: When Left Bank was set up, we took an investment with BBC Worldwide, so they are twenty-five per cent owners of the company. For that, they have an exclusive five-year distribution deal on all our programmes, with *Wallander* being one of the first. The BBC has been very helpful in putting the shows together, and in terms of pre-sales and marketing. Ole, for Yellow Bird, was able to bring German finance and commercial interest to the project. Then there were American pre-sales to WGBH, and the BBC assisted with pre-sales around the world. Left Bank brought the production expertise to the project. We use primarily British directors, with a Swedish crew, and the editing takes place in the UK. Branagh is very involved, too, approving directors and key casting.

SP: There are now multiple versions of *Wallander* ...

AH: Though they are very different. The Swedish version was made for the local and German markets. And it may never have been screened in the UK without the success of the British/Scandinavian *Wallander* series. After their success, BBC Four acquired the Swedish series. Prior to Sky buying all the rights to output from AMC, HBO and Showtime, a lot of American programming was shown on the BBC, such as *24* [dir. various, 2001–2010] and *Curb Your Enthusiasm* [dir. various, 2000–ongoing]. These programmes disappeared from the BBC about three years ago. This led to the idea to bring European television to the schedules, and BBC Four bought *Spiral* [*Engrenages*, dir. various, 2005] from France, *Romanzo Criminale* [dir. various, 2008–2010] from Italy, *The Killing* [2011–ongoing] from Denmark, and *Wallander* from Sweden. This is a real institutional sea-change, as previously foreign language programming was seen as comparable to foreign films – playing to a tiny art-house audience. There had never before been any foreign language series on UK TV channels positioned in popular slots. In my view, the British/Scandinavian *Wallander* provided a bridge, presenting the audience with a fundamentally Swedish series in the English language. The idea was for the series to be like a translated novel. We found a visual equivalence: when a character picks up a newspaper, it is in Swedish. When they turn on the television, it is in Swedish. The signposting will be in Swedish, but the characters will talk English to each other. You have to decide, in television, what the rules of your narrative world are. You have to believe you are in Sweden.

SP: It is interesting that you talk in terms of the construction of a fictional world and the decision-making process behind that. One of the elements I find very striking in the British/ Scandinavian *Wallander* programmes is the use of HD [High Definition] technology.

AH: We were one of the very first shows in the UK to use the RED digital camera, which is technologically very interesting and innovative. Using a 35mm lens, it clearly provides a big step towards feature-film style aesthetics. If you look at the first shot of the first episode [*Sidetracked*] – it is of Ken as Wallander in the field – it was Ken's idea to open with this image: a brilliant analogy of the rape field and the young girl's assault, and also in terms of the impact of the yellow and blue colours – those of the Swedish flag. You are announcing, through the composition of the very first image of the series, that you are in Sweden, coupling this with the colours of the credit sequence and the use of Swedish typography. We had a brilliant director [Philip Martin] and Director of Photographer [Anthony Dod Mantle], fresh from his work on *Slumdog Millionaire*. The series is [in terms of pace] provocatively and deliberately slow – I felt this was a good opportunity to make television in a slightly different way, with a little touch of 'indie' cinema, a series fitting somewhere in its aesthetics and appeals between BBC One and BBC Two.

SP: You're now making the third series?

AH: Yes, and the interesting thing about the third series is that we are filming for the first time in winter. One of the films will be *The Dogs of Riga* – an updated version in terms of the book's political scenarios – and another will be the story of Wallander's daughter Linda, *Before the Frost* reworked from the position of Wallander himself. The other one is a short story Mankell wrote called 'The Grave', which was only ever published in Holland. We will then make one more series, with *The White Lioness* completely reworked, as the novel is set in South Africa, and *The Troubled Man* as a two-part film.

SP: Why have we as a country got a current fascination with Scandinavian crime fiction?

AH: I think the recent tragic killings in Norway [the attack in 2011 by right-wing extremist Anders Behring Breivik on an AUF summer camp on the island of Utoya, Buskerud] tell us quite a lot here. I spend a lot of time in Scandinavia, and they are lovely people, but there is a darkness there. Whilst shocking, the recent news has historical precedents in the region: the shooting of Olof Palme in Sweden, for example.

SP: There are so many fascinating paradoxes at play in Scandinavian society.

AH: *Festen* [dir. Thomas Vinterberg, 1998] is one of my favourite films – fantastically powerful in its presentation of a patriarchal gathering breaking down – there is a real darkness running right the way through their art. And then there is the unspoken complicity occurring in the Second World War – there were hidden groups of pro-Nazi, pro-fascist people ...

SP: Which is part of the plot of *The Girl with the Dragon Tattoo* ...

AH: And it runs through Henning Mankell's works. The first novel we adapted – *Sidetracked* – features a plotline which has shades of fascist undertones in the crimes presented.

SP: And by contrast, the novels of Sjöwall and Wahlöö are Marxist works. Some have suggested that there is 'just enough' difference between the British people and the Scandinavians to allow us this fascination ...

AH: And that might be partly why we had problems when trying to repeat the successful 'trick', so to speak, of *Wallander* with adaptations of *Zen* [dir. various, 2011, from the novels by British writer Michael Dibdin featuring Italian detective Aurelio Zen]. Culturally, the Italian people are very different, and so the series was a bit more of a challenge. It was more difficult to conjure up the narrative world.

SP: Apart from the third series of *Wallander*, what else is Left Bank working on?

AH: We also make *Mad Dogs* [dir. various, 2011–2012] for Sky One, with the third series of the franchise now in production. We also make films, having just completed *The Lady* [dir. Luc Besson, 2011] – the story of Aung San Suu Kyi and her role in Burma's democratic movement.

Interview C: Johan Theorin

Interviewee Johan Theorin (JT). Online interview, 18 August 2011.

SP: There is a huge recognition of, and current fascination with, Scandinavian crime fiction. The form has a rich history, but why, in your opinion, is the genre particularly popular now, and on such a global scale?

JT: Well, I hope it partly is because we writers produce crime novels of high quality. But of course there are other explanations. One is that the interest is just part of a bigger wave of recognition and popularity of things Scandinavian in the world, such as Ikea, Volvo, H&M, the Swedish and Norwegian Royal families, the music of Abba, the Danish films of Susanne Bier and Lars von Trier etc, which has been growing and growing in the last twenty years or so. There is a curiosity about these countries and their culture, and more and more foreign visitors come to Sweden each year, according to statistics I just heard. Having said that, I also think that the Scandinavian crime writers have done one thing well, and that is to write about their own countries and fellow countrymen, nothing else. I get the feeling that too many writers in countries like Spain, France, and the UK dream about making it big in the United States, and therefore set their stories in America, or at least Americanise their own countries too much in their novels, turning them into weak imitations of US thrillers.

SP: How much is the genre particularly suited to exploring matters of Sweden's national identity? To what extent do they reflect a 'Swedish-ness' in terms of a national social and cultural disposition? Are there other themes and matters examined particularly closely in works of Scandinavian/ Swedish crime fiction?

JT: I am too close to Sweden to answer questions about our identity, I think. A book called *Fishing in Utopia: Sweden and the Future that Disappeared* [London: Granta, 2009], written by an English journalist [Andrew Brown] who has spent many years in Sweden, was an eye-opener because it made me look at Sweden from a new perspective while reading it last year. But the silence of the landscape and of the characters are culturally very Scandinavian in the crime fiction, I think. The terse rhythm of the language in our novels is another feature, perhaps inspired by the old Norse and Icelandic prose poems.

SP: What are your thoughts on the legacy of Sjöwall and Wahlöö's *Beck* books? And of Henning Mankell's *Wallander* mysteries?

JT: Sjöwall and Wahlöö were the two crime authors who (to paraphrase what someone wrote about Dashiel Hammett) took murder out of the parlour and put it in the alleys of Sweden where it belongs. They made Swedish crime and police work feel real. Before them, Swedish crime fiction had been elegant, bourgeois and non-political, 'Agatha Christie-stories' if you like by writers such as Maria Lang and Stieg Trenter, but Sjöwall and Wahlöö brought a gritty realism and a leftist perspective to their crime stories. They were a huge influence on later Swedish crime writers such as Mankell, Åke Edwardson, Leif G. W. Person, Kjell Eriksson, Roslund and Hellström, to name a few. I like the Sjöwall and Wahlöö novels and the *Wallander* mysteries very much, but I wrote my Öland novels almost as counter-reaction to their novels. I did not want my stories to be realistic city police procedurals.

SP: What do the books (in this genre) say about local matters: regional, or in relation to the links between Nordic countries?

JT: Again, I think I'm too close to this region of the world to say much about this. But of course, the Scandinavian countries are very highly organised. We expect the police to show up when a serious crime has been committed, and doing their jobs without taking any bribes. We have relatively few guns here, or at least few handguns. That is why tragedies like the Palme assassination in 1986 or the Oslo terror attacks this summer [2011] are such national traumas. We think they can't happen here.

SP: How much translates to a global audience, i.e. tapping into global (rather than local) concerns?

JT: Well, we are all people in the world. We should basically all have the same concerns for ourselves and others. Fear and hate and grief and love and trust are universal things, and also the conflicts between cities and rural areas. I write about those things, and it is a pleasure to know that my books will be sent overseas and might end up with some reader in America or Japan or Brazil and perhaps connect with them.

SP: Many historians suggest that Sweden is a country in constant tension between its 'isolationist' past and its place in a transnational era (in relation to say, membership to the EU). Would you agree with this assertion?

JT: I'm not sure we ever have been very isolationist. Sweden has always been influenced by larger countries; France in the 1700s, Germany in the 1800s and now England and the US after World War Two. But I think there has been both an arrogance (bad) and idealism (good) in us Swedes, because we have gone abroad in the last fifty years and tried to help smaller and poorer countries to become more like Sweden.

SP: How much of an impact on Swedish culture and society would you say the shooting of Prime Minister Olof Palme had, and, in turn, on the development of the crime drama as a format?

JT: I think the Palme assassination was crucial for the writing of Swedish crime fiction, because it destroyed our innocence and we had to deal with this trauma somehow – one way was to write and read crime stories in much greater numbers and of a higher quality than we had done before. Just a few years after Olof Palme was shot, Henning Mankell came along with his socialistic policeman Kurt Wallander who quietly longs for the return of the welfare state. The *Wallander* novels quickly became bestsellers in Sweden – after previous crime novels in the early 1980s had not – and I don't think that is a coincidence.

SP: Does the model of the welfare state remain a mainstay of contemporary Swedish life (in terms of collectivism and solidarity), and/or how is it reflected in the works of crime fiction?

JT: The Swedish welfare state has dwindled the last twenty years or so, but I think it can be found as a certain optimism in our crime fiction, where there is an underlying assumption that if the police and the politicians and teachers and social workers just organise things well enough and take good care of everyone from the cradle to the grave there will be no more crime in Sweden.

SP: One of the aspects I admire most of your own work is the way they reveal a clear understanding and handling of generic conventions (of crime drama and horror/the supernatural), and how they combine elements (of for example the police procedural, the detective thriller, the ghost story)

JT: Well, I have read these different genres all my life, and I like them all. For me it was fun to try write crime stories and weave in strands of folklore and the supernatural. But Selma Lagerlof did the same thing a hundred years ago – and [Arthur Conan Doyle's] *The Hound of the Baskervilles* is also a combination of genres – so it is nothing new.

SP: Are there particular writers (Swedish, Scandinavian, or further afield) that you class as being particularly influential to your own works?

JT: I have read a lot of the crime fiction of Ruth Rendell and Karin Fossum, who both explore human relationships in their novels, and I like their work and try to care as much about my characters as they do about theirs. I also like the novels of Peter Straub and Shirley Jackson, who do the same thing as Fossum and Rendell in the supernatural genre.

SP: To what extent do you think the qualities of crime fiction can be translated into visual form for film and television, and how many are 'medium-specific' (singular to the written form of the novel)?

JT: Film and television stories are like express trains where everybody must get aboard at point A and leave at point B and things must run very smoothly for the whole journey and be very clearly presented. Crime movies tend to be loud and aggressive, with very little room for character studies and subtle details. (Still, when they work they are great – I like crime films like *The Usual Suspects* [dir. Bryan Singer, 1995], *Lock Stock and Two Smoking Barrels* [dir. Guy Ritchie, 1998], *Sea of Love* [dir. Harold Becker, 1989] and *One False Move* [dir. Carl Franklin, 1992] very much.)

SP: Are you involved in any plans re the adaptations of your novels for film or television? Would this be something you would be interested in?

JT: The film rights have been sold to the same company [Yellow Bird] that produced the three films based on the Stieg Larsson books.

SP: Your books reveal a particularly skilful handling of time (in terms of narrative structure) and memory, as well as an interest in the act of storytelling. If possible, please could you expand on these elements a little.

JT: I think we live our whole lives in the past, present and future simultaneously – and also in our dreams and nightmares – and I try to show that in my fiction. Also, I have discovered a lot of things about the past of my own family on Öland when I have written these novels, when people have told me memories of my dead relatives – not just good memories, because there was a lot of poverty on the island, and some of my relatives seem to have been rather mean – and that has affected the stories as well. But of course we seldom remember things correctly. And I would like to write more about distorted and untrustworthy memories, but this is very hard to do without completely confusing the reader.

SP: How much of your exploration of the professional group-ings of the police and of journalism/the news media (such as the Ölands-Posten) are regionally and/or nationally minded, and how much are universal in their analysis of these two interconnecting professional institutions? Do you draw on your own previous experience as a journalist? Is there a particular freedom of the press in Sweden and/or Scandinavia?

JT: I worked as a journalist for twenty years, but have so far never used a journalist as a main character – perhaps because it has been so popular for other crime writers to do so. The freedom of the press is solid here in Scandinavia. But there are other concerns – I think a journalist always has to grapple with reality, because he or she can only catch small bits of it in their articles. That always bothered me as a jour-nalist – all the small things that have to be left out – and I am much happier making things up as a novelist.

SP: Would you consider your novels to be politically minded? In what ways? The events of the World War are particularly resonant in *Echoes from the Dead* – how much of this re-flects or comments on Sweden's own past?

JT: No, I don't think they are political. At least not party po-litical. I am interested in politics as a person and think it is important that we all vote and protect our democracy, but as an author I don't have any particular political message in my novels, and I don't put the blame on any system, capi-talistic or socialistic, for the criminal activities of individual persons. I had enough of political messages and propaganda in the Swedish children books of the 1970s, which was read to me when I was little.

SP: Certain themes and motifs are patterned across your novels in particularly striking ways: the family, childhood, and gen-erations; specifics of the landscape (such as rock formations, fog, and the water) and island life; the outsider (against an insider community); transformation (of nation and of the individual). What draws you to explore these particular areas?

JT: This is the landscape of Öland where my mother and her family comes from, and I have been to this island in the Baltic sea ever since I was a baby, but always as a visitor. As an adult, I can sense myself as a child there and see the landscape with both new and old eyes. I try to use this in my novels.

SP: You set the quartet on Öland, and state (on your website), that 'The goal was to write a novel for each of Öland's seasons – an Öland quartet where the weather and the atmosphere of the landscape affect the characters of the story.' Please could you expand on this structural decision, and how it affected the poetics and themes of the novels.

JT: I just got the idea for two novels which I realised had to take place in the autumn (*Echoes from the Dead*) and in the winter (*The Darkest Room*) and thought; Well, why not make it a quartet then? The island of Öland changes so much between the season when it comes to the weather and the population (few people in the winter, many tourists in the summer) that I thought a seasonal approach would make the four novels very different from each other. A year on Öland in four installations. I enjoy writing about landscapes, and how they are perceived by people. But when I started this Four Seasons project, I found out that the British writer Ann Cleeves (who is a keen Scandinavian crime fiction reader, by the way) was doing the same thing on the Shetland Islands. Great minds think alike!

SP: Revelations of truth (in terms of plot) are essential to most crime novels – how do you decide what and when to make the reader aware of particular pieces of information, and when to withhold?

JT: Revelations of hidden and painful truths are a powerful thing in a novel, and a thing that makes me enjoy both reading and writing crime stories. The revelations in *The*

Murder of Roger Ackroyd [Agatha Christie, 1926] or in *A Kiss before Dying* [Ira Levin, 1953] for example – they shook me deeply when I read them in my teens. I think it is great fun when a surprising twist can be pulled off, but it can also become very contrived and the twist shouldn't be the main goal of a crime story. I don't write whodunits.

SP: In connection to the above question, narrative agency and access to characters' thoughts (especially of the killer and the detective or investigating protagonist) is equally key in the mapping of a crime fiction. Please could you talk a little about your decisions in this area, too?

JT: In a whodunit, you can of course never present the killer and his thoughts to the reader. At the same time you have to make the reader understand sooner or later what the motive of the murderer is, usually by having the detective give a lecture at the end. It is hard to vary this model. As I said, I don't really write whodunits – but the art of exposition is always a challenge in crime novels. Not too much, not too little.

SP: How do you decide on the 'modus operandi' of the killer, and how much is the (particular) act of murder integrated to the thematic concerns of the novel?

JT: I am actually not interested in the murders at all. *Se7en* was a good film fifteen years ago, but these days I am sick of all novels and films about serial killers who try to devise new ways of killing and torturing their victims – almost as if the authors were in a gore competition. I'm just interested in the mystery and the consequences of a murder, not the technical details. Most real murderers don't have a modus operandi anyway – they just kill a person with the nearest available weapon and will have to live with that sudden move the rest of their lives.

Interview D: Mari Jungstedt

Interviewee Mari Jungstedt (MJ). Online interview, 11 December 2011.

SP: Why is Nordic noir particularly popular now?

MJ: Of course the remarkable success with the *Millenium* trilogy has had a great impact on the interest of Swedish crime right now. But even before that, we have a long tradition on crime literature in Sweden which began with the international success of Sjöwall/Wahlöö in the sixties. They also introduced social criticism as an important element in their books and this has had an effect on Swedish crime writers. They inspired many authors, big names after them like Henning Mankell, Håkan Nesser, and Åke Edwardsson. Then women started to write crime novels and they contributed to new elements that have broadened and widened the genre – first Liza Marklund, Karin Alvtegen, Inger Frimansson, Karin Wahlberg, etc. The women put more of everyday life into the genre and the relationships between people became even more important; between man and woman, parents and children, etc.

And then almost ten years ago came a new sort of 'boom' when Åsa Larsson, Camilla Läckberg and myself debuted the same year in 2003. Shortly after us came also Mons Kallentoft, Johan Theorin, Viveka Sten, Jens Lapidus, etc. and there was a new boom of Swedish crime literature. A new element now was the exotism of getting to know small places throughout the country of Sweden: the environment in which the story takes place became very important, as exemplified by the relationship between writers and places such as Åsa Larsson and Kiruna, Camilla Läckberg and Fjällbacka, Johan Theorin and Öland, Mons Kallentoft and Västerås, Viveka Sten and Sandhamn, myself and Gotland. I think all these factors have contributed to the success alongside others like the fact that the quality of the Swedish literature is high, and that people in general are curious about Sweden, partly because of the Swedish welfare system – the idea that Sweden is the ideal society where everything is working so perfectly, with equality between men and women, high living standards, and all appearing to be so clean and well-organised.

Also people are interested in Sweden because we do have many famous people and events that are known world-wide even though Sweden is such a small country in terms of population, with only nine million inhabitants in this big country. Examples include the Nobel Prize, Ingmar Bergman, Volvo, Saab, Olof Palme, Björn Borg, Ingrid Bergman, Pippi Longstocking and Astrid Lindgren, Abba, Roxette, Zlatan Ibrahimovic, etc, etc.

Another factor that promotes interest in Sweden is that we are situated so far north and it makes us exotic, so close to the North Pole, the coldness, the dark winters and the land of the midnight sun. Furthermore, there are the typical Swedish 'trademarks': everything from beautiful Swedish girls, to the right of common access.

SP: Do your works and others of Swedish crime fiction reflect aspects of 'Swedish-ness'?

MJ: Of course, it is very hard to avoid when you are a Swedish author and the Swedish-ness influences the literature in every aspect, whether we do it consciously or not.

SP: What are your thoughts on the *Millennium* trilogy as books and films?

MJ: I loved the books, especially the character of Lisbeth Salander (a modern Pippi Longstocking!), the author's feminism and criticism of society, but also of course the stories and that the books are very entertaining and suspenseful. I must admit, though, that I smiled a little by myself when I read about Mr Blomqvist's success in getting all women into bed – sometimes worse than James Bond! I think maybe that reflected a little bit Stieg Larsson's own dreams ... I also loved the Swedish films, first and foremost the fantastic, unforgettable portrait of Lisbeth Salander, by the actress Noomi Rapace.

SP: What are your thoughts on Sjöwall and Wahlöö, and Mankell's *Wallander* mysteries?

MJ: I love them all! I have read every book and they have inspired me a lot of course. They manage to combine interesting characters, suspense, narrative efficiency, intrigue, and social critique.

SP: Which writers influence your own works?

MJ: I have always read a lot, ever since I was little. Books have always been an important part of my life. I have always read all kinds of books, but ever since I was a child I have loved mysteries and detective stories; Agatha Christie, Sir Arthur Conan Doyle's Sherlock Holmes stories, Enid Blyton with the Famous Five books. Later I read all the Mankell, Sjöwall Wahlöö and other Swedish crime writers. But I really read all kinds of books and I think I am being influenced by them all somehow – I read everything from Herta Muller to Toni Morrison, Dennis Lehane, Joyce Carol Oates, Håkan Nesser and a bunch of Swedish authors you might not know.

SP: How involved are you in the adaptations of your novels, on both the Swedish and German productions?

MJ: Absolutely nothing. I was asked in the beginning to write the scripts for the German films, but I said no. I love film, but I want to write my books, that's all I want to do and if I start to mix up with a lot of other things I won 't have time for my stories!

SP: Your books reveal a particular interest in time and memory – are they important concerns to you?

MJ: After having published nine novels over the past nine years and now [at the time of publication] working on my tenth, I can see a pattern in my writing, I have never had a plan for my writing, how many books I will write in this series and so on. I think every book is unique, every story is unique, so for me I cannot say that I will write ten books or fifteen books in this series ... I cannot say a number. There might be one more book or twenty-five more books about Knutas on Gotland – I have no idea! As long as I can come up with good stories I will write and as long as I think it gives me pleasure.

But I can see a red line throughout my writing – a theme that keeps coming back, more or less, in every book. And it is our childhood and how it affects us in different ways; the vulnerability during childhood, the exposure, the fragility and how things that happen when we grow up can have such an impact on our adult lives. I think this is really the explanation why I am writing and this is my 'driving force'. I want my books to be entertaining, suspenseful and a joy to read, integrating the environment of Gotland and Sweden and also focused in depicting relationships between people, which are central in my books. But also I want to tell a deeper story, something that can affect the reader in a deeper way.

SP: Would you consider your novels to be politically minded?

MJ: I am sure they are, even though my prime ambition is not one of social criticism, rather trying to say something about relationships between people, how childhood affects us and trying to understand how a person can commit the worst of crimes.

But of course, as a former journalist (I worked as a news anchor in the Swedish Television for ten years before I started writing full-time) I am very interested in society and I also spend a great deal of time on research. I think almost fifty per cent of the work with the books is research. And the research takes me to all kinds of places where I also bring the reader of course; it has taken us for instance, into a clinic for anorexic women, the world of motorcycle gangs, the fashion world behind the scenes of the catwalk, the art world, archaeological excavations, once I had to sneak into a secretive club where men meet to have sex with other men, and so on.

SP: How do you decide on the 'modus operandi' of the killer?

MJ: It all depends on the story and who the killer is. And the modus operandi is not the most interesting thing – all the circumstances have to decide the modus operandi – even though I enjoyed it a lot when, during the writing of my sixth novel (*The Dark Angel*) I could dust off the old modus operandi from Agatha Christie in her novel *Sparkling Cyanide* [1945]!

Interview E: John Ajvide Lindqvist

Interviewee John Ajvide Lindqvist (JAL). Interview conducted at FantasyCon, Brighton, 1 October 2011.

SP: From the use of song lyrics in your work, especially *Harbour* and via the title of *Let the Right One In*, you obviously have affection for [British band] The Smiths, for Morrissey, and for British pop music of a particular kind from a particular era. To give another example, there is a moment early on in your novel *Little Star* where you talk about David Bowie and 'Life on Mars'.

JAL: In my stories I use my personal obsessions, and I use the lyrics and the quotes to try and get an emotional equivalent to the thing I'm trying to describe. Often I can play a song to myself over and over and over again – like for example when I was writing *Harbour* I was listening to 'Nobody Loves Us', this Morrissey B side – I think I played that 200 or 300 times, sometimes I would have it running all day on repeat, until I can no longer hear it, and I am in the atmosphere of that song because that's how I want certain parts of the book to feel. I would like the person reading to have the same relation to the music as I do, so when they see these lines they hear the song, and they get into that mood that I want. Oftentimes, the music I want to hear in the story – so to speak – comes before the story itself. For example, for my latest project is a 'zombie massacre' story I wrote in thirty-five days, I wanted the soundtrack to be music by Modern Talking – a horrible German pop band from the eighties that basically wrote the same song over and over and over again, with squeaky voices: the perfect soundtrack of a zombie massacre. In the story, the group has this old mix tape with them when they go out onto the island, and when the zombies start coming, the boom-box gets left there, and continues to pump out this horrible synth music! The music is essential to the writing and the story.

SP: Yes, it is clearly integral to the atmosphere of your work. To continue with the Morrissey example a little longer, it seems there may be a similarity between what people say about his music, and what people say about Sweden. Whether flippantly or in making serious critical points, Morrissey's music is often described as sad, depressing, and depressive. Similarly, the first thing people have said to me when they hear I am writing a book about Swedish crime fiction is to invoke the idea of Scandinavian gloom – the melancholy at the heart of the country. Obviously this is a generalisation and a cultural stigma, but is there a grain of truth in terms of 'the Scandinavian mood'?

JAL: I'm sure there is, and also because of physical, practical reasons, as we have a lot of darkness in Sweden – there is a period of at least four months a year when it is constantly dark, snowy, and cold, and you don't really go out – we don't get enough light! So it is very different to California in that respect – you sit in your house and you get to think a little bit too much! And of course there is also our language – the words we use develop from that basic geographical fact of what Sweden is like, and so in our language, our expressions, the way that we think, a certain level derives from the fact that there is so much darkness in Sweden. I don't know where the particular, Swedish mental structure comes from, but this is definitely a part of it.

SP: The relationship between the landscape and the language is closely intertwined.

JAL: Yes, and there is definitely a certain Swedish mentality, one we share with the Norwegian, Finnish and Icelandic people … the Danes seem to be a little bit different … but they have other problems!

SP: Turning to the key idea of 'darkness in the woods' in your novels, I'm struck by the way your work is adjacent to that of Henning Mankell in the evocation of different Swedish landscapes: the landscape of *Let the Right One In* – the city setting and the insularity of a block of flats, and then you move to the landscape of *Harbour*, which becomes a character in its own right.

JAL: Some of this comes from my own experience – now I live in a landscape similar to that of *Harbour*, but before that I spent some time in the setting of *Let the Right One In* and a great deal of time in the Stockholm setting of *Handling the Undead*. In terms of the sense of place – I don't think I'm very good at describing nature – but the sense of place is very important to me. I often make up maps of the fictional settings while writing the novels. It is very important for me to know exactly what it looks like around the characters, when they are walking, how the air feels when something bad is going to happen, when the wind's blowing, and the sounds of the sea – these are very important, too. Without them, the stories wouldn't be scary. So the sense of place is like that of the music – the music has a certain emotional impact or resonance in you, and being part of a landscape has another. This is part of the problem I'm having with my next novel – *X* – because there is no landscape in the story, none whatsoever: it is just this short-cut grass in every direction.

SP: As you have mentioned the new project X: do you think that, unconsciously or otherwise, you have set yourself this task in knowing how important landscape is to your work (and I beg to differ – I think you are very good at describing nature, especially in *Harbour*) – setting yourself a challenge by taking this element away in the latest book. It sounds like an experiment that you have set yourself.

JAL: Yes, and I don't even know what is going to happen! At this stage, I have just thought up forty people to whom this event is going to happen, and their relationships become fundamental to the narrative. I'm not even sure yet if it is going to be a horror story – which is very unusual.

SP: Do you think it is might be a coincidence that you have moved into this territory just as you find international success – your name is very well-known now, both by fans of the horror genre and those in literary circles, and there are the successful adaptations of *Let the Right One In*.

JAL: No, I don't think so – I don't care much about this sort of thing, otherwise I wouldn't have just written a straight out zombie massacre novel. Ordinarily I try to write three-dimensional characters; they are one-and-a-half dimensional at most in the zombie story: you only get to know them a little bit before they are eaten! So now I have the spirit to do something complicated again, and this is simply the idea that I have: people being transported to this non-place.

SP: Perhaps, then, isolation is an important theme here? Returning to the idea of landscape, the characters' isolation in the landscape – where you put them – seems very significant. I was struck in this way by the set-up to *Little Star*, as the little girl is found in a bag, placed in a cellar. The characters in *Let the Right One In* suffer their own forms of isolation, and *Harbour* presents a particular, insular community. And people have spoken of Sweden as an isolationist place – a country struggling to find its place in the world following the advent of globalisation.

JAL: But we're not isolationist – I don't think that's true, because especially during the time of Olof Palme, Sweden was an extremely international country. It was one of the places taking a stand against the problems of the third world, and against dictatorships in other countries. There is a legacy then of Sweden in the seventies – many townships in third world countries having town squares dedicated to Olof Palme, and so on. When you speak to people in India, or in Vietnam, they will raise his name. I don't think Sweden is isolationist – I think Denmark is now – it is really closing its borders. Sweden, as a Scandinavian country, takes more refugees per capita from other countries.

SP: What, to you, was the impact of Olof Palme's death on Swedish society?

JAL: I don't think that the impact at the time was so big, but I think he has become a mythological figure whose death is seen as causally linked to Sweden's fortunes on a psychological and sociological level. His death is seen as *the point* at which things started to go wrong, when the solidarity of the Social Democratic society broke apart, when it really started seven or eight years before his death, on a serious scale. So Palme's death was not, in actuality, a watershed moment. Nowadays, however, it is seen that way, taking on the force of mythology. It is also true, for example, that Sweden allowed German soldiers to train in the country [during the Second World War] – and this too is part of our shame, our mythology, our self-image. Palme's death is part of a slow decay.

SP: Do you believe that the welfare state, and that particular model of life, still has resonance in Sweden today?

JAL: Yes, it does, also as a mythological character. Sweden as a welfare society: OK, it didn't work very well, doesn't work any more, but we have this proud past where everything was working well, everyone was paying their taxes to care for the poor and the weak – this is also a part of our self-image … a Golden period that defined what Sweden is. And a lot of people around the world still have this image of Sweden, even though it isn't really like that anymore – we are now a standard European country with a right-wing government for the last two elections. We should also remember that a lot of the demonisation of the welfare state was done by the Social Democrats in the Eighties.

SP: Would you say there is a political element at work in your novels, in the writing?

JAL: I never set out to write a social or political commentary; Henning Mankell, on the other hand, has a very specific political agenda – he wants to talk about Sweden in his novels, about society, about what is happening here. I don't. But because of my working-class background and upbringing, this creeps into my stories. And if you take, for example *Little Star*, if you take your horror stories seriously, and place it within its society, then it becomes automatically a sort of social criticism. Because you are portraying something terrible happening in a believable way, you are saying that something must be wrong with society, a society in which this could happen, at all. Of course, this doesn't go for *Handling the Undead*, because the dead do not wake up, but even then, I think that the way the dead get treated, incarcerated, has a certain political resonance. So even though I don't set out to write social commentary or criticism at all, it comes as a side effect because of my own background and the fact that horror, if taken seriously, becomes a form of criticism.

SP: I would agree; you don't impose political thought onto the narrative. That can sometimes be the case in other writers' work, and can seem rather forced, especially when they have an agenda that they want to press – it becomes a kind of polemic. I think Mankell is very good at integrating the two. We should also mention here Sjöwall and Wahlöö, who many people see as representing the apogee of Swedish crime fiction. They obviously had a very strong, very forthright left-wing political agenda that they wanted the books to promote.

You mention horror and its effects when taken seriously. Your works demonstrate a sophisticated understanding of the horror genre. I don't think you're interested in subverting the genre; there is a great affection for horror in the works.

JAL: Yes, I'm very fond of the horror genre as such. I don't read a lot of horror, but I do watch quite a few horror movies – most of them, of course, are not very good. As I have a genuine affection for the genre, I want to give something to it, and I'm very proud to be a part of it. This is something that some journalists don't seem to be able to understand. They say: you are a very good writer; why do you need these horrific elements in your work? But that is where I start: I start with the horror elements, and then I construct the story around them, so it would be nothing without them.

SP: On the back of *Millennium*, there is currently a cultural 'hipness' about Scandinavia. With your own success, with the film adaptations *Let the Right One In* and *Let Me In*, with Stieg Larsson's work, with Mankell's works and the British adaptations of *Wallander*, and the Danish *Forbrydelsen*: all of these cultural artefacts coming out of Scandinavia have led to a particular point of impact.

JAL: Yes, a particular phenomenon right now that will inevitably pass away in a few years, and then it will be, say, Kenya! I haven't the slightest idea why Sweden should be hip – maybe the influence of Stieg Larsson is key here.

SP: What is your take on the Larsson phenomenon, and the works themselves?

JAL: I really liked the first book [*The Girl with the Dragon Tattoo*] a lot, because I thought it was such a generous work. Usually, in the crime novels I have read, you can have four or five original ideas to develop through the story – in the worst cases they only have one original idea to last five hundred pages. But the first Stieg Larsson novel is full of ideas! So it is very generous in that way. And then of course there is the heroine, Salander: she is perfect, a great character. And the first film was unusually good, too.

SP: That leads us to the film adaptations of your book, *Let the Right One In*, and your screenplay for the Swedish version. *Let the Right One In* is a very striking film, and especially distinctive in its look.

JAL: Yes, Tomas Alfredson is a very talented director, bringing a particular look to both *Let the Right One In* and his later film *Tinker Tailor Soldier Spy*. But we should also remember the cinematographer on both pictures, Hoyte Van Hoytema: he has a very distinctive vision in mind – how to frame the shots, how to move the camera – so it is very much a collaborative process, achieving the visual feel of these movies.

SP: It strikes me, too, that the US version – *Let Me In* – is doing something very different to the Swedish version, and that a lot of reviewers and journalists did not appreciate this, seeing it as a mere 'Americanisation' of the Swedish film, and of your source novel as well. My understanding of *Let Me In* is different, that is doing something else in terms of genre.

JAL: I feel the same. The general response to the American film has been very unfair. I can see of course that it has borrowed quite a lot from Tomas's film, and some scenes are very similar. But there are also considerable, discernible differences, even within scenes, in terms of how they play out; for example, the scene between Abby and the father where he strokes her – there is a very different emotional resonance at work. And also the way the film starts: focusing on the ambulance going to the hospital – it gives the thing a completely different tone. It is very much its own movie. I know how passionate the director [Matt Reeves] was for this story, and for making this movie.

SP: That comes across to me as a viewer of the film, and there are certainly different emotional and stylistic registers. Reeves is working in a much more melodramatic mode. His understanding of different genres, and combining them, is prevalent in his earlier film, too, in *Cloverfield*.

JAL: One big difference between them is that Tomas has hardly watched any horror films, whereas Matt Reeves is an aficionado!

SP: I look forward to seeing the other films of your novels. I know that you are involved in the making of the film version of *Harbour*?

JAL: Yes, Tomas will be directing that, eventually!

SP: And we know that *Handling the Undead* is in production.

JAL: Hopefully we will start shooting next summer.

SP: Do you ever write with cinema in mind?

JAL: No, because, for example, *Little Star* would not then have been possible: I feel this book is more or less unfilmable. I think I have a sort of cinematic imagination, because I start out with very strong images, and then I try to make paths between them to make a story. In that manner I am very visual in my thinking – maybe that is one reason why the books work quite well as movies.

AFTERWORD

This book has aimed to show how particular films and television programmes, all deriving from Swedish crime novels, convey the cultural, historical and psychological depths of which the form is capable. As has been demonstrated over five chapters, it combines considerations of adaptation, historical documentation, genre, and cultural critique with close textual analysis (or stylistic criticism). It's my belief that a *combination* of these methodological approaches – of binding debates about history, industry, and form with the practice of interpretation – is still rare in Film and Television Studies and provides fresh readings of the various texts under scrutiny. The work of Antoine de Baecque in *Camera Historica* provides an exemplary account of the possibilities to be found in fusing considerations of film form and historical detail, of 'focusing on what the cinematic art reveals about a society at any given moment' *without losing sight of* 'the film-object itself'.[222] My book has followed strands of de Baecque's approach, moving towards and away from the film-object and television-object at particular points, to gain a series of interpretative perspectives. These adjustments of critical viewpoint are facilitated and encouraged by film's own stance towards history. As de Baecque puts it, echoing Kracauer's words from *History: The Last Things Before the Last*, 'cinema hovers above history like a helicopter or a plane taking topographical photographs, yet not as high as theory, whose obsession with regular patterns and concepts blinds it to the contours of the landscape below'.[223]

As my Introduction states, 'this approach aims to uncover the texts' significance and appeals from both inside (in terms of points of style such as camerawork, performance, and décor) and outside (surrounding political climates and social circumstances) the work itself.' By now, I hope it has become clear that the internal structures and stylistic elements of the films and programmes are not separate from external factors, but that rather the *mise-en-scène* develops a particular vision of society, in synthesis. There is an impossibility of isolation in terms of the concrete object (the novel, the film or TV series), its medium, and its location in contemporary society. Political discourse is deeply embedded in the pieces, as they raise pertinent questions of international responsibility, civic duty, humanism, and humanitarianism. After the current craze for all things Scandinavian – from *The Girl with the Dragon Tattoo* to *The Killing* and the knitted jumpers worn by its central protagonist Sarah Lund, to Michelin-starred Danish restaurants – has inevitably died away, Sweden's place in the world as expressed artistically in film and television (or film-as-television) will, I predict, remain tantalisingly inviting in its complexities.

Two thoughts from Kurt Wallander to close, both taken from *The Man Who Smiled*, binding matters together. Pondering Harderberg's hold over multiple industries, a new aspect dawns for Wallander: 'What I'm looking at is really an atlas of the world, he thought. National boundaries have been replaced by ever-changing demarcation lines between different companies whose turnover and influence are greater than the budgets of many whole countries.'[224] And yet, in Sweden, in Skåne, in Ystad, climatic particularities of the far country create an ethereal, all-encompassing fog, often cloaking the landscapes. The first words of the novel present us with Wallander's thoughts about it, as 'A silent, stealthy beast of prey. Even though I have lived all my life in Skåne, where fog is forever closing in and shutting out the world, I'll never get used to it.'[225] It is familiarly unknowable, opaque, and oppressive. It encapsulates the murky confusions of local, global, personal, and private spaces, in these Swedish crime dramas. It shuts out the world, but only for a while.

NOTES

1 An earlier version of this opening account of Nordic noir on British television can be found in Steven Peacock (ed.), *Stieg Larsson's Millennium Trilogy: Interdisciplinary Approaches to Nordic Noir on Page and Screen* (London: Palgrave Macmillan, 2012), pp. 5–7 and 103–104.

2 Henning Mankell's *Wallander* novels (1991–2009) are enormously popular in his native Sweden, Scandinavia, Germany, and the UK, and have won many awards including the German Crime Prize and the British 2001 CWA Gold Dagger Award for *Sidetracked*. The novels, in order of publication, are *Mördare utan ansikte* (1991; English translation by Steven T. Murray: *Faceless Killers*, 1997); *Hundarna i Riga* (1992; English translation by Laurie Thompson: *The Dogs of Riga*, 2001); *Den vita lejoninnan* (1993; English translation by Laurie Thompson: *The White Lioness*, 1998); *Mannen som log* (1994; English translation by Laurie Thompson: *The Man Who Smiled*, 2005); *Villospår* (1995; English translation by Steven T. Murray: *Sidetracked*, 1999); *Den femte kvinnan* (1996; English translation by Steven T. Murray: *The Fifth Woman*, 2000); *Steget efter* (1997; English translation by Ebba Segerberg: *One Step Behind*, 2002); *Brandvägg* (1998; English translation by Ebba Segerberg: *Firewall*, 2002); *Pyramiden* (1999; short stories; English translation by Ebba Segerberg with Laurie Thompson: *The Pyramid*, 2008); *Den orolige mannen* (2009; English translation by Laurie Thompson: *The Troubled Man*, 2011).

3 First series: *Sidetracked* (aired 30 November 2008); *Firewall* (aired 7 December 2008); *One Step Behind* (aired 14 December 2008). Second series: *Faceless Killers* (aired 3 January 2010); *The Man Who Smiled* (aired 10 January 2010); *The Fifth Woman* (aired 17 January 2010). Third series: *An Event in Autumn* (1 April 2012); *The Dogs of Riga* (8 April 2012); *Before the Frost* (15 April 2012).

4 www.radiotimes.com/news/2011–11–18/the-killing-knit-your-own-sarah-lund-jumper (accessed 06/03/2012).

5 See for example Janet McCabe, 'Nothing Like a Dane' for *CST Online*, http://cstonline.tv/nothing-like-dane (accessed 06/03/2012), and Sam Wollaston's review for *The Guardian,* www.guardian.co.uk/tv-and-radio/2012/jan/07/tv-review-borgen-sherlock (accessed 06/03/2012).

6 Sam Wollaston, television review for *The Guardian*, 26 May 2012, www.guardian.co.uk/tv-and-radio/2012/may/26/tv-review-kingdom-of-plants (accessed 29/05/2012). In 2013, the British fascination with Swedish crime fiction increased further. The Saturday night slot for Nordic noir on BBC Four was filled by *Arne Dahl* – a TV series based on the 'Unit A' novels by Jan Arnald (under the pseudonym Arne Dahl), about a team of maverick detectives. The impact and popularity of Scandinavian crime drama were marked in other ways, too. In April 2013, Krister Henriksson (*Wallander*) took the lead role in a production of *Doktor Glas* at Wyndham's Theatre in London, performed in Swedish with English subtitles. British television channel ITV sought to attract the audience of *Forbrydelsen* and *Wallander* by crafting a homegrown crime drama – *Broadchurch* – that borrowed liberally from Nordic noir: heavy on melancholic atmosphere, intricate family ties, and emotional angst.

7 Stieg Larsson's *The Girl with the Dragon Tattoo* was the best-selling novel in Europe in 2008, and then debuted at number four on the *New York Times* best-seller list in 2009, subsequently spending months near the top of the trade paperback list.

8 See, for example, Mark Bould, *Film Noir: From Berlin to Sin City* (London and New York: Wallflower, 2005), Mark T. Conrad (ed.) *The Philosophy of Film Noir* (Lexington, KY: The University of Kentucky Press, 2006), Andrew Spicer, *Film Noir* (London and New York, Toronto Pearson Education Limited, 2002), and

Nicholas Christopher, *Somewhere in the Night: Film Noir and the American City* (New York: The Free Press, 1997).

9 There are notable exceptions. As David Cairns eloquently suggests of *The Lost Weekend* (dir. Billy Wilder, 1947) – the tale of alcoholic Don Birnam's desperate attempts to beat the bottle – 'The flavour of a film noir crime flick comes from [a] focus on deceit, not from Birnam's actual thefts (a botched bag-snatch; a liquor store hold-up conducted with nothing more than a mean scowl), but from the way it treats drinking as a criminal career, to be pursued secretly and obsessively, the tools of the trade hidden and smuggled and covered up with lies. The stylistic mix of urban realism with hints of German expressionism merely confirms the film's genre qualifications.' David Cairns, 'The Lost Weekend', a film essay presented in the booklet accompanying the 2012 'Masters of Cinema' blu-ray release of *The Lost Weekend*, p. 6.

10 Michael W. Boyce, *The Lasting Influence of the War on Postwar British Film* (London: Palgrave Macmillan, 2012), p. 80.

11 Bould, *Film Noir*, p. 3.

12 Boyce, *The Lasting Influence of the War on Postwar British Film*, p. 80.

13 Robert B. Pippin, *Fatalism in American Film Noir: Some Cinematic Philosophy* (Charlottesville, VA and London: University of Virginia Press, 2012), p. 95.

14 Karen Klitgaard Povlsen, 'Gender and Geography in Contemporary Television Crime Fiction', in Paula Arvas and Andrew Nestingen (eds), *Scandinavian Crime Fiction* (Bangor: University of Wales Press, 2011), p. 89.

15 Nestingen and Arvas (eds), *Scandinavian Crime Fiction*, p. 1.

16 The series' remit reads, 'The Nordic Film Classics series offers in-depth studies of key films by Danish, Finnish, Icelandic, Norwegian, and Swedish directors. Written by emerging as well as established film scholars, and where possible in conversation with relevant film practitioners, these books help to shed light on the ways in which the Nordic nations and region have contributed to the art of film.' See also my review of the series in *Journal of Adaptation in Film and Performance* 5: 1 (2012), pp. 93–96.

17 There are, of course, noteworthy predecessors demonstrating a similar approach. See Raymond Durgnat, *A Mirror for England:*

British Movies from Austerity to Affluence (London: Faber & Faber, 1970), Charles Barr, *English Hitchcock* (London: Movie, 1999), and Robin Wood, *Hitchcock's Films Revisited* (New York: Columbia University Press, 1998). More recent publications combining close textual analysis and sociocultural criticism to particularly illuminating effect include Boyce, *The Lasting Influence of the War on Postwar British Film* and Antoine de Baecque, *Camera Historica: The Century in Cinema* (New York: Columbia University Press, 2012).

18 Jonathan Bignell, 'The Police Series', in John Gibbs and Douglas Pye (eds), *Close-Up 03* (London: Wallflower Press, 2009), pp. 63–64.

19 Edward Docx, 'Stieg and Dan: two of a bad kind?', The New Review, *The Observer*, 12 December 2010, p. 36.

20 Heather O' Donoghue, 'New Wine in Old Bottles: Innovation and Tradition in Stieg Larsson's *Millennium* Trilogy' in Peacock (ed.), *Stieg Larsson's Millennium Trilogy*, p. 45.

21 See Sarah E. H. Moore's more precise discussion of the trilogy's presentation of European court proceedings in 'Storytelling and Justice in *The Girl Who Kicked the Hornets' Nest*', Peacock (ed.) *Stieg Larsson's Millennium Trilogy*, pp. 144–163.

22 Eva Gabrielsson with Marie-Francoise Colomban, *'There Are Things I Want You to Know': About Stieg Larsson and Me* (Seven Stories Press, 2011).

23 See for example Elaine Sciolino, 'A Word From Stieg Larsson's Partner and Would-Be Collaborator', *New York Times*, 17 February 2011, http://artsbeat.blogs.nytimes.com/2011/02/17/a-word-from-stieg-larssons-partner-and-would-be-collaborator/ (accessed 06/03/2012).

24 Sarah Niblock, 'Journalism and Compassion: Rewriting the On-Screen Crusader for the Digital Age', Peacock (ed.) *Stieg Larsson's Millennium Trilogy*, p. 136.

25 A good example of the ho-hum stance of critics towards Fincher's film is Keith Uhlich's position in *Time Out (New York)*, 13 December 2011, seeing the movie's slick visual style as noteworthy, but cautioning that 'lurid it remains ... delighting the franchise junkie above all other considerations', www.timeout.com/us/film/the-girl-with-the-dragon-tattoo (accessed 30/08/2012). A more positive and thoughtful response is found in David Denby's review

for *The New Yorker*, 12 December 2011, www.newyorker.com/arts/
critics/cinema/2011/12/12/111212crci_cinema_denby (accessed
30/08/2012).

26 See Owen Williams, 'Murder Ink', *Empire* (London: Bauer Media),
December 2010, p. 52.

27 See for example Jakob Stougaard-Nielsen's description in 'Nordic
Noir – a short history': 'Sjöwall and Wahlöö had translated several
of Ed McBain's 87th precinct novels, and found in his pioneering
police procedurals a formula of their own markedly Scandinavian
crime fiction, wherein police officers' private lives and personal
struggles are mirrored in the larger social landscape of Sweden.
From *Roseanna* (1965) to *The Terrorists* (1975), we follow Martin
Beck and his homicide squad from a sex murder of an American
tourist to the murder of the prime minister in a Swedish police
state, anticipating the murder of the Swedish prime minister Olof
Palme by a decade. In their investigations, Beck and his team are
constantly faced with an impenetrable police bureaucracy, representing a brutal society that gradually overshadows the idyllic
Swedish welfare state.' Printed in Arrow Films' 'Nordic Noir' DVD
booklet, 2012.

28 *Ibid.*

29 *The Laughing Policeman* (also known as *An Investigation of
Murder*), 1973, dir. Stuart Rosenberg (Twentieth Century Fox
Film Corporation).

30 *De gesloten kamer*, 1993, dir. Jacob Bijl, starring the famous Belgian
actor Jan Decleir as Martin Beck (Film Case, Prime Time).

31 For example, *Carambole* (full title *Nesser's Van Veeteren: Carambole*)
was filmed in 2005, dir. Daniel Lind Lagerlöf, starring (as all the
films do) Sven Wollter as Detective Chief Inspector Van Veeteren.
The film and series (or TV series of films) is a co-production between
Sweden, Denmark, Germany, Norway, and Finland (ARD Degeto
Film, Canal +, Degeto Film, Film på Gotland, Svensk Filmindustri,
TV2 Norge, Yleisradio).

32 http://yellowbird.se/index.php?option=com_seyret&Itemid=4&
task=videodirectlink&id=308 (accessed 25/03/2012).

33 As Jakob Stougaard-Nielsen writes in 'Nordic Noir – a short history',
'In the late 1980s and in the 1990s, the Nordic international thriller
gained attention with Swede Jan Guillou's Coq Rouge series (1986–

2006) featuring the Swedish spy, Carl Hamilton, a noble man with socialist leanings ... Adaptations of Guillou's thrillers for film and TV have appeared periodically since *Code Name Coq Rouge* in 1989 starring Stellan Skarsgård; *Hamilton – In the Interest of the Nation* (2012) is the latest Swedish film featuring the popular super-agent.' Printed in Arrow Films' 'Nordic Noir' DVD booklet, 2012.

34 For a wider appraisal of my methodological interest in the stylistic criticism of films, see Steven Peacock, *Hollywood and Intimacy: Style, Moments, Magnificence* (London: Palgrave Macmillan, 2011), and *Colour* (Manchester: Manchester University Press, 2010).

35 Henning Mankell, 'Foreword', *The Pyramid* ('Pyramiden'), English translation by Ebba Segerberg and Laurie Thompson (London: Vintage Books, 2009), p. 1.

36 I have elsewhere examined related concerns in the relationship between the Danish television drama *Riget* (*The Kingdom*, dir. Lars von Trier, 1994) and its US remake *Kingdom Hospital* (dir. Craig Baxley, 2004), in Steven Peacock, 'Two *Kingdoms*, Two Kings', *Critical Studies in Television* 4: 2 (Autumn 2009), pp. 24–36.

37 Shane McCorristine, 'The Place of Pessimism in Henning Mankell's Kurt Wallander Series', in Nestingen and Arvas (eds) *Scandinavian Crime Fiction*, p. 81.

38 Mankell presents a characteristic scenario in the novel *One Step Behind* (*Steget Efter*), as the murderer makes his move through the expansive woodlands surrounding the town Ystad: 'He stepped out and shot each of them once in the head ... It was over so quickly that he barely had time to register what he was doing. But now they lay dead at his feet, still wrapped around each other, just like a few seconds before. He turned off the tape recorder that had been playing and listened. The birds were chirping. Once again he looked around. Of course there was no one there. He put his gun away and spread a napkin out on the cloth. He never left a trace', Henning Mankell, *One Step Behind,* trans. Ebba Segerberg (London: Vintage Books, 2008) digital edition, Kindle location 194.

39 Lars Trägårdh, 'Sweden and the EU: Welfare State Nationalism and the Spectre of "Europe"', in Lene Hansen and Ole Wæver (eds), *European Integration and National Identity: The Challenge of the Nordic States* (London and New York: Routledge, 2002), p. 150.

40 Erik Hedling, 'Ingmar Bergman and Modernity: Some Contextual Remarks', in Mariah Larsson and Anders Marklund (eds), *Swedish Film: An Introduction and Reader* (Nordic Academic Press, 2010), p. 225.

41 'The history of translation theory can be in fact be imagined as a set of changing relationships between the relative autonomy of the translated text, or the translator's actions, and two other categories: equivalence and function. Equivalence has been understood as "accuracy", "adequacy", "correctness", "correspondence", "fidelity" or "identity"; it is a variable notion of how the translation is connected to the foreign text. Function has been understood as the potentiality of the translated text to release diverse effects, beginning with the communication of information and the production of a response comparable to the one produced by the foreign text in its own culture. Yet the effects of translation are also social, and they have been harnessed to cultural, economic, and political agendas: evangelical programs, commercial ventures, and colonial projects, as well as the development of languages, national literatures, and avant-garde literary movements. Function is a variable notion of how the translated text is connected to the receiving language and culture.' Lawrence Venuti (ed.), *The Translation Studies Reader* (2nd edition, New York and London: Routledge, 2004), pp. 5–6.

42 Gayatri Chakravorty Spivak, 'The Politics of Translation', in Venuti (ed.), *The Translation Studies Reader*, pp. 369–371. Originally published in Gayatri Spivak, *Outside in the Teaching Machine*, London and New York: Routledge, 1993).

43 Such keystone works include George Bluestone, *Novels into Film* (Berkeley, CA: University of California Press, 1957); Sarah Cardwell, *Adaptation Revisited: Television and the Classic Novel* (Manchester: Manchester University Press, 2002); Deborah Cartmell and I. Whelehan (eds) *The Cambridge Companion to Literature on Screen* (Cambridge: Cambridge University Press, 2007); Christine Geraghty, *Now a Major Motion Picture: Film Adaptations of Literature and Drama* (London: Rowman and Littlefield, 2008); Thomas Leitch, *Film Adaptation and Its Discontents* (Baltimore, MD: John Hopkins University Press, 2007).

44 Thomas Leitch, 'Vampire Adaptation', *Journal of Adaptation in Film and Performance* 4: 1 (2011), pp. 5–16 (pp. 5, 11).

45 *Ibid.*, p. 11.

46 *Ibid.*

47 Jonas Frykman, 'Nationalla ord och hangligar', in Billy Ehn, Jonas Frykman and Orvar Löfgren, *Försvenskningen av Sverige – det nationellas förvandlingar* (Stockholm: Natur och Kultur, 1993), p. 123. Cited in Allan Pred, *Recognizing European Modernities: A Montage of the Present* (London: Routledge, 1995), p. 257.

48 Steve Blandford, Stephen Lacey, Ruth McElroy and Rebecca Williams, 'Editorial: Television Drama and National Identity – the Case of "Small Nations"', *Critical Studies in Television* 6: 2 (Autumn 2011), p. xiv.

49 Francis Sejersted, *The Age of Social Democracy: Norway and Sweden in the Twentieth Century* (New York: Princeton University Press, 2011), pp. 1–6.

50 *Ibid.*, p. 307.

51 John Gilmour, *Sweden, the Swastika and Stalin: The Swedish Experience in the Second World War* (Edinburgh: Edinburgh University Press, 2010), p. 1.

52 Sejested, *The Age of Social Democracy*, pp. 185–188.

53 Cited in Anders Isaksson, *Per Albin* (Stockholm: Wahlström & Widstrand, 2000), pp. 365–366.

54 Gilmour, *Sweden, the Swastika and Stalin*, p. 17.

55 *Ibid.*, p. 18.

56 *Ibid.*, p. 48.

57 *Ibid.*, p. 270.

58 Thord Lindell and Herbert Lagerström, *Svensk historia* (Stockholm, 1967), pp. 164–70. Cited in Gilmour, *Sweden, the Swastika and Stalin*, p. 270.

59 Stieg Larsson, *The Girl with the Dragon Tattoo*, trans. Reg Keeland (London: MacLehose Press, 2008), digital edition, Kindle location 1425.

60 *Ibid.*, digital edition, Kindle location 2745.

61 *Ibid.*, digital edition, Kindle location 3063.

62 Deborah Orr discusses the salience of exploring such a system's challenges in 'Can Scandinavian Crime Fiction Teach Socialism?': 'The socialist left and the liberal left have little in common, with Blairism a shining example of how difficult it is to "triangulate" them. Hard work and compromise is needed before social freedom and state

welfare can be shackled together. Even then, perhaps, the resulting beast is an impossible chimera.' Orr, 'Can Scandinavian Crime Fiction Teach Socialism?', Guardian.co.uk, 24 February 2011, www.guardian.co.uk/commentisfree/2011/feb/24/can-scandinavian-crime-fiction-teach-socialism (accessed 19/04/2011).

63 Sejersted notes how, 'The demand to adapt was considered by many in the immigrant communities as a lack of understanding of the needs of immigrants to maintain their own identity. If there was anything that the former emigration countries of Sweden and Norway ought to have understood, it was the need of the immigrants to retain their own culture ... Equality and freedom thus emerged once again as possible contradictions.' Sejersted, *The Age of Social Democracy*, p. 403.

64 Andrew Brown, *Fishing in Utopia: Sweden and the Future that Disappeared* (London: Granta, 2009), p. 126.

65 *Ibid.*, p. 128.

66 *Ibid.*, p. 130.

67 The sense of conspiracy and cover-ups haunting the case continues into the present day. In August 2012, Ben Quinn for *The Guardian* broke the news that, 'Eva Rausing, who was found dead in July at the London home she shared with her husband, an heir to the TetraPak fortune, had passed on information about the unsolved 1986 murder of Swedish prime minister Olof Palme, Swedish prosecutors have revealed ... She claimed she had learned that Palme had been killed by an entrepreneur who feared the politician was a threat to business', *The Guardian*, 29 August 2012, p. 8.

68 Brown, *Fishing in Utopia*, pp. 129–130.

69 Lars Trägårdh, 'Sweden and the EU: Welfare State Nationalism and the Spectre of "Europe"', in Hansen and Wæver (eds), *European Integration and National Identity*, p. 130.

70 Mette Hjort, *Small Nation, Global Cinema: The New Danish Cinema* (Minneapolis and London: University of Minnesota Press, 2005), p. 25.

71 Pred, *Recognizing European Modernities*, p. 217.

72 Paul Britten Austin, *On Being Swedish: Reflections Towards a Better Understanding of the Swedish Character* (London: Secker and Warburg, 1968), p. 9.

73 Peter Cowie, *Swedish Cinema: from Ingeborg Holm to Fanny and Alexander* (Stockholm and London: The Swedish Institute, 1985), p. 39.

74 *Ibid.*, p. 90.

75 *Ibid.*, pp. 90–91.

76 Sarah E. H. Moore, 'Storytelling and Justice in *The Girl Who Kicked the Hornets' Nest*', in Steven Peacock (ed.), *Stieg Larsson's Millennium Trilogy*, p. 145.

77 John Scaggs, *Crime Fiction* (New York and London: Routledge, 2010), p. 1.

78 P. D. James, *Talking About Detective Fiction* (Oxford and London: Bodleian Library and Faber and Faber, 2010), pp. 13–14.

79 *Ibid.*, pp. 19–20.

80 *Ibid.*, p. 20.

81 *Ibid.*, p. 72.

82 David Thomson, *The New Biographical Dictionary of Film*, 4th edition (New York: Little, Brown, 2002), p. 574.

83 John Scaggs, *Crime Fiction*, pp. 87–89.

84 *Ibid.*, pp. 3–4.

85 Robert Kolker, *A Cinema of Loneliness: Penn, Stone, Kubrick, Scorsese, Spielberg, Altman* (3rd edition, Oxford: Oxford University Press, 2000), p. 183.

86 Kerstin Bergman, 'The Well-Adjusted Cops of the New Millennium: Neo-Romantic Tendencies in the Swedish Police Procedural', in Nestingen and Arvas (eds), *Scandinavian Crime Fiction*, pp. 34–45.

87 *Ibid.*

88 http://thesusanne.com/post/17712009633/the-scandinavian-gloom (accessed 01/04/2012).

89 Ibsen Stage Company, www.artsjobs.org.uk/arts-news/post/talk-scandinavian-gloom-or-room-for-something-new/ (accessed 01/04/2012).

90 Hjort, *Small Nation, Global Cinema*, p. ix.

91 *Ibid.*, pp. ix–x.

92 *Ibid.*

93 *Ibid.*

94 *Ibid.*

95 *Ibid.*, pp. 31–32.

96 Anders Marklund, 'The New Generation of the 1960s: Introduction', in Larsson and Marklund (eds), *Swedish Film: An Introduction and Reader*, p. 239.

97 Cowie, *Swedish Cinema: from Ingeborg Holm to Fanny and Alexander*, pp. 64–66.

98 www.bbc.co.uk/news/entertainment-arts-16495095 (accessed 01/04/2012).

99 Anders Marklund, 'Genre Filmmaking in a Difficult Film Climate: Introduction', in Larsson and Marklund (eds), *Swedish Film: An Introduction and Reader*, pp. 182–183.

100 Hjort, *Small Nation, Global Cinema*, p. 162.

101 *Ibid.*, pp. 164–165.

102 Trevor G. Elkington and Andrew Nestingen, 'Introduction', in Trevor G. Elkington and Andrew Nestingen (eds), *Transnational Cinema in a Global North: Nordic Cinema in Transition* (Detroit, MI: Wayne State University Press, 2005), pp. 8–9.

103 Yellow Bird's industrial status is also indicative of the flow and impact of globalisation. The company was acquired in 2007 by the Swedish production group Zodiak Television. Alongside Yellow Bird, Zodiak bought media companies from other countries, including the Netherlands, Belgium, Russia, and the UK. In turn, it expanded from being a Scandinavian group into a pan-European group. In 2008, Zodiak Television was acquired by Italian media conglomerate De Agostini, merging with two other production groups, Marathon and Magnolia (from France and Italy respectively). In 2010 De Agostini also bought the UK/US-based media group RDF and merged all the companies together, becoming what is now called Zodiak media group, with the headquarters in London.

104 Mikael Wallén, Managing Director, Yellow Bird Productions, interviewed by Steven Peacock, Stockholm, 30 March 2011.

105 Examples include *The X Files: I Want to Believe* (dir. Chris Carter, 2008), *Sex and the City* (dir. Michael Patrick King, 2008), and *In the Loop* (dir. Armando Iannucci, 2009, based on the BBC comedy-drama *The Thick of It* 2005–ongoing). This pattern is different to a growing (if still niche) marketing strategy of providing films with simultaneous release dates at the cinema and on digital television (for example, Ken Loach's film *Route Irish* was shown at the cinema

and on Sky Television's pay-TV box office service at the same time, in March 2011).

106 Mikael Wallén interview, 30 March 2011.

107 As Roberta Pearson explains in the introduction to *Reading Lost*, TV3 'emerged roughly from the late 1990s and is characterised by fragmented, not to say splintered, audiences, distribution through digital technologies and industry panic over audience measurement and advertising strategies.' Roberta Pearson (ed.), *Reading Lost: Perspectives on a Hit TV Show* (London: I. B. Tauris, 2009), p. 1.

108 A similar set of stylistic decisions can be seen at work in the US serial drama *House* (NBC/Universal Media Studios 2004–ongoing) and, more overtly, in serial-killer drama *Dexter* (Showtime, 2006–ongoing). As I note in *Dexter: Investigating Cutting Edge Television*, 'Some of the most compelling designs of the series stem from the way the surface materials of the external world – settings, decor, landscapes, look – reflect Dexter Morgan's synthetic sensibility .' Steven Peacock, '*Dexter*'s Shallow Designs', in Douglas L. Howard, *Dexter: Investigating Cutting Edge Television* (London: I. B. Tauris, 2010), p. 49.

109 Michael Hjorth and Hans Rosenfeldt, *Sebastian Bergman*, trans. Marlaine Delargy (London: Trapdoor, 2012), Kindle digital edition, location 337.

110 www.huffingtonpost.co.uk/2012/06/04/sebastian-bergman-review_n_1568167.html (accessed 26/07/2012).

111 Lars Trägårdh, 'Sweden and the EU: Welfare State Nationalism and the Spectre of "Europe"', in Hansen and Wæver (eds), *European Integration and National Identity*, p. 131.

112 de Baecque, *Camera Historica*, p. 16.

113 Brown, *Fishing in Utopia*, p. 28.

114 Cowie, *Swedish Cinema*, pp. 72–73.

115 Brown, *Fishing in Utopia*, p. 139.

116 Jens Lapidus, *Snabba Cash*, translated from the Swedish by Astri von Arbin Ahlander (London: Macmillan, 2012), digital edition, Kindle location 399.

117 Brown, *Fishing in Utopia*, pp. 28–29.

118 Maj Sjöwall and Per Wahlöö, *The Abominable Man* (London: Harper Perennial, 2005), digital edition, Kindle location 175.

119 Brown, *Fishing in Utopia*, p. 236.

120 Henning Mankell, *One Step Behind* (London: Vintage, 2008), digital edition, Kindle location 164.

121 Elkington and Nestingen (eds), *Transnational Cinema in a Global North*, p. 15.

122 Sejersted, *The Age of Social Democracy*, p. 403.

123 Brown, *Fishing in Utopia*, p. 137.

124 *Ibid.*, pp. 246, 252.

125 Peacock, '*Dexter*'s Shallow Designs', p. 78.

126 Larsson, *The Girl with the Dragon Tattoo*, digital edition, Kindle location 546.

127 Brown, *Fishing in Utopia*, pp. 112–113.

128 See the official site of the Leveson Inquiry at www.levesoninquiry. org.uk/ (accessed 11/09/2012).

129 Austin, *On Being Swedish*, p. 34.

130 Liza Marklund, *The Bomber* (first published 1998, Transworld digital edition 2011), Kindle location 389.

131 *Ibid.*, Kindle location 465.

132 Larsson, *The Girl with the Dragon Tattoo*, Kindle location 828.

133 Sarah Niblock, 'Journalism and Compassion: Rewriting an On-Screen Crusader for the Digital Age', in Peacock (ed.), *Stieg Larsson's Millennium Trilogy*, p. 79.

134 *Ibid.*, p. 80

135 *Ibid.*, pp. 85–86.

136 Larsson, *The Girl with the Dragon Tattoo*, Kindle location 3192.

137 Scaggs, *Crime Fiction*, pp. 94–95.

138 *Wallander Country* (2010), cited in Anne Marit Waade, 'BBC's *Wallander*: Sweden Seen through British Eyes', *Critical Studies in Television* 6: 2 (Autumn 2011), p. 55.

139 Helene Tursten, *Torso* (Soho Crime Digital Edition, 2007), Kindle location 6041.

140 Daniel Brodén, 'The Criminal and Society in *Mannen på taket*', in Larsson and Marklund (eds), *Swedish Film: An Introduction and Reader*, p. 199.

141 Maj Sjöwall and Per Wahlöö, *The Laughing Policeman* (Harper Perennial Digital Edition, 2009), Kindle location 221.

142 *Ibid.*, Kindle location 232.

143 Mankell, *The Pyramid*, p. 333.

144 Waade, 'BBC's *Wallander*: Sweden Seen Through British Eyes', p. 219.

145 Karsten Wind Meyhoff, 'Digging into the Secrets of the Past: Rewriting History in the Modern Scandinavian Police Procedural' in Nestingen and Arvas (eds), *Scandinavian Crime Fiction*, p. 70.

146 Throughout his directorial career, from *Alien 3* (1992) to *Panic Room* (2002) and *The Social Network* (2010), Fincher has been attracted to projects that allow him to explore modernity's impact on the individual, as an obstacle to human intimacy (wanted or otherwise).

147 Pippin, *Fatalism in American Film Noir*, p. 7.

148 Henning Mankell, *Before the Frost*, translated from the Swedish by Ebba Segerberg (London: Vintage, 2009), back cover.

149 See, for example, Paul Gallagher's article for *The Observer* in December 2009: www.guardian.co.uk/uk/2009/dec/27/wallandar-hemming-mankell-tv-books-detective (accessed 17/09/2012).

150 At the same time, from the outset, the episode declares its interest in a complication of viewpoint. It opens with 'documentary' footage without making clear the time, place or identity of the participants. We will later learn that the film is of the Jonestown massacre in Guyana in the 1970s. The footage wrong-foots us: we are lost without the mainstay presence of familiar protagonists, amidst a sea of different voices. Some of those involved deliver their accounts direct to camera, and there is the documentary film-maker's voiceover. This is the recording which will later be discovered in Anna's flat by Linda, a find which not only 'drives the narrative' but also links this character to the multiplicity of voices in the episode, *and* brings her centre stage in terms of the plot.

151 Mankell, *Before the Frost* (Vintage Digital Edition, 2008), Kindle location 181.

152 Nicole Rafter and Michelle Brown, *Criminology Goes to the Movies: Crime Theory and Popular Culture* (New York: New York University Press, digital edition 2011), Kindle location 1651.

153 Shane McCorristine, 'The Place of Pessimism in Henning Mankell's Kurt Wallander Series', in Nestingen and Arvas (eds), *Scandinavian Crime Fiction*, p. 77.

154 Tytti Soila, 'Sweden', in Tytti Soila, Astrid Soderbergh Widding and Gunnar Iversen (eds), *Nordic National Cinemas* (London: Routledge, 1998), p. 160.

155 Scaggs, *Crime Fiction*, pp. 50–51.

156 Slavoj Žižek, 'Henning Mankell, the Artist of Parallax View', in *Parfume*, www.lacan.com/zizekmankell.htm (accessed 04/04/2012).

157 Austin, *On Being Swedish,* p. 59.

158 Brown, *Fishing in Utopia*, p. 182.

159 Bo Tao Michaëlis (ed.), *Copenhagen Noir*, trans. Mark Kline (New York: Akashic Books, 2011), p. 17.

160 Kristian Lundberg, 'Savage City, Cruel City', trans. Lone Thygesen Blecker, in Bo Tao Michaëlis (ed.), *Copenhagen Noir*, pp. 168–175.

161 *Ibid.*, p. 166.

162 Richard Hill and David Haworth, *The Newcomers: Austria, Finland, Sweden* (Brussels: Euro Publications, 1995), pp. 132–133.

163 Brown, *Fishing in Utopia*, p. 6.

164 Hakan Nesser, *Borkmann's Point* (London: Pan Books, digital edition 2010), Kindle location 133.

165 Ian McEwan, *Saturday* (London: Vintage, 2006).

166 *Ibid.*, Preface.

167 Hjorth and Rosenfeldt, *Sebastian Bergman*, Kindle location 92.

168 Nesser, *Borkmann's Point*, Kindle location 154.

169 Henning Mankell, *The Man Who Smiled* (London: Vintage, 2010), pp. 11–12.

170 Shane McCorristine, 'The Place of Pessimism in Henning Mankell's Kurt Wallander Series', in Nestingen and Arvas (eds), *Scandinavian Crime Fiction*, p. 81.

171 Mankell, *The Pyramid: The Kurt Wallander Stories*, trans. E. Segerberg and L. Thompson (London: Harvill Secker, 2008), p. 115.

172 Mankell, *The Pyramid*, p. 295.

173 *Ibid.*, p. 296.

174 *Ibid.*, p. 322.

175 *Ibid.*, p. 373.

176 *Ibid.*, p. 432.

177 *Ibid.*, pp. 344–345.

178 Larsson, *The Girl with the Dragon Tattoo*, Kindle location 179.

179 *Ibid.*, Kindle location 407.

180 Lapidus, *Snabba Cash*, Kindle location 450.

181 An earlier version of this description of the film's opening sequence can be found in Peacock (ed.), *Stieg Larsson's Millennium Trilogy*, pp. 1–2.

182 Charles Taylor, 'The James Bond Title Sequences', www.salon. com/2002/07/29/bond_titles/ (accessed 30/08/2012).

183 Waade, 'BBC's *Wallander*: Sweden Seen Through British Eyes', p. 47.

184 Interview with Andy Harries conducted by the author, London, 8 December 2011.

185 Waade, 'BBC's *Wallander*', p. 54.

186 Lapidus, *Snabba Cash*, Kindle location 303.

187 Larsson, *The Girl with the Dragon Tattoo*, Kindle location 2475.

188 Michaëlis (ed.), *Copenhagen Noir*, p. 14.

189 Daniel Brodén, 'The Criminal and Society in *Mannen på taket*', in Larsson and Marklund (eds), *Swedish Film: An Introduction and Reader*, p. 200.

190 Scaggs, *Crime Fiction*, pp. 70–71.

191 Sjöwall and Wahlöö, *The Laughing Policeman*, op. cit., Kindle location 155.

192 Lapidus, *Snabba Cash*, Kindle location 166.

193 Larsson, *The Girl with the Dragon Tattoo*, Kindle location 1224.

194 Åsa Larsson, *Sun Storm* (also known as *The Savage Altar*, London: Penguin, 2008), digital edition, Kindle location 667.

195 *Ibid.*, Kindle location 764.

196 *Ibid.*, Kindle location 818.

197 *Ibid.*, Kindle location 828.

198 Trägårdh, 'Sweden and the EU', in Hansen and Wæver (eds), *European Integration and National Identity*, p. 149.

199 Brown, *Fishing in Utopia*, p. 30.

200 Marklund, *The Bomber*, Kindle location 320.

201 Sarah Casey Benyahia, 'Salander in Cyberspace', in Peacock (ed.), *Stieg Larsson's Millennium Trilogy*, pp. 74–76.

202 *Ibid.*

203 James, *Talking About Detective Fiction*, p. 17.

204 Mankell, *The Pyramid*, p. 1.

205 *Ibid.*, p. 299.

206 Nestingen, *Crime and Fantasy in Scandinavia*, p. 232.

207 Mankell, *The Man Who Smiled*, p. 288.

208 Larsson, *Sun Storm*, Kindle location 273.

209 Larsson, *The Girl with the Dragon Tattoo*, Kindle location 614.

210 Brown, *Fishing in Utopia*, p. 50.

211 Forshaw, *Death in a Cold Climate*, p. 21.

212 Cowie, *Swedish Cinema*, pp. 79–80.

213 Mariah Larsson, 'Contested Pleasures', in Larsson and Marklund (eds), *Swedish Film: An Introduction and Reader*, p. 205.

214 *Ibid.*, p. 205.

215 Tursten, *Torso*, Kindle location 2609.

216 *Ibid.*

217 Barry Forshaw, 'The Larsson Phenomenon: Sales Figures and Sexual Abuse', in Peacock (ed.), *Stieg Larsson's Millennium Trilogy*, pp. 24–26.

218 *Ibid.*

219 Andrew Nestingen, 'Realism, Melodrama and Scandinavian Crime Fiction in Transition', in Nestingen and Arvas (eds), *Scandinavian Crime Fiction*, p. 177.

220 *Ibid.*, p. 172.

221 *Ibid.*, p. 179.

222 de Baecque, *Camera Historica*, p. 12.

223 *Ibid.*, p. 29.

224 Mankell, *The Man Who Smiled*, p. 391.

225 *Ibid.*, p. 1.

BIBLIOGRAPHY

Fiction

Austen, Jane, *Emma* (Wordsworth Editions, 2000)

Christie, Agatha, *The Mousetrap and Other Plays* (William Morrow, 2012)

——, *The Murder of Roger Ackroyd* (Harper, 2007)

——, *Sparkling Cyanide* (Collins, 2012)

Conan Doyle, Arthur, *The Hound of the Baskervilles* (Penguin Classics, 2001)

Easton Ellis, Brett, *American Psycho* (Picador, 1991)

Hjorth, Michael and Hans Rosenfeldt, *Sebastian Bergman* (Trapdoor, 2012)

Jungstedt, Mari, *The Gotland Cycle* (Corgi, 2009–ongoing)

Lapidus, Jens, The *Stockholm Noir* Trilogy (Macmillan, 2012)

Larsson, Åsa, *The Savage Altar* (*Solstorm*) (Delta, 2006)

Larsson, Stieg, *The Girl with the Dragon Tattoo* (Quercus, 2009)

——, *The Girl Who Played with Fire* (Quercus, 2009)

——, *The Girl Who Kicked the Hornet's Nest* (Quercus, 2010)

Levin, Ira, *A Kiss Before Dying* (Corsair, 2011)

Lindqvist, John Ajvide, *Handling the Undead* (Quercus, 2009)

——, *Let the Right One In* (Quercus, 2009)

——, *Harbour* (Quercus, 2011)

——, *Little Star* (Quercus, 2012)

Mankell, Henning, *The Pyramid* (Vintage, 2009)

——, The *Wallander* series (Vintage, 2008–2009)

Marklund, Liza, The *Annika Bengzton* Series (Transworld, 2011–ongoing)

McEwan, Ian, *Saturday* (Vintage, 2006)

Nesbo, Jo, *Headhunters* (Vintage, 2012)

——, The *Harry Hole* Series (Vintage, 2005–ongoing)

Nesser, Håkan, The *Van Veeteren* Series (Pan, 2007–2010)

Palahniuk, Chuck, *Fight Club* (Vintage, 1996)

Sjöwall, Maj and Per Wahlöö, The *Martin Beck* Series (Harper Perennial, 2002–2010)

Theorin, Johan, The *Öland* Quarter (Black Swan 2009–2012)

Tursten, Helene, The *Irene Huss* Series (Soho Crime, 2007–ongoing)

Non-fiction

Austin, Paul Britten, *On Being Swedish: Reflections Towards a Better Understanding of the Swedish Character* (Secker and Warburg, 1968)

Badley, Linda, R. Barton Palmer and Steven Jay Schneider (eds), *Traditions in World Cinema* (Edinburgh University Press, 2006)

Barr, Charles, *English Hitchcock* (Movie, 1999)

de Baecque, Antoine, *Camera Historica: The Century in Cinema* (Columbia University Press, 2012)

Bignell, Jonathan, 'The Police Series', in John Gibbs and Douglas Pye (eds), *Close-Up 03* (Wallflower Press, 2009)

Bignell, Jonathan and Stephen Lacey (eds), *Popular Television Drama: Critical Perspectives* (Manchester University Press, 2005)

Blandford, Steve, Stephen Lacey, Ruth McElroy and Rebecca Williams, 'Editorial: Television Drama and National Identity – the Case of "Small Nations"', *Critical Studies in Television* 6: 2 (Autumn 2011)

Bluestone, George, *Novels into Film* (University of California Press, 1957)

Bluestone, Natalie Harris, *Double Vision: Perspectives on Gender in the Visual Arts* (Associated University Press, 1995)

Boozer, Jack (ed.), *Authorship in Film Adaptation* (University of Texas, 2008)

Bordwell, David, *The Way Hollywood Tells It: Story and Style in Modern Movies* (UCA, 2006)

Bould, Mark, *Film Noir: From Berlin to Sin City* (Wallflower, 2005)

Boyce, Michael W., *The Lasting Influence of the War on Postwar British Film* (Palgrave Macmillan, 2012)

Brown, Andrew, *Fishing in Utopia: Sweden and the Future that Disappeared* (Granta, 2009)

Butler, Jeremy G., *Television Style* (Routledge, 2010)

Cardwell, Sarah, *Adaptation Revisited: Television and the Classic Novel* (Manchester University Press, 2002)

Cartmell, Deborah and I. Whelehan (eds), *The Cambridge Companion to Literature on Screen* (Cambridge University Press, 2007)

Chalaby, Jean (ed.), *Transnational Television Worldwide* (I. B. Tauris, 2005)

Chaudhuri, Shohini, *Contemporary World Cinema* (Edinburgh University Press, 2005)

Christopher, Nicholas, *Somewhere in the Night: Film Noir and the American City* (The Free Press, 1997)

Collins, Richard, *Media and Identity in Contemporary Europe: Consequences of Global Convergence* (Intellect, 2002)

Conrad, Mark T. (ed.), *The Philosophy of Film Noir* (University of Kentucky Press, 2006)

Cowie, Peter, *Swedish Cinema: from Ingeborg Holm to Fanny and Alexander* (The Swedish Institute, 1985)

Creeber, Glen, *Serial Television* (BFI, 2004)

Dixon, Wheeler Winston, *Film Genre 2000: New Critical Essays* (UNY, 2000)

Docx, Edward, 'Stieg and Dan: two of a bad kind?', The New Review, *The Observer*, 12 December 2010, p. 36

Dowd, Gavin, *Genre Matters* (Intellect, 2006)

Durgnat, Raymond, *A Mirror for England: British Movies from Austerity to Affluence* (Faber & Faber, 1970)

Ehn, Billy, Jonas Frykman and Orvar Löfgren, *Försvenskningen av Sverige – det nationellas förvandlingar* (Natur och Kultur, 1993)

Elkington, Trevor G. and Andrew Nestingen (eds), *Transnational Cinema in a Global North: Nordic Cinema in Transition* (Wayne State University Press, 2005)

Forshaw, Barry, *Death in a Cold Climate: A Guide to Scandinavian Crime Fiction* (Palgrave Macmillan, 2012)

Gabrielsson, Eva with Marie-Francoise Colomban, *'There Are Things I Want You to Know': About Stieg Larsson and Me* (Seven Stories Press, 2011)

Geraghty, Christine, *Now a Major Motion Picture: Film Adaptations of Literature and Drama* (Rowman and Littlefield, 2008)

Gibbs, John and Douglas Pye (eds), *Style and Meaning: Studies in the Detailed Analysis of Film* (Manchester University Press, 2005)

Gilmour, John, *Sweden, the Swastika and Stalin: The Swedish Experience in the Second World War* (Edinburgh University Press, 2010)

Hammond, Michael and Lucy Mazdon (eds), *The Contemporary Television Series* (Edinburgh University Press, 2005)

Hansen, Lene and Ole Wæver (eds), *European Integration and National Identity: The Challenge of the Nordic States* (Routledge, 2002)

Havens, Timothy, *Global Television Marketplace* (BFI, 2006)

Hill, Richard and David Haworth, *The Newcomers: Austria, Finland, Sweden* (Euro Publications, 1995)

Hjort, Mette, *Cinema and Nation* (Taylor and Francis, 2000)

——, *Small Nation, Global Cinema: The New Danish Cinema* (University of Minnesota Press: 2005)

Howard, Douglas L., *Dexter: Investigating Cutting Edge Television* (I B Tauris, 2010)

Isaksson, Anders, *Per Albin* (Wahlström & Widstrand, 2000)

James, P. D., *Talking about Detective Fiction* (Bodleian and Faber & Faber, 2010)

Kolker, Robert, *A Cinema of Loneliness: Penn, Stone, Kubrick, Scorsese, Spielberg, Altman* 3rd edition (Oxford University Press, 2000)

Larsson, Mariah and Anders Marklund (eds), *Swedish Film: An Introduction and Reader* (Nordic Academic Press, 2010)

Leitch, Thomas, 'Vampire adaptation', *Journal of Adaptation in Film and Performance Intellect*, 4: 1 (2011), pp. 5–16.

——, *Film Adaptation and Its Discontents* (John Hopkins University Press, 2007)

Lindell, Thord and Herbert Lagerström, *Svensk historia* (Stockholm, 1967)

Lury, Karen, *Interpreting Television* (Hodder Arnold, 2005)

McCabe, Janet and Kim Akass (eds), *Quality TV: Contemporary American Television and Beyond* (I. B. Tauris, 2007)

McFarlane, Brian, *Novel to Film* (Clarendon, 1996)

Michaëlis, Bo Tao (ed.), *Copenhagen Noir*, trans. Mark Kline (Akashic Books, 2011)

Miller, Toby, *Global Hollywood* (BFI, 2001)

Moran, Albert, *Understanding the Global TV Format* (Intellect, 2006)

Naremore, James (ed.), *Film Adaptation* (Athlone, 2000)

Neale, Steve, *Genre and Contemporary Hollywood* (BFI, 2002)

Nelson, Robin, *State of Play: Contemporary 'High End' TV Drama* (Manchester University Press, 2007)

Nestingen, Andrew, *Crime and Fantasy in Scandinavia: Fiction, Film, and Social Change* (University of Washington Press; University of Copenhagen: Museum Tusculanum Press, 2008)

Nestingen, Andrew and Paula Arvas (eds), *Scandinavian Crime Fiction* (University of Wales Press, 2011)

Newcomb, Horace (ed.), *Television: the Critical View*, 7th edition (Oxford University Press, 2007)

Peacock, Steven, *Colour* (Manchester University Press, 2010)

——, 'Two *Kingdoms*, Two Kings', *Critical Studies in Television* 4: 2 (2010), pp. 24–36

——, *Hollywood and Intimacy: Style, Moments, Magnificence* (Palgrave Macmillan, 2011)

—— (ed.), *Stieg Larsson's Millennium Trilogy: Interdisciplinary Approaches to Nordic Noir on Page and Screen* (Palgrave Macmillan, 2012)

Pearson, Roberta (ed.), *Reading Lost: Perspectives on a Hit TV Show* (I. B. Tauris, 2009)

Pippin, Robert B., *Fatalism in American Film Noir: Some Cinematic Philosophy* (University of Virginia Press, 2012)

Pred, Allan, *Recognizing European Modernities: A Montage of the Present* (Routledge, 1995)

Priestron, Martin, *The Cambridge Companion to Crime Fiction* (Cambridge University Press, 2003)

Rafter, Nicole and Michelle Brown, *Criminology Goes to the Movies: Crime Theory and Popular Culture* (New York University Press, 2011)

Scaggs, John, *Crime Fiction* (Routledge, 2010)

Sejersted, Francis, *The Age of Social Democracy: Norway and Sweden in the Twentieth Century* (Princeton University Press, 2011)

Skelton, Tracey and Tim Allen, *Culture and Global Change* (Routledge, 1998)

Soila, Tytti, Astrid Soderbergh Widding and Gunnar Iversen (eds), *Nordic National Cinemas* (Routledge, 1998)

Spicer, Andrew, *Film Noir* (Toronto Pearson Education Limited, 2002)

Spivak, Gayatri, *Outside in the Teaching Machine* (Routledge, 1993)

Thomson, David, *The New Biographical Dictionary of Film*, 4th edition (Little, Brown, 2002)

Venuti, Lawrence (ed.), *The Translation Studies Reader* (Routledge, 2004)

Vighi, Fabio, *Sexual Difference in European Cinema* (Palgrave, 2009)

Waade, Anne Marit, 'BBC's *Wallander*: Sweden Seen through British Eyes', *Critical Studies in Television* 6: 2 (Autumn 2011), pp. 51–62.

Williams, Owen, 'Murder Ink', *Empire* (December 2010), pp. 51–54

Wood, Robin, *Hitchcock's Films Revisited* (New York: Columbia University Press, 1998)

Film and television

24 (Imagine Entertainment, 20th Century Fox Television, Real Time Productions, 2001–2010)

491 (dir. Vilgot Sjöman, 1964)

Absolutely Fabulous (BBC, 1992–ongoing)

Arne Dahl (Filmlance International AB, Sveriger Television, Zweiter Deutscher Fernsehen, 2011–2012)

Annika Bengzton (Yellow Bird, 2012–ongoing)

Beck (Nordisk Film and TV Fond, Rialto Film, Svensk Filmindustri, 1993–2009)

Bomber, The (*Sprängaren*, dir. Colin Nutley, 2001)

Bonnie and Clyde (dir. Arthur Penn, 1967)

Borgen (DR Fiktion, 2010–ongoing)

Bridge, The (Filmlance International AB, Nimbus Film Productions, Sveriges Television, 2011)

Broadchurch (ITV/Kudos, 2013)

Cats, The (*Kattorna*, dir. Henning Carlsen, 1965)

Children of Men (dir. Alfonso Cuarón, 2006)

Close Encounters of the Third Kind (dir. Steven Spielberg, 1977)

Cloverfield (dir. Matt Reeves, 2008)

Conversation, The (dir. Francis Ford Coppola, 1974)

CSI: Crime Scene Investigation (CBS, 2000–ongoing)

Curb Your Enthusiasm (HBO Films, Production Partners, 2000–ongoing)

De gesloten kamer (dir. Jacob Bijl, 1993)

Deal, The (dir. Stephen Frears, 2003)

Deep Throat (dir. Gerard Damiano, 1972)

Dexter (Showtime/John Goldwyn Productions, 2006–ongoing)

Dirty Harry (dir. Don Siegel, 1971)

Double Indemnity (dir. Billy Wilder, 1944)

Dream of Freedom, A (*En dröm om frihet*, dir. Jan Halldoff, 1969)

Dr. No (dir. Terence Young, 1962)

Easy Money (*Snabba Cash*, dir. Daniel Espinosa, 2010)

Easy Money II (*Snabba Cash II*, dir. Babak Najafi, 2012)

Experiment, The (*Das experiment*, dir. Oliver Hirschbiegel, 2001)

Eyes Wide Shut (dir. Stanley Kubrick, 1999)

Festen (dir. Thomas Vinterberg, 1998)

Fight Club (dir. David Fincher, 1999)

French Connection, The (dir. William Friedkin, 1971)

Girl Who Kicked the Hornets' Nest, The (*Luftslottet som sprängdes*, dir. Daniel Alfredson, 2009)

Girl Who Played with Fire, The (*Flickan som lekte med elden*, dir. Daniel Alfredson, 2009)

Girl With the Dragon Tattoo, The (*Män som hatar kvinnon*, dir. Niels Arden Oplev, 2009)

Girl With the Dragon Tattoo, The (dir. David Fincher, 2011)

Godfather, The (dir. Francis Ford Coppola, 1972)

Greed (dir. Erich von Stroheim, 1924)

Headhunters (*Hodejegerne,* dir. Morten Tyldum, 2011)

House (NBC/Universal Media Studios, 2004–ongoing)

I am Curious – Yellow (dir. Vilgot Sjöman, 1967)

Inspector Morse (ITV, 1987–2000)

In the Loop (dir. Armando Iannucci, 2009)

Irene Huss Mysteries, The (Yellow Bird, Illusion Films, Kanal 5, Film I Vast, 2005–ongoing)

Killing, The (*Forbrydelsen*, DR/NRK/SVT, 2007–ongoing)

Killing, The (AMC, 2011–ongoing)

Kingdom, The (*Riget*, Arte, DR, Sveriges Television/Zentropa, 1994)

Kingdom Hospital (Touchstone Television, Mark Carliner Productions, Sony Pictures Television, 2004)

Kommissar und das Meer, Der (Network Movie Film und Fernsehproduktion, 2006–2010)

Lady, The (dir. Luc Besson, 2011)

Laughing Policeman, The (also known as *An Investigation of Murder*) (dir. Stuart Rosenberg, 1973)

Let Me In (dir. Matt Reeves, 2010)

Let the Right One In (*Låt den rätte komma in*, dir. Tomas Alfredson, 2008)

Lewis (Granada Media, ITV Productions, 2007–2012)

Licence to Kill (dir. John Glen, 1989)

Lock, Stock, and Two Smoking Barrels (dir. Guy Ritchie, 1998)

Locked Room, The (*De Gesloten kamer,* dir. Jacob Bijl, 1993)

Longford (dir. Tom Hooper, 2006)

Loving Couples (*Älskande par,* dir. Mai Zetterling, 1964)

Mad Dogs (Left Bank Pictures, Sky Television, 2011–2012)

Mad Men (Lionsgate/AMC 2007–ongoing)

Maltese Falcon, The (dir. John Huston, 1941)

Man on the Roof, The (*Mannen på taket,* dir. Bo Widerberg, 1976)

M*A*S*H (dir. Robert Altman, 1970)

Millennium (Yellow Bird Films/Sveriges Television, 2010)

Murder, My Sweet (dir. Edward Dmytryk, 1944)

Nesser's Van Veeteren (ARD Degeto Film, Canal +, Degeto Film, Film på Gotland, Svensk Filmindustri, TV2 Norge, Yleisradio, 2000–2006)

Night Games (*Nattlek,* dir. Mai Zetterling, 1966)

North by Northwest (dir. Alfred Hitchcock, 1959)

One False Move (dir. Carl Franklin, 1992)

Orpheus (*Orphée,* dir. Jean Cocteau, 1950)

Paradise (*Paradiset,* dir. Colin Nutley, 2003)

Pelle the Conqueror (*Pelle erobreren,* dir. Bille August, 1987)

Punishment Park (dir. Peter Watkins, 1971)

Queen, The (dir. Stephen Frears, 2006)

Romanzo Criminale (Cattleya, Sky Italia, 2008–2010)

Roseanna (dir. Hans Abramson, 1967)

Roseanna (dir. Daniel Alfredson, 1993)

Route Irish (dir. Ken Loach, 2011)

Safe House (dir. Daniel Espinosa, 2012)

Salò or the 120 Days of Sodom (*Salò o le 120 giornate di Sodoma,* dir. Pier Paolo Pasolini, 1971)

Sea of Love (dir. Harold Becker, 1989)

Sebastian Bergman (Tre Vänner Produktion AB, Sveriges Television, 2012–ongoing)

Se7en (dir. David Fincher, 1995)

Sex and the City (dir. Michael Patrick King, 2008)

Silence of the Lambs, The (dir. Jonathan Demme, 1991)

Slumdog Millionaire (dir. Danny Boyle, 2008)

Spiral (*Engrenages*, Canal +, Son et Lumière, 2005)

Sun Storm (*Solstorm*, dir. Leif Lindblom, 2007)

Suspiria (dir. Dario Argento, 1977)

Taking of Pelham One Two Three, The (dir. Joseph Sargent, 1974)

Taxi Driver (dir. Martin Scorsese, 1976)

Thick of It, The (BBC/YLE, 2005–ongoing)

THX1138 (dir. George Lucas, 1971)

Tinker Tailor Soldier Spy (dir. Tomas Alfredson, 2011)

Torment (*Hets*, dir. Ingmar Bergman, 1944)

Touch of Frost, A (ITV Productions, Excelsior, Yorkshire Television, 1992–ongoing)

Usual Suspects, The (dir. Bryan Singer, 1995)

Wallander (DR, Nordiska TV-Samarbetsfonden, SVT, 1995–2007)

Wallander (Canal+, DR, Degets Film, Film i Skåne, SF, TV2 Norge, TV4 Sweden, Yellow Bird Films, 2005–2010)

Wallander (Yellow Bird Films, Zodiak, ARD Degeto Film, BBC Scotland, Film i Skåne, Left Bank Pictures, TV4 Sweden, 2008–ongoing)

West Wing, The (NBC, Warner Bros., 1999–2006)

X Files, The: I Want to Believe (dir. Chris Carter, 2008)

Zen (Left Bank Pictures, RTI, ZDF, 2011)

Websites

www.artsjobs.org.uk/arts-news/post/talk-scandinavian-gloom-or-room-for-something-new/ (accessed 01/04/2012)

Denby, David, *The New Yorker*, 12 December 2011, www.newyorker.com/arts/critics/cinema/2011/12/12/111212crci_cinema_denby (accessed 30/08/2012)

Gallagher, Paul, *The Observer*, 27 December 2009, www.guardian.co.uk/uk/2009/dec/27/wallandar-hemming-mankell-tv-books-detective (accessed 17/09/2012)

www.huffingtonpost.co.uk/2012/06/04/sebastian-bergman-review_n_
1568167.html (accessed 26/07/2012)

www.levesoninquiry.org.uk/ (accessed 11/09/2012)

McCabe, Janet, 'Nothing Like a Dane', for *CST Online*, http://cstonline.
tv/nothing-like-dane (accessed 06/03/2012)

Orr, Deborah, 'Can Scandinavian crime fiction teach socialism?', 24
February 2011, www.guardian.co.uk/commentisfree/2011/feb/24/can-
scandinavian-crime-fiction-teach-socialism (accessed 19/04/2011)

www.radiotimes.com/news/2011-11-18/the-killing-knit-your-own-
sarah-lund-jumper (accessed 06/03/2012)

Sciolino, Elaine, 'A Word From Stieg Larsson's Partner and
Would-Be Collaborator', *New York Times*, 17 February 2011, http://
artsbeat.blogs.nytimes.com/2011/02/17/a-word-from-stieg-
larssons-partner-and-would-be-collaborator/ (accessed 06/03/2012)

Taylor, Charles, 'The James Bond Title Sequences', www.salon.
com/2002/07/29/bond_titles/ (accessed 30/08/2012)

http://thesusanne.com/post/17712009633/the-scandinavian-gloom
(accessed 01/04/2012)

Uhlich, Keith, *Time Out (New York)*, 13 December 2011, www.timeout.
com/us/film/the-girl-with-the-dragon-tattoo (accessed 30/08/2012)

Wollaston, Sam, *The Guardian*, www.guardian.co.uk/tv-and-
radio/2012/jan/07/tv-review-borgen-sherlock (accessed 06/03/2012)

——, *The Guardian*, www.guardian.co.uk/tv-and-radio/2012/may/26/
tv-review-kingdom-of-plants (accessed 29/05/2012)

http://yellowbird.se/index.php?option=com_seyret&Itemid=4&task=
videodirectlink&id=308 (accessed 25/03/2012)

INDEX